HOLISTIC LANGUAGE INSTRUCTION

Dr Jaime Hoerricks

HOLISTIC LANGUAGE INSTRUCTION

Addressing Literacy in Standard and Non-Standard Populations

The Education Studies Collection

Collection Editor
Dr Janise Hurtig

First published in 2024 by Lived Places Publishing

All rights reserved. No part of this publication may be reproduced, stored in a retrieval system, or transmitted in any form or by any means, electronic, mechanical, photocopying, recording, or otherwise, without prior permission in writing from the publisher.

The authors and editors have made every effort to ensure the accuracy of information contained in this publication, but assume no responsibility for any errors, inaccuracies, inconsistencies, and omissions. Likewise, every effort has been made to contact copyright holders. If any copyright material has been reproduced unwittingly and without permission the Publisher will gladly receive information enabling them to rectify any error or omission in subsequent editions.

Copyright © 2024 Jaime Hoerricks

British Library Cataloguing in Publication Data
A CIP record for this book is available from the British Library

ISBN: 9781916704466 (pbk)
ISBN: 9781916704480 (ePDF)
ISBN: 9781916704473 (ePUB)

The right of Jaime Hoerricks to be identified as the Author of this work has been asserted by them in accordance with the Copyright, Design and Patents Act 1988.

Cover design by Fiachra McCarthy
Book design by Rachel Trolove of Twin Trail Design
Typeset by Newgen Publishing UK

Lived Places Publishing
Long Island
New York 11789

www.livedplacespublishing.com

Abstract

Guided by a lived experience point of view, Holistic Language Instruction reveals a flaw in an assumption that underpins many of the world's educational systems: that there is only one way that humans learn language. The data show that this flaw has left about 40 per cent of the world's English language learners behind in the development of their language skills. Are these students disabled? Or does the system disable them when it does not address the way in which their brains acquire and process language? When these learners begin to fall behind their peers in their educational journey, they may be placed in a special education program, assigned to a speech and language professional, or simply ignored. Given that language processing differences have no connection with intellect, what if these learners could be easily accommodated within the general population of students and progress through school with their peers? This book first informs the reader of the issue, explains why the current paradigm fails so many learners, presents the different language processing models, then charts a path forward for current and future educators, parents, and caregivers to support the growth of English language literacy in all learners.

Key words

English Language Instruction; English Language Learner; Science of Reading; Natural Language Acquisition; Gestalt Language Processing; Non-Verbal Autism; Disability Studies; Special Education & Teaching Studies.

Contents

Chapter 1	Introduction	1
	Learning objective	1
Chapter 2	Deconstructing the Science of Reading	35
	Learning objective	35
Chapter 3	Early childhood literacy	75
	Learning objective	75
	Exercises and activities for analytic language processors	109
	Exercises and activities for gestalt language processors	114
Chapter 4	Young adult literacy	127
	Learning objective	127
Chapter 5	Adult literacy	171
	Learning objective	171
Chapter 6	Cross-curricular literacy	207
	Learning objective	207
Chapter 7	Summary	239
References		248
Index		297

1
Introduction

Learning objective

Students will be able to synthesize the elements of the Natural Language Acquisition model and its relation to learning English in standard and non-standard learner populations.

> "I hear and I forget. I see and I remember. I do and I understand." – Kong Fuzi (孔夫子).

Rationale

The learning goal requires students to synthesize information about the Natural Language Acquisition model from multiple sources and contexts (standard and non-standard learner populations). Students must integrate this information to demonstrate understanding of how the model relates to teaching and learning the English language across different groups.

This aligns well to the Common Core standards (e.g., CCSS.ELA-LITERACY.RST.11-12.7) which require integrating information from multiple formats / media to address a question or problem. Students must pull together information about the model itself as well as examples from different populations to synthesize how the model applies in various contexts. This demonstrates the ability to integrate and evaluate multiple sources to address the underlying question.

When designing the chapters of this book, I have intentionally incorporated instructional approaches encouraged by the Common Core standards. These include emphasizing nonfiction texts, analytical writing, cross-curricular skills, and utilizing technology / media. In essence, university instruction can be partially shaped by the approaches championed by the Common Core as academics bring aspects of those pedagogical shifts into their own teaching and course design even without formal adoption of the standards in a particular setting. The Common Core has rippled into higher education by influencing the instructional materials, activities, and structural decisions made by instructional designers seeking to build key transferable skills.

Meet the author

Hello and welcome to Holistic Language Instruction. My name is Dr Jaime Hoerricks, the author of this text and your guide through this journey. By way of introductions, many professional cultures ask participants to share a fun fact about themselves. I'll begin. I happen to be autistic, a gestalt language processor (aka, non-verbal), and was functionally illiterate when I graduated from high school in Southern California in 1988. These elements of my identity have a lot to do with the fact that I am the proud owner of the International Classification of Diseases (ICD) diagnostic code 6A02.2, "Autism Spectrum Disorder without disorder of tellectual development and with impaired functional language" (WHO, 2021a, 2021b), information that wasn't available to me when I was going through school as a child. Back then, I was just "different", perhaps a bit "odd".

To me, this isn't some random or trivial point. It is an important factor in this text. You see, for many years various communities have asked that future work focus on those areas that improve their members' day-to-day lives. Also, that there needs to be more involvement from members of the targeted communities in research as well as in the creation and publication of materials that are offered to or for them. This work is an attempt to do just that, to feature someone who was failed by the traditional educational system yet found a path to a sustainable and happy life. In doing so, it features the work of a now special education teacher with a diverse range of lived experiences. These experiences reinforce the central premise of this text: that how, when, and where one learns language, particularly the English language, depends entirely upon how one's language acquisition and processing centers function. This implies, of course, that there is more than one way in which humans can learn the English language. I'll get to that shortly. But first, a bit more about me and what brought me to write this book.

My educational background

In my almost six decades on this planet, I've managed to earn both a Bachelor and a Master degree in Organizational Leadership from Woodbury University, a Master of Education – Instructional Design, from Western Governors University, a Master of Education – Special Education, from Loyola Marymount University, and a PhD in Education from Trident University. I've earned a 150-hour certificate in Teaching English as a Foreign Language from the University of Toronto's Ontario Institute for Studies in Education. I've earned a 40-hour certificate from my school district's training and development division in the Orton-Gillingham method. I've also earned a 90-hour Early Literacy certificate from Atlanta's Rollins Center for Language and Literacy. I did all of this, beginning when I was 36 years old and was supporting my rather large family working as a forensic scientist for the City of Los Angeles.

How I got there, or how I came to be in the employ of the City of Los Angeles as a functionally illiterate adult, and how it is that I am now a special education teacher and literacy specialist is an interesting story. The path, and the lessons learned, will be woven throughout this text. I will use them to illustrate the points of what holistic language instruction can look like at various stages of one's life. I thus offer myself as the exemplar, as well as a few of my willing former students, to provide the "mass" of the item under study. In this way, topics become less abstract and more practical.

What does it mean to be illiterate?

First, let's dive into the difference between illiterate and functionally illiterate. Illiterate generally refers to someone who lacks basic reading and writing skills and is unable to understand written text or write coherently. They may struggle with recognizing letters, forming words, or comprehending written information. Illiteracy, in this sense, is often associated with a lack of formal education or limited access to quality education (Vágvölgyi et al., 2016), though it can find its roots in language deficits in the brain.

Functionally illiterate, on the other hand, usually describes people who have some basic reading and writing skills but still struggle to use these skills effectively. While they may be able to read simple texts or even write basic sentences, they may have difficulty comprehending complex instructions, filling out forms, or engaging in tasks that require advanced literacy skills often found in adult life. The functionally illiterate often have wide gaps in their reading and writing abilities that hinder their overall literacy proficiency (Semingson and Kerns, 2021).

My having been functionally illiterate is separate from my being a gestalt language processor, also known in the autistic community as being "non-verbal". Non-verbal is not the same as non-vocal or non-speaking, though many confuse these two concepts. The term non-verbal speaks to the way the human brain acquires, learns, and / or processes language. Gestalt language processing (GLP) is the big technical term for the way the "non-verbal" brain processes language (Prizant, 1982; Blanc, 2012). This language processing style is not unique to autistic people, though many of us use GLP. The other way humans process language is called analytic language processing (ALP). We'll cover both in more detail later. Here, I just wanted to introduce the terms.

With these ideas in mind, how does one graduate from school functionally illiterate? It's easier than you might think. Let me explain.

Taking a step back – traditional language instruction in elementary schools in the US

I attended elementary school in the 1970s in the United States. Then and there, schools favored the "traditional" approach to language instruction. The "traditional", grammar-based approach featured vocabulary building and the development of the four main skills of listening, speaking, reading, and writing. It was, and still is, a teacher-centered instructional approach that relies heavily upon lectures (also called modeling), memorization, and drills. Assessments are given and scores received. Then, students move on (Lightbown and Spada, 2021). Students moved on, not because they were necessarily ready to move on, but because the schedule dictated the pace. I saw the results of this practice in my own life manifest in gaps in my language skills, one that built gap upon gap (Mason and Sinha, 1992) over the course of my schooling.

We would say today that those teachers taught to the center of the room. Assessment data really didn't inform instruction in any way that I can remember. There was a certain plan and pace that teachers meant to keep, and we kept it (Juel, 1988). A student like me could easily hide in a large classroom, relying upon eager peers to provide cover when a teacher would ask for a student to demonstrate their proficiency to the class (Davidson, 2021).

When I would occasionally get called upon, I would panic. This time was long before the world would come into an awareness of the traits, strengths, and limitations that now place me on the autism spectrum. I didn't have free-flowing conversational skills like my peers. I didn't have the decoding skills needed to decipher what was on the page. I would wait, then the teacher would prompt, and then I would improvise using my mental bank of language scripts (gestalts) – a behavior known as delayed echolalia (Prizant and Rydell, 1984), which is common among autistic people (Fay, 1969).

My improvisation relied upon a mind that processed chunks of language scripts, gestalts. It didn't do so letter by letter, understanding all the rules of the English language. Rather, it absorbed how the chunks of language sounded and felt, as well as the contexts in which they were discovered. My alexithymia assisted, unconsciously, in gathering the emotions of the speaker as they spoke their words (Taylor, 1984), and the feelings within the room as they were spoken (Kinnaird, Stewart, and Tchanturia, 2019). In my panic at a request to read aloud or respond to a question, my brain would assemble a reply that it believed would satisfy the request. Early on, I was comically inept. My replies tended toward the nonsensical, never seeming to correlate with the requests. Later, with practice and as my storehouse of sounds, words, and feelings developed, they became more coherent. In short, as I grew up, I become more adept at using my delayed and immediate echolalia to communicate (Prizant, 1982, 1983; Prizant and Duchan, 1981; Prizant and Rydell, 1984; Stiegler, 2015).

Early echolalia

Much of what was known in the West about autism and communication then was guided by the works of Leo Kanner and Hans Asperger. A few generations ago, only the most profound cases of communication deficits were referred to specialists. Unknown in the West were the works of the early Soviets; Sukhareva, Vygotsky, and their compatriots (Smagorinsky, 2013; Vasileva and Balyasnikova, 2019; Vygotsky, 2012). Sadly, the western countries would only learn of their work after the fall of the "Iron Curtain". I say sadly because their work seems to my mind more humane, more holistic. While Asperger, for example, studied autism to determine the functioning levels of autistic children and adults as part of Nazi scientific racism, and thus who would live and who would be "relieved of their suffering" for the good of the family and the Volk (Hoerricks, 2023), the work of the Soviet scientists seemed to look for root causes so appropriate supports could be given (New and Kyuchukov, 2022; Simmonds, 2019).

These early Soviet doctors looked at autism in a systemic fashion. They noted that autistic children often displayed motor disorders, including problems with muscle tone and coordination. They wondered if there was a connection between the severity of motor disorders and the child's emotional state. They studied how language and speech were also affected in autism, with prosody (pace, rhythm, and voice modulation) often being disrupted. In severe cases, they observed, children may experience either selective or total mutism. However, they observed, when the child's emotional condition improved, there was often a transition from repeating words and phrases (echolalia) to more meaningful communication (New and Kyuchukov, 2022). The later, and seemingly unconnected, work of Prizant (1981, 1982, 1983, 1984, 1985) and Blanc (2012) would show them to be completely spot-on.

For me, echolalia combined with alexithymia meant that I was pretty good at mimicry. When I ingested language from others, it came with the emotional content, tone, tenor, and intonation. In my multi-ethnic and multilingual melting pot of city and schools, I had built an assortment of phrases in English, Spanish, German, Russian, and Armenian. Some of these languages seemed to go better together, like English and German, with similar sounds and meanings. Others seemed light years away from what I knew of

English, like Russian and Armenian (Bodmer, 1944). I worked hard at sounding correct in each language and dialect that I repeated in response to questions and requests, trying to match what was coming out of my mouth with how the words sounded and felt in the theater of my mind. Sometimes, the languages got confused in delivery, a German response to a Spanish prompt or the wrong word / phrase returned, much to the endless delight of my peers.

Middle school years

In the US, it's assumed that by the time one leaves the primary grades and heads off to middle school that one knows how to read and comprehend the English language. I didn't. I knew some sight words and could string some words together when asked to read aloud, but I had no comprehension skills. When I would be tasked with reading a passage aloud, I would struggle mightily if I had never encountered the words before. Often, the teachers would get impatient and move on to a student who could keep pace with their schedule for the day. At no time did any of my teachers attempt to intervene to find out if I could read or try to teach me the fundamentals of reading.

Middle school, for me, was a rough time. It's embarrassing when you have severe gaps in your skills. I was the butt of jokes and received a ton of teasing and bullying. Puberty was hitting. The last thing that I wanted to do was to stay at school and work on my reading. In fact, I couldn't wait to get out each day.

California had seemingly invested a lot of money in its schools and reading programs. In 1965, its governor signed the Miller-Unruh

Act into law. According to the Act, the intent and purpose of the law was "the prevention of reading disabilities and the correction of reading disabilities at the earliest possible time in the educational career of the pupil". (Sparks, 1968) The Act was directed toward what it called "reading success" for students in the primary grades. It provided funds for the salaries of reading specialists, as well as for scholarships to develop new specialists and librarians (Sparks, 1968). I saw no evidence that any of the programs funded by the Act were present at my school in suburban Los Angeles County.

Diving into reports from that time frame, 1982–1984, one finds that the situation in public schools mirrors what we see today. There were teacher shortages. There were funding shortages. There was a disconnect between what the state aspired to and the results that it managed to deliver. The data showed that California students were average readers in primary school but slipped below the national average in middle and high school. Not much can be found in the literature about what was meant to be done about this. So many of us slipped through the cracks (Guthrie and Kirst, 1985).

In a general sense, we were presented with a range of literature, including novels, short stories, poems, and plays. Through lecture, we were instructed on how to analyze the literary elements, such as plot, character development, theme, and figurative language. The curriculum aspired to foster a love for reading and develop critical thinking skills in us. It was long on aspiration and short on results.

Thinking back, I can recall a time when we were going to analyze Shakespeare's *Julius Caesar* in the eighth grade. I panicked at the thought of having to read that twisted English aloud. A few days and nights of panic gave way to a ray of sunshine. I remembered that there were lots of these classic stories on the local public broadcasting channel. I wondered if the local library had copies of these films. I managed to string together a query to the library staff. Somehow, they arranged to have the 1953 Marlon Brando version of the film made available at the library for me to watch. The film was amazing. The dialogue, thankfully, was very close to the original play. I was able to absorb some of it as I sat and watched, building what I thought might be helpful scripts for later use in the classroom. I tried to focus on those scenes that felt very impactful. If only I could know ahead of time which parts I would have to read.

Alas, it didn't matter. The teacher, perhaps sensing that I wouldn't do well, never called upon me to participate in the table reads. But I learned a valuable lesson. The library staff would be vital to my ability to move through school. That, and in the days before plagiarism checking software, I had my own "William Forester" (Davis-McElligatt and Roth, 2012). There, I had a whole building full of sentence and paragraph starters. As a hint towards my later work with "mentor texts", the writings of the world's best authors were there for me to sample and build any paper that might be required (Chidiac, 2019). All I had to do was ask the staff where to find books on the subject at hand.

High school years

The teachers at my high school were a mix of those nearing retirement, and young, eager, and passionate 20-somethings. Class sizes were quite large. In most of my classes, it was easy to sit in the back of the room and not participate. There were no "checks for understanding". There were very few lively discussions on topics of our choosing. There were the texts and the assignments. There were monologues from our teachers and quiet time for work. There was no such thing as "student voice" or "windows and mirrors" in the 1980s in Southern California's public schools.

When I entered high school, I was 13 years old. I was also 6'2" and quite athletic. I was encouraged to join the freshman basketball team, later becoming its star. Given my size, I frequently practiced with the varsity squad. With this bit of popularity came friends. These friends were a source of academic help. I could ask them questions after practice. I could meet them on weekends to "study together". I had become quite adept at social engineering.

Of course, I had no idea what social engineering was or that I was engaged in it. My pattern-recognizing autistic mind, paired with the way it processed, stored, sorted, and utilized language scripts, worked out ways in which to ask questions that seemed to get the responses I was after. Contrary to the view that all autistics lack social skills or miss social cues, it turns out that some of us can develop this social engineering skill to a fine art (Scullin-Esser, 1988; Simpson, Ganz, and Mason, 2012).

I had a few "go-to" scripts. Usually, I would ask a friend from class, "Man, [teacher's name]. What are we going to do?" They might respond, "I know. It's crazy. Let's meet at [location] and work on it. Hopefully, we can finish in time." We'd meet. They'd verbally process their anxiety over the project. I'd gather the information they were sending out verbally and do my best to throw together what they were saying on a page of my own. Perhaps it was coherent. I doubt that it was. I soon found that few of my teachers read what we submitted. Armed with that information, my course through high school was set.

Over the four years, I made friends with the smart kids. I did my best to organize study sessions where I could mine them for helpful information. During tests, I cheated as best as I was able. When I couldn't, I failed the tests miserably. On balance, I did well enough to graduate towards the top of my class and left with a 3.8 grade point average (GPA). That fact alone is why I place little value on GPAs to this day.

Before you judge my use of "mentor texts", social engineering, and cheating on tests, consider that how one views cheating depends upon one's point of view. Was I not the one being cheated out of a "free and appropriate public education", what we now call FAPE? After all, it's often the case that younglings lack the moral judgment to fully comprehend why cheating on exams might be wrong, even if they feel the system itself is treating them unfairly. Their underdeveloped faculty for ethical reasoning, combined with a penchant for self-interest, and peer pressure in adolescence, can lead them to rationalize unethical actions they would later regret. (Side bar: I don't regret it.) However, rather than condemn, we must seek to educate. Which is my point here. Never mind. Let's move on.

Adult, and illiterate in college

It is expensive to be illiterate as an adult (Lal, 2015). When I speak on the subject now, I ask the audience if they can name the most expensive thing on the planet. The answers range from cyber-currencies to precious metals. I say simply that it's ignorance. Ignorance is expensive.

Being a successful athlete in high school, my grades and test scores didn't matter. All that was required of me to play my first semester of college football was a 2.0 GPA in high school. Standardized tests like the SAT and ACT weren't considered if one had over a 3.0 GPA. With a 3.8 high school GPA, I was considered ready to play. Yet, something was missing. I had never taken a foreign language in high school. The thought terrified me, so I avoided it. I had trouble enough learning one language, why would I want to torture myself learning another at school (Krashen, 1981)? Besides, it wasn't needed for graduation. However, I found out during my senior year that my lacking this "core requirement" meant that I would not be eligible to receive any of the five Division 1 scholarship offers I had received to play football – and go to college for free. Thus, it was off to community college.

Though it was a community college, my first destination after high school was a "football school". None of the classes I attended were rigorous. All were packed with football players. Nothing much was expected of us, save for showing up. Yet, as an illiterate student, I struggled to succeed even in those classes. After an injury in my first semester and a cross-state transfer, I couldn't handle the rigorous college classes at a "regular school". I was left to fend for myself in regular classes. I didn't do well.

I liked being on campus, however. I wanted to stay. I managed to figure out that I could take short-term courses, withdraw at the last moment without penalty, then register for other short-term courses, and eventually make it to the end of the school year. But, in doing this, I earned very few credits. Eventually, I found classes that didn't feature much reading or writing. For example, I took wine tasting, twice. I received credit for an internship. Thus, I was able to string together enough credits over four years of trying to earn an associate degree in Political Science.

The thought of transferring to a four-year university course frightened me. I did not see a way to duplicate what I had done in community college at the local state school. Besides, I needed a break. I worked as a construction laborer for a bit. Then I worked as a security guard. Then in a warehouse. Then as a janitor. Another job had me as driver and bodyguard to a women's sport fashion magnate. None of these jobs paid much. None required me to read. I know now that all my past employers took advantage of the fact that I couldn't read to cheat me out of wages, overtime, and some benefits.

It's safe to say that every single employer from the time that I left college in 1992 until I returned to college 13 years later took advantage of the fact that I couldn't comprehend what was put in front of me to read. This caused me problems with the Internal Revenue Service. This caused me problems with my banks. I signed up for an auto loan that I couldn't really afford. I made just about every financial mistake that one could make because I didn't understand the adult world, I didn't have someone looking out for me anymore, and I couldn't read.

Seeing the light

In the late 1990s, I was back in California after wandering and working across the US, then wandering and working across western Europe; finally living and working in rural southwestern Germany. I was attempting to put an adult life together. After the death of my grandmother, I was trying to connect with my extended family. I was introduced to the head of my Scottish kindred or clan, the Clan MacFarlane, who happened to live in Southern California. He was a few years older than me and lived a rock-star lifestyle. At the time, I was 6'7" and almost 400lb, and was winning championships in the Scottish Highland Games. I was a giant. He offered me a job as his ghillie.

A ghillie, in traditional Scottish culture, handles the Laird's affairs outside of the house. They supervise and act as steward to the lands and all that live on the estate. They can be a hunting or fishing guide. They can also serve as bodyguard and collection agent. It was this latter function that my new employer had in mind for me. With me by his side, he feared no man. With me leading the way into his customers' businesses, he left no debt uncollected. It was decent work. And it didn't require that I read.

As I got to know him and his family, I met his grandmother and his aunt who were in business together. I found out that they were quite famous. They were Dottie and Lilly Walters of Speak and Grow Rich fame, and the Walters' Speaker Service. They knew absolutely everyone. They were excellent businesspeople. And, more importantly, they had the knack of sizing up people in an instant.

Dottie quickly recognized that something wasn't quite right with me. When she would ask me to go get a box of books for shipping, for example, I struggled to find the right one. She asked me about the errors. I trusted her enough to tell her of my struggles.

She cared enough to take some time out of her very busy schedule to get me started on my path to literacy. Again, she knew absolutely everyone in so many professional spaces and connected me with some of her clients whom she believed would be a great fit to mentor and tutor me to a functional literacy.

It was around this time that my employer, and now friend, became a Freemason. At first, the nights that he would attend Lodge were nights off for me. He didn't need help or protection in Lodge. Plus, as a non-member, there wasn't much that I would be able to do there. That all changed about six months later when he invited me to join him at their monthly dinner.

Walking in the door of North Hollywood Lodge for the first time was like the splitting of the atom for me. As I stepped into the foyer and looked around, my eyes feasted upon a visual treasure trove. Much like the stained glass works of the world's finest cathedrals, Masons have instructional artworks called Tracing Boards (Rees, 2019). Adorning the walls of this amazing temple to knowledge were beautiful panels that depicted the symbols, and thus the lessons, of the Degrees of Freemasonry.

I stood for what seemed like forever, soaking it all in. At once, I felt welcome and included. Here, this ancient fraternity seemed to take the time to support their lessons with beautiful visual aids. A dozen questions popped into my mind. Then hundreds. Then … meltdown. It was very overwhelming to my autistic system to be confronted with all this wisdom and beauty without any warning and preparation. My problems with functional language conspired against me. My panic and anxiety worked together with my fight / flight / freeze response to render me almost catatonic.

Yet, inside, my synapses were exploding joyfully at the possibilities found within this new space. One lone thought managed its way through the chaos, "I'm home."

Order from chaos

Over dinner, I didn't have the headspace or the scripts to engage in meaningful conversations. I could manage my name and the fact that I worked for one of the Lodge's new members. I found out that, contrary to popular belief, membership in an American Masonic Lodge is not all that exclusive. In fact, Lodges do not invite people to membership. All that is necessary is for the person to ask for an application. Now, to be sure, there's a bit of a vetting process. But it's a lot easier to join Freemasonry than people think (Hoerricks, 2010).

Sensing my excitement, and my lack of words, Michael handed me an application. The rest of the evening was a multisensory blur, an overload to my autistic system. 20 years later, I can still feel the joy and relief of finding a place that seemed to get me.

I brought the application home. My wife had a ton of questions. I had few answers. I struggled to describe what happened and how I felt. I think she sensed that it was a positive thing and trusted me enough to let me explore this new avenue. After all, we autistics often lack opportunities to socialize. Here, with Freemasonry, the Lodges were filled with serious men – mature, masculine men. Men who believed that the improvement of oneself was a desirable goal and helped each other selflessly towards its attainment.

I didn't think too much about the downsides of joining such a venerable institution. I was caught up in the joy of the moment.

I turned in my application, paid my fees, and reported to the Lodge for my initiation. It was an amazingly transformational night (Hoerricks, 2010).

The highs of the night's events were countered by the crushing low of the knowledge of a task given to each Mason. To progress through the Degrees of Freemasonry in California, one must memorize a portion of the preceding ritual's dialogue and recite it back to the membership in open Lodge. Indeed, this is how one demonstrates one's "proficiency" in most US-based Lodges.

Panic! Terror! What have I gotten myself into? Me? Memorize a script and recite it back? I was crushed.

My panic and terror were informed by a life unsupported. Yet there, in my new home, I would have all the support that I would need. Brotherly love meant that my new Lodge brothers would find a way to help me accomplish my obligations. Relief meant that they had already encountered this issue and had a solution. In fact, the solution was hundreds of years old, hidden within the phrase "the instructive tongue, and the attentive ear" (Hoerricks, 2010; Rees, 2019). This meant that the instructional staff, my new brothers, would vocalize the lines I was to retain and recite. I would listen and repeat. We would practice on Lodge nights in the comfort of the Lodge's lounge. I could watch the ritual performance as many times as I needed. We could take as long as necessary, the ancient fraternity being in no hurry. This system would help me build the bank of gestalts necessary to succeed and progress.

On the night that I was to deliver my first proficiency, again, panic and terror. Yet, within the membership was a brother who was new, like me. He happened to be a psychiatrist. In getting to know me over the preceding months, he recognized the signs that I might have functional language difficulties and other mental processing problems, then known as Asperger's Disorder. He made referrals and got me on the path to an eventual diagnosis (Hoerricks, 2023). But more importantly, on that night he sat with me as I gave my recital. He quietly prompted me when I would miss a line or stall in my recollection. In doing so, he helped me get through one of the more terrifying moments of my adult life. He would do it twice more over the next year as I made my progress towards becoming a Master Mason.

Lessons learned

When I was raised a Master Mason in early 2004, I was finally beginning to use originally created basic grammar. I was beginning to piece together appropriate vocabulary and respond to questions coherently when surprised with an unanticipated vocal exchange. Where before I had relied upon echolalia and heavy mental scripting, I could now operate more extemporaneously. I practiced my new skill in those small talk situations at the monthly Lodge dinners and other Masonic social events. Gradually, I branched out into other spaces with my newly developed skill, even exploring the occupational therapy aspects of improv theater at the suggestion of my care team.

Reflecting upon this journey, I can see the stages in my language development as an unsupported non-verbal autistic (Prizant, 1982, 1983). For years, decades almost, I was stuck around level three or level four of my development, relying upon a couple of words or some simple, trusted phrases to communicate. With my new diagnoses, and the emerging internet, I set about developing my newfound skills as well as finding out why it had all gone so terribly wrong for me. Why did my teachers not recognize that I was struggling with language? Why was I allowed to graduate high school with no comprehension skills and only a minimal vocabulary? Why didn't my teachers know this Natural Language Acquisition model (Blanc, 2012)?

It wouldn't be until I became a teacher myself that I would come across the answers to these questions. Teachers are generally taught in their preparation programs that there is one way in which humans learn language. We're drilled on the so-called Science of Reading. We're counseled that if a child isn't keeping up with instruction, they must have disordered language acquisition. Meetings are convened. Parents are counseled. And students are assigned eligibility for special education services, generally under the Specific Learning Disability designation. With that, the child is offered the services of a speech and language pathologist. The child will get about 60 minutes of therapy per month during their schooling but gradually fall behind their peers in terms of their academics.

While I didn't have access to special education services as such when I was a child, I could see myself in many of the students I faced in my first year as a teacher. I felt their frustration, their struggles with the rigorous language load of modern American education. I saw that my upper elementary grade level students were already falling behind. I saw a student with beautiful, almost rhythmic prosody not have a clue about what he had so eloquently just read. I saw a student freeze in response to the simplest questions. I recognized the signs. I resolved to help them using what had worked for me. At the end of my first year, despite the pandemic, my kids' comprehension scores increased by double digits. I was certainly on to something. In my new career, I was once again … home.

Human language acquisition

Reflecting upon my hundreds of hours spent learning about language acquisition and learning in my teacher preparation at Loyola Marymount University, at the University of Toronto's Teaching English as a Foreign Language program, and at the Rollins Center for Language and Literacy at the Atlanta Speech School, one theme kept popping up in discussions – our students need "windows and mirrors". The phrase "windows and mirrors" can be traced to Emily Style's 1988 book *Curriculum as Window and Mirror*. This phrase is commonly used when discussing representation in education and the curriculum. "Windows" refers to the need for students to be able to look out at and learn about other people's experiences, perspectives, and worlds that may be different than their own. In this view, the curriculum should provide diverse "windows" into other cultures, identities, stories, and histories. "Mirrors", on the other hand, refers to the need for students to also see themselves and their own experiences, culture, and identity reflected in the curriculum and materials with which they engage. Students should be able to see themselves mirrored not only in **what** they read and learn, but in **how** they read and learn it. The problem was, I saw none of the autistic or GLP experience of language represented in the content with which I engaged. When I pushed back or asked questions, I was greeted with either puzzled stares and silence or condescending replies that I, as a student, should just remain quiet and learn what was being presented. My experiences during this time have given rise to the creation of this book, as well as my previous book, *No Place for Autism?* (2023).

You see, not all humans acquire or learn language in the same way. Sukhareva and Kanner were the first to comment about the peculiarities of autistic people's relationship with language (Hoerricks, 2023). Later, Prizant (1982, 1983) was seemingly the first academic to posit that the autistic style wasn't necessarily defective or disordered, rather just different. Prizant and his associates, and later Blanc (2012) perhaps more completely, documented this difference of language acquisition in autistic populations. While these efforts were generally restricted to autistic populations, the documentation of language development has been happening in the West since at least the 1950s.

B. F. Skinner published his seminal work *Verbal Behavior* in 1957. In it, he outlined a behavioral theory of language that focused on conditioning and reinforcement. He viewed language as a set of behaviors shaped by reinforcement and conditioning. He focused on breaking down language into small units and using reinforcement to teach those units. We can still see his beliefs and theories in modern English language instruction.

Largely unknown in the West during this time was Lev Vygotsky and his sociocultural theory from the 1920s and 1930s (Berk and Winsler, 1985; Kozulin et al., 2003; Vygotsky, 1962; 1978; Wertsch, 1985). He viewed language as emerging from social interactions and shaped by culture. He focused on the meaning and communicative functions of language. He saw language development as the internalization of cultural tools for thinking and communicating.

Where Skinner emphasized external conditioning shaping language behaviors, Vygotsky emphasized social learning and internal cognitive processes. Skinner broke language into small behavioral units, Vygotsky focused on contextualized meaningful learning. Where Skinner saw reinforcement as key, Vygotsky saw social interaction as key. In general, Vygotsky placed more emphasis on an active role in language acquisition through social learning, while Skinner again saw learning language as a product of external conditioning. In examining the literature on the comparative results of the approaches, one can see the more humane approach to development traced from the early Soviet scholars, as opposed to the more rigid and structured style of western nations, resulting in better rates of literacy within their respective populations (Arnove and Graff, 1987; Comings, 1999; Graff, 1987; Jones, 1988;). We've known about these results for at least a generation, yet we've made no changes or adjustments to our approaches.

We can see the wisdom in Vygotsky's view in relation to so-called "hip-hop culture", which emerged in the 1970s in predominantly Black and Hispanic urban areas of the United States. It's hard to argue that it hasn't had a significant influence on language. As hip-hop music and its associated artistic expressions like breakdancing, DJing, and graffiti art rose in popularity, so too did the linguistic conventions of its creators and fans. Terms originally used by hip-hop pioneers, like "fo sho", " mos def", and "24 /7", became ingrained in slang vernacular. The competitive lyrical sparring of rap battles birthed new forms of wordplay and rhetorical flair. Over time, as hip-hop culture gained wider appeal, its original slang and idioms filtered through to the speech patterns of young people more broadly. The fact that certain terms and linguistic styling carry the cachet of sounding "cool" or "streetwise" has seen their use spread well beyond those original artists. In Vygotsky's theory, we can view hip-hop terminology and phrasing as culturally contingent tools for thinking and communicating among youth that have been widely internalized. So, while hip-hop originated within specific subcultures, its language now shapes mainstream dialogue.

Reflecting upon this information, the old Soviet ideas on language instruction would be entirely more fit for purpose in educating classrooms with all types of learners. Unfortunately, it's bad form in the West to mention the former Soviet Union or its constituent nations and satellites in a positive light.

Yet we must acknowledge that there are different ways in which humans acquire, learn, and use language, and that these types will be present in a single classroom. We must identify and understand these types so that we can design appropriate instruction. This is, after all, one of the hallmarks of Universal Design for Learning (UDL) – knowing your students. The more recent works of Prizant and Blanc have given us the names of these types of language learners: analytic and gestalt processors. Can we not acknowledge that they are both valid and need support within a single classroom, rather than assign the "normal" label to one and push the other into language therapy?

Natural language acquisition and development

Summarizing from the literature, natural language acquisition and development are the processes by which humans progress from basic language skills to fluent, flexible language through a series of predictable developmental stages, guided by their innate abilities. There are two main processing patterns that can drive this development:

- ALP involves breaking down language into individual blocks and components and learning rules to combine them. ALP learners build language from the "bottom up". Most within the neurotypical population are ALP learners. By contrast, a minority of the neurodivergent population are ALP learners (Blanc, 2012).
- GLP relies on absorbing language "wholes" (gestalts or scripts from sources such as songs or phrases) and then segmenting them into smaller units that are recombined in novel ways. GLP learners build language from the "top down". A majority of the neurodivergent are GLP learners, while a minority of the neurotypical population are (Blanc, 2012).

While the processing patterns differ, both ALP and GLP learners progress through predictable stages, capitalizing on their natural strengths. With the right support, both processing patterns can lead to fluent, original language production as well as comprehension. The question becomes, why not approach language instruction in the same classroom that supports both in a holistic way? That, again, is the point of this book.

Outline

Here's how we will work our way forward.

- **Introduction:** The case for this book is made in the introduction, outlining the present problem and the path to a solution.

- **Deconstructing the Science of Reading:** In the West, we teachers are all made to jump on the so-called Science of Reading bandwagon. We will deconstruct the Science of Reading to find out why it works (sometimes) and why it fails so many students.
- **Early childhood literacy:** What does an inclusive classroom look like for the early grades? How can teachers assess students for learning? What assessments are available to help teachers get to know their students?
- **Young adult literacy:** With so many students falling behind in the early grades, what does a holistic literacy program look like for young adults? Is it possible to bring them up to grade level and beyond alongside their grade level peers?
- **Adult literacy:** With adult literacy in the West at an all-time low, what can be done? Can local public schools provide literacy programs that support the whole family, or the whole community?
- **Cross-curricular literacy:** No, most elective subject teachers have no desire to teach literacy. But they must support efforts to increase their students' reading, comprehension, and writing skills. There is a sane path forward.
- **Summary:** We reflect upon the journey to creating a holistic program of language instruction that works wherever English is taught. A charge is given for you to take what you've learned here into your community and effect positive change.

Why study the path to literacy in this way?

Think again about the concept of "windows and mirrors". This idea encourages educators to evaluate their curriculum, materials, and practices to ensure they provide windows into diverse experiences as well as mirrors students can relate to and see themselves in. Courses of instruction with both "windows" and "mirrors" have been linked to greater student engagement, empathy, and learning outcomes. If students remain unengaged, will they learn such vital skills as reading, writing, and comprehending language?

Let us consider what such a classroom might look like for the early grades. The focus there would be on language and literacy as tools for communication and thought, not just isolated skills that are reinforced through mindless repetition. In such a class, authentic social uses of language are prioritized over decontextualized drills. As students interact, teachers and staff can add scaffolding of more complex language through their own social interactions with the students.

Activities would include collaborative projects where peers learn together, like group story creation. Fun, play-based scenarios that involve using language purposefully in imaginary contexts help to reinforce the words and phrases that students learn. During read-aloud sessions, teachers ask open-ended questions and expand on student responses. Teachers incorporate culturally and linguistically relevant language experiences in the stories and songs they bring to the class. And, again, teachers model more advanced language use through their own interactions with students and staff.

Assessment in such a class involves a holistic evaluation of a child's ability to use language for thinking and communicating across a variety of contexts. Here, identifying each student's zone of proximal development (ZPD) helps to provide them with optimal challenges (Gredler, 2012). Finally, student development is tracked through social, collaborative tasks rather than isolated skill tests and standardized assessments.

Working in this way, the class and curriculum support students' social and emotional growth.

- Collaborative projects build skills in teamwork, communication, and perspective-taking as students work together.
- Play scenarios allow safe opportunities to act out social situations and emotions, practicing appropriate responses.
- Teachers can model and reinforce positive social behaviors like sharing, listening, and cooperation when facilitating group work.
- Discussing culturally and linguistically relevant texts can validate students' identities and backgrounds and promote self-esteem.
- Scaffolded interactions with peers and the teacher provide a supportive environment for risk-taking.
- Mistakes are framed as learning opportunities rather than failure, reducing anxiety.
- Open-ended dialogue encourages students to express ideas and feelings in their own words, and, in the case of English language learners / emerging bilinguals, in their own home languages. For those without the gestalts yet, the classroom interaction helps students build up their bank of words, phrases, and feelings.
- Individual perspectives are welcomed, fostering a sense of belonging.
- Tasks are designed to be achievable but still challenging within each student's ZPD to build confidence.

Overall, the social focus, collaborative activities, culturally responsive teaching, and scaffolded support inherent in such a framework create an environment that promotes students' social-emotional wellbeing along with their language and literacy development. As the students progress in grade and age, the work gets more complex. But the supportive structures remain the same.

Preparing to study

Pause here and reflect on your own language background and experiences as a learner. What images come to mind. Are your memories happy or sad? Do you even remember learning to operate in your culture's dominant language? If you're new to English, how did learning English as a second or foreign language work for you?

Having taken a moment to collect our thoughts, let's jot a few things down in our notebooks. Here, you might write a summary of your journey to literacy in the English language. If you need help getting started, consider the following questions in your reflection.

- What language(s) did you grow up speaking at home? What language(s) were you educated in?
- If English was not your first language (your L1), what messages did you receive about your L1 and culture in school? Were your L1 and culture valued and affirmed?
- Did you ever feel isolated, misunderstood, or unsupported because of language differences? Explain.
- How did your language experiences shape you socially, emotionally, and academically?

- What could teachers have done to better support you as a language learner?
- How might your language background and experiences shape your approach to working with diverse students?
- What strengths do you bring as a teacher because of your language experiences? What potential biases or blind spots do you need to address?
- How might you apply principles of the Natural Language Acquisition model to build on the language assets of your students?

The goal of this writing prompt is to have you reflect deeply on your personal experiences as a language learner, even if it only includes English, and how that impacts your role as a teacher of language. Please feel free to share your open and honest thoughts.

During our studies

As we work through this book, you will be asked to do research. Please bear in mind that the bulk of the academic world considers ALP the default and GLP a defect requiring therapy. Thus, as you research, you will find more sources on ALP language instruction in so-called mainstream sources, while information on GLP learners will be found in areas around speech and language pathology / therapy and special education. It's all there. We just need to know where and how to look for it.

Check for understanding

How are you getting on? I hope you are managing all right and that the material is making sense so far. Were there any words or terms in the chapter you have just read that you did not fully understand or recognize? There can often be unfamiliar vocabulary when learning new subjects. Take a moment to look up any unfamiliar terms and add them to your notes or include them in the margins. Indeed, my books are full of notes and scribbles. Going over the materials in this active way—by paraphrasing, summarizing, and identifying problem areas, looking up solutions, and integrating new information into your knowledge—will help enhance your retention and grasp of the key concepts.

Some things that might trip you up

There are some common issues that teachers come upon. Exploring the Natural Language Acquisition model and its implications for inclusive teaching could potentially cause cognitive dissonance in a few ways for someone new to the concept.

- One may hold misconceptions or biases about how language should be used in the classroom that conflict with the principles of the model; for example, believing that requiring Standard Academic English is always best practice.
- One's own experiences as a native English speaker who did not face language struggles could clash with recognizing the needs of English language learners and emerging bilinguals.
- One may not have considered one's language privilege before or reflected critically on one's monolingual upbringing. In the previous reflection activity, one may have discovered and acknowledged these potential blind spots.
- Applying the model requires letting go of control and allowing for a range of language use and expression in the classroom. This could be uncomfortable for some.

- Concepts of equity and social justice embedded in the model may challenge strongly held beliefs about meritocracy, color-blindness, etc.
- One is being asked to apply a new model that may conflict with previous training or assumptions about effective teaching. This may require changing existing schemas.
- If one's actions have previously marginalized students, this model requires honest reckoning and change. The realization could cause discomfort.

If this book is being used in a formal course, the facilitator should anticipate cognitive dissonance and equip teacher candidates to work through it constructively. The goal is expanding awareness and promoting inclusive practices. If working independently, it will be best to pause again to reflect upon these points and plan next steps accordingly.

Summary

In closing, this chapter has explored differing perspectives on how humans acquire and learn language, centering on the dichotomy between analytical and gestalt processing patterns. While the former pattern has historically been privileged in English language teaching, evidenced in the predominance of phonics and grammar-based approaches, the latter, which is common among neurodivergent groups, has too often been pathologized or simply left unsupported.

The key takeaway going forward is that both analytical and gestalt pathways represent valid, natural means of developing linguistic aptitude, albeit via different mechanisms. Rather than impose a one-size-fits-all model derived from neurotypical norms, truly inclusive pedagogy must acknowledge and nurture the strengths of divergent learners.

As we'll discover in the chapters that follow, practical steps toward this vision include using scaffolded social interaction, play-based learning, and multisensory environmental print to build essential language scripts and vocabulary. Ongoing formative assessment should emphasize authentic, context-driven communication over decontextualized subskills. Most crucially, neurodiverse students require patient accommodation of their learning timeline, capitalizing on strengths like visual-spatial skills and verbal memory.

With concerted effort, education systems can shift toward celebrating both windows and mirrors in the journey toward English fluency, leveraging varied perspectives to advance literacy for all. This ultimately promises a more empowered, skilled generation equipped to transpose their gifts into lifelong success.

2
Deconstructing the Science of Reading

Learning objective

Students will analyze the principles of the Science of Reading (SOR) and evaluate how its structured, skills-based approach supports or challenges language learners.

> "The limits of my language mean the limits of my world."
> – Ludwig Wittgenstein, in *Tractatus Logico-Philosophicus*, Proposition 5.6.

Rationale

The learning objective aligns to the Common Core standard CCSS.ELA-LITERACY.SL.11-12.4, which provides a relevant framework for learners to present their evaluation of the Science of Reading approach for language learners. This standard stresses presenting information and evidence in a way that conveys perspective while still addressing opposing views in an organized, substantive style appropriate for the audience and task. To meet this standard, students could create a presentation that clearly outlines their perspective on how the Science of Reading's approach supports or challenges language learners. They would need to support this perspective with specific evidence and findings from their analysis of texts and research on the Science of Reading as well as key principles for language acquisition. The presentation would need to follow a logical reasoning progression and address counter-perspectives or critiques regarding use of the Science of Reading. Students would need to develop the content with sufficient depth and detail, using an objective, academic tone suited to an education audience. In these ways, the Common Core Speaking and Listening standard provides a framework for a presentation that requires students to synthesize and evaluate evidence to convey their perspective in an organized, reasoned, and cognizant manner regarding the implications of the Science of Reading for language learners. The standard aligns closely to the learning goal's emphasis on analysis and evaluation.

Introduction

If you are veteran teacher, a new teacher, an aspiring teacher, or a parent of a school-aged child, you've likely heard of the Science of Reading (SOR). Indeed, in my journey to the classroom, and in professional development sessions since (Hoerricks, 2023c), this so-called science is often presented rather uncritically as gospel. The SOR is often paired with terms like "evidence-based" or "research-based" in reporting or in marketing statements. Unfortunately, very little discussion or questioning is ever allowed as to just what type of evidence or research underpins the SOR. Yet, it's vital that we ask such questions. As such, it's there where we'll start our exploration.

Elsewhere in my professional life, I happen to be the founder and CEO of an autism support charity known as the Towcester Abbey Praeceptory, or the Abbey for short. There, one of the many services we provide to the community is a free and independent Institutional Review Board (IRB). An IRB is a committee that reviews and approves or rejects research involving human subjects to ensure the research aligns with ethical standards.

Traditional IRBs are internal committees at research institutions, while independent IRBs like the Abbey's operate externally without institutional pressure or bias. This allows an independent IRB to better prioritize ethical considerations and provide more rigorous protections for human research subjects.

To legally approve and monitor biomedical and behavioral research in the US, an independent IRB needs authorization from the Department of Health and Human Services, which involves developing strong policies and procedures, ensuring expertise in various disciplines, and demonstrating capacity to thoroughly review research protocols and informed consent.

Me being me, with my naturally curious autistic brain, and being the Abbey's trained and certified IRB Chairperson, I approached the whole discussion of the SOR as actual science with a ton of skepticism. What I discovered shocked me – in every case, I found that companies had conducted behavioral research on students outside of IRB guidance.

Now, you might be thinking, "So what? What's the problem with these vendors conducting their research without someone like you poking about?" It turns out there's a very good reason IRBs exist, especially independent IRBs, with people like me asking tough questions.

Consider the premise that underpins the evidence in these so-called evidence-based interventions. The evidence, in every case, was a behavioral research study conducted with human subjects to ascertain if the intervention had the desired effect – an increase in some skill or other. To do this scientifically, control groups are established, students are randomly assigned, and the groups are assigned the intervention under consideration or either no intervention or a treatment known to researchers to be not "as good" as the one proposed.

Now put yourself in a parent's shoes. Your child's teacher sends a note home. The note explains that your consent is needed for your child to participate in a behavioral research study investigating the efficacy of a particular reading intervention. In legal / scientific language, the note lists the potential harms to your child. In this case, the harm is that they may be assigned randomly to the control group and thus be mal-educated for the study's duration. Would you sign such a form (Hoerricks, 2023c)? As an IRB Chairperson, there's no way I would let such a research study's design touch actual human subjects—children—with our approval.

The legal landscape

Thus it is, with this information in mind, that we begin our journey towards holistic language instruction with a deconstruction of the so-called SOR. Rather than rely upon my own authority as an IRB Chair, or my lived experience, to structure and perform this deconstruction, we will rely upon the frameworks and methods of one of the world's foremost philosophers and semioticians. But more on that later in the chapter.

The SOR refers to methods for teaching reading, with a focus on phonics, phonemic awareness, fluency, vocabulary, and comprehension (Hall, 1976; Kingston, 1968; Stammer, 1979). It is certainly not new. However, it has gained significant popularity and influence in English-speaking education systems in the last few decades.

In the United States, the SOR has been promoted by various national advisory panels and advocacy groups since at least the mid-1960s (Chall, 1977). Many US states have passed laws or policies requiring teachers to be trained in the SOR's techniques and practices. Mississippi, for example, passed the "Mississippi Literacy-Based Promotion Act" in 2013, which mandated training in research-based reading instruction for K-3 teachers. This includes training in phonics, phonemic awareness, fluency, vocabulary, and comprehension (Jackson Public School District, 2023). Ohio passed a dyslexia screening and intervention bill in 2021 that requires teachers to complete a reading instruction training program based on the SOR (Ohio Department of Education, 2023). Tennessee passed a law in 2021 requiring elementary teacher preparation programs to include instruction in "reading science" and dyslexia. New elementary teachers must pass a test on knowledge and practices of "scientific reading" instruction (Tennessee Department of Education, 2023). Arkansas passed Act 1063 in 2017 requiring teachers to be trained in the SOR and which includes explicit, systematic phonics instruction. New teachers must pass a foundations of reading exam (Arkansas Department of Education, 2018).

Several other states like Florida, Connecticut, and Oregon have also passed bills or policies aimed at improving teacher training in the SOR and structured literacy methods in recent years. The focus, according to policymakers, is on making sure teachers are well versed in proven, research-based reading instruction practices.

In my state, California, there is not currently a state-wide law that mandates teacher training in the SOR as such. However, there are some relevant efforts and policies here. In 2018, the California State Board of Education approved a comprehensive literacy framework for K-12 public schools. It highlights research on how children learn to read and calls for all teachers to be knowledgeable in SOR instruction. However, there is no mandate tied to this framework (California Department of Education, 2018). In 2019, a bill was introduced in the California legislature called the California Right to Literacy Act. It would have required preservice and in-service training for K-3 teachers in reading instruction grounded in scientific research on literacy. This bill did not pass. It did, however, result in a lawsuit that questioned whether students have a right to literacy. That lawsuit was eventually settled with moneys promised to improve the state of reading instruction in the state, but no "right" was enshrined in law (California School Boards Association, 2020; Cano, 2020).

We do, however, have a section of our Education Code that requires the California Commission on Teacher Credentialing (CTC) to "develop, adopt, and administer a reading instruction competence assessment ... to measure an individual's knowledge, skill, and ability relative to effective reading instruction" (FindLaw, 2023). That mandate became the Reading Instruction Competence Assessment®, or RICA® test. The stated purpose of the RICA®, from its publisher, is "to ensure that California candidates for Multiple Subject Teaching Credentials and Education Specialist Instruction Credentials (special education) possess the knowledge and skills important for the provision of effective reading instruction to students" (California Teacher Credentialing Examinations, 2023).

Anecdotally, the RICA® is the most feared of all the standardized tests that teachers must pass in California. As I write this, I am studying to take this test as part of the final steps towards attaining a lifetime, or Clear teaching credential (Level 2). I've used text-based study materials (Rossi and Schipper, 2012; Zarrillo, 2017) as well as web-based solutions. The materials make the RICA sound quite matter of fact. Yet, the first-time passing rate is a mere 66 per cent (Lindenmuth., 2023). I've sat in preparation sessions hosted by my employer with fellow teachers who have failed the test multiple times and are in a panic around the deadline to pass this test. Teachers in California have five years to progress from their Level 1 teaching credential to the Level 2, Clear credential. Failure to complete all the elements in those five years results in a return to the beginning of the process and another trip through internship.

I know my own struggles with studying for this test lay in the disconnect between what I know works for me as a GLP learner and my GLP students and how I must answer questions for the test. The best test prep service I've been able to find contains tons of disclaimers like, "This is how they want you to respond on that kind of question". Added to my struggles of memorizing inaccurate information to respond to purposefully tricky multiple-choice questions are the written response questions. There, the test presents case files of struggling students, with the test taker asked to evaluate the problems and suggest solutions from the SOR marketplace. I've been told that I read too much into the questions, and thus get them wrong when I don't offer a superficial response that notes the appropriate application of the SOR for the student. Might there be a validity problem with such a test?

Elsewhere in the world, the 2016 Rose Report in the United Kingdom recommended systematic synthetic phonics as the primary approach for teaching reading (Department for Education, 2006). Phonics screening checks for all Year 1 students were introduced in 2012. The use of phonics is widespread in the UK, though some debate exists around ensuring a balanced literacy curriculum (Double et al., 2019). In Australia, the SOR has been promoted by organizations like MultiLit (MultiLit, 2023). There, the government initiated a phonics test for all Year 1 students in 2021. Explicit phonics instruction is part of the national English curriculum (NSW Education Standards Authority, 2023). However, approaches vary between states and schools. In Canada, there is also an increased focus on the SOR led by researchers like Dr Timothy Shanahan (Shanahan, 2012). Several provinces have implemented phonics screening (Hobbs, 2022). However, whole language approaches remain common, creating disagreements like the so-called "reading wars" in the US (Kim, 2008).

With all this emphasis on reading instruction and literacy, one would think that literacy rates in the western world would be near 100 per cent. Unfortunately, this is not the case. With all the money spent, and all the emphasis placed on literacy, the US, for example, has only reached an overall literacy rate of 86 per cent (World Atlas, 2023). This number, and my lived experience, hint at an underlying problem with the methods used to address literacy. More on that later. But first, let's explore the SOR and get to know it at face value before beginning our deconstruction.

The Science of Reading

According to the literature, the SOR refers to the vast body of research that has accumulated over decades from various scientific fields to attempt to understand how the ability to read develops, why some struggle, and how reading is best taught. It involves elements of cognitive psychology, developmental psychology, educational psychology, linguistics, neuroscience, genetics, intervention science, classroom teaching experiments, and literacy assessments. Here in the US, most teachers learn about the SOR in relation to an evolution of thought on the subject that seemingly began with the Simple View of Reading (SVR). This term was first described by Gough and Tunmer (1986), and later supported with data by Hoover and Gough (1990). The SVR's influence has been building in educational policy and practice around the west. It's been cited in well over 5,000 papers (Nation, 2019). But more importantly, it gave rise to the work of Scarborough and the creation of Scarborough's Reading Rope (Duke and Cartwright, 2021).

Scarborough's Reading Rope

Dr Hollis Scarborough (2001) built upon Gough and Tunmer's model, expanding upon the explanation of the types of skills involved in decoding and comprehension, to create her Reading Rope. Her rope metaphor and graphics convey her theory of the integrated, intertwined nature of reading subskills. The Reading

Rope and the SOR are often used interchangeably in professional development sessions and teacher training classrooms. Both models fall on the structured literacy side of the "reading wars" argument (Kerns, 2021).

Scarborough's 2001 article "Connecting early language and literacy to later reading (dis)abilities: Evidence, theory, and practice," published in the *Handbook of Early Literacy Research*, reviewed research on the developmental precursors and pathways related to skilled reading and reading disabilities. It discussed links between early language development, pre-literacy skills, and later literacy outcomes. It suggested that strong early language and verbal abilities facilitate later reading acquisition. It highlighted phonological awareness as a pivotal precursor skill for decoding. Deficits in phonological awareness, she noted, are often associated with early reading difficulties. The article outlines the multiple "strands" involved in skilled reading as depicted in her Reading Rope model while emphasizing that reading relies on the integration of the "strands", or the many cognitive and linguistic skills.

With the emphasis on solving reading problems, Scarborough reviewed evidence that deficiencies in any "strand" can impede a student's reading development. Early difficulties in language, phonological awareness, or print concepts, for example, may foreshadow later reading problems, in her view.

She pointed to effective early instruction and intervention as the key components that can promote successful reading acquisition and help prevent reading disabilities. To that end, she advocated for early identification of at-risk children and targeted instruction in early literacy skills as the path to skilled reading for all children.

Overall, her article synthesized the available research at the time in the West on connections between early skills, later literacy, and effective instruction, underscoring the importance of a comprehensive early literacy curriculum.

Putting the typical graphic that is used in training into words, the Reading Rope is made up of multiple "strands" that are woven together, each representing a different skill (Scarborough, 2001). The strands are grouped first into Language Comprehension (usually shown as the upper group) and Word Recognition (the lower group).

Language Comprehension strands

- Background knowledge – using what you already know about a topic to help you understand what you're reading.
- Vocabulary – understanding the meanings of words.
- Language structures – understanding grammar rules and sentence structures.
- Verbal reasoning – being able to get meaning from context clues.
- Literacy knowledge – understanding features of print, like reading left to right.

With the Language Comprehension strands, Scarborough notes that learners become increasingly strategic in their use of these skills as they become more proficient in this area.

Word Recognition

- Phonological awareness – being able to hear and manipulate the sounds in words. This includes rhyming, blending sounds, and breaking words into syllables.

- Decoding – being able to sound out written words by knowing the relationships between letters and sounds. This involves skillfully using the rules of phonics.
- Sight recognition – being able to automatically recognize familiar words by sight.

With the Word Recognition strands, Scarborough notes that learners become increasingly automatic in their use of these skills as they become more proficient in this area.

All these strands are said to work together seamlessly in skilled readers. A weakness in any strand, she notes, can hinder overall reading ability. The rope graphic is meant to represent how readers integrate and coordinate the different skills.

When it all goes wrong

Having now taught across the K-12 grades in the US, as well as having my own experiences as a student, I've seen what happens when students fall behind their grade-level peers in their reading abilities. Teachers, sometimes using data to inform instruction, double down on the SOR and implement approved interventions in the hope of bringing students back to par. Intervention after intervention is applied, testing is performed, and time marches on. Yet a large segment of the student population in systems that use a structured reading approach continue to get left behind.

In the US, if the student continues to struggle, they may receive an evaluation by a team of specialists and be assigned an Individualized Educational Plan (IEP). Usually, problems with language learning are assigned to the Specific Learning Disability (SLD) category. SLD means a person has trouble with basic skills like reading, writing, math, listening, or speaking. This is because of the way in which their brain works, not because of something else like poor eyesight, hearing issues, or emotional problems (each of those have their own eligibility criteria). Students with the SLD eligibility for special education services might have trouble with things like dyslexia (reading), dyscalculia (math), or dysgraphia (writing) (Grigorenko et al., 2020).

It's important to note that special education eligibilities are not diagnoses. In the US, school staff cannot provide diagnoses. Here, as elsewhere in the world, only doctors and certain other professions can legally provide a diagnosis of a disorder. The types of professionals that can diagnose disabling conditions vary by country. It's also important to note that a student generally receives a single eligibility for services. That eligibility is usually based upon what is causing the system the most issues at the time of the evaluation. In my case, given my medical history, with ADHD, autism, and being a GLP learner, I could conceivably receive an Other Health Impairment (OHI) for my ADHD, Autism, (AUT), or SLD eligibility for services if I were a K-12 student now. But I would only get one eligibility. If I was given the AUT eligibility because of behavioral / communication issues, I wouldn't be eligible to receive the language services that the SLD eligibility provides. It's a huge problem, but one I hope will be remedied—at least for language issues—by properly informing teachers and engaging in actual science in developing students' reading skills.

Where's the science in the Science of Reading?

You see, if the SOR was in fact science, some uncomfortable conversations would have taken place decades ago. In science, inquiry usually starts with discovering and exploring. Data get collected and interpreted. Assumptions get tested and improved. Conflicting information gets investigated. Feedback from stakeholders is received and gets processed. All this activity aims to refine the expected result of the inquiry (Hoerricks, 2023b). In scientific research involving human subjects, IRBs are necessarily involved to protect participants. As we've seen, that doesn't seem to happen with the research around the SOR (Hoerricks, 2023c).

The SOR doesn't seem to follow a recognizably scientific pattern. It starts with a fairly solid view of language acquisition, then throws out one of the two types of human language acquisition to focus exclusively on ALP. GLP learners are assigned the "(dis) abled" label and largely ignored as problematic in the general education classroom. Those with the privilege of place or wealth may get an IEP that addresses their "deficits" and offers some support. Others, like me in my youth, are simply promoted through graduation … remaining largely functionally illiterate.

Considering that gestalt processing has been known and studied in the West since at least the early 1980s (Prizant, 1983), there's no excuse for the current paradigm. The Reading Rope and the SOR describe a process that about 60 per cent of the student population can use effectively (Blanc, 2012). What about the other 40 per cent? How and why does the SOR fail the GLP learners, like me? Questions like these require a thorough deconstruction of its underlying premises and assumptions, before we embark on a path towards improvement.

To accomplish this, we'll first examine how and why things go wrong for GLP learners engaging with the SOR. Then, the rest of the book will focus on how to make things right for all our language learners.

What is deconstruction?

The SOR is often put forward as the best model for teaching reading. However, it should be examined critically as a conceptual framework rather than solid science. The SOR did not come from controlled experiments – it is Scarborough's framework based on her experience. So, it serves more as a teaching guide than a proven theory.

Using ideas from French-Algerian philosopher Jacques Derrida (2020) allows us to challenge the assumptions and binary oppositions in the SOR. This involves looking at the historical background and metaphors like the Reading Rope, which highlight some aspects of reading while hiding others. We can question the SOR's focus on speech over writing and its search for external "quick fixes" rather than meaning-making. The goal is to establish new, more inclusive views on reading teaching.

Derrida's semiotic view of language as an unstable system of signs is relevant too (Chandler, 1994). Standardized reading tests assume right and wrong answers, which clashes with how meaning happens in context through cultural codes. Critiquing the SOR should challenge how such tests define reading ability from a narrow perspective.

The SOR puts forth a particular philosophical stance on reading instruction, falsely presenting itself as scientifically authoritative. Examining it critically using Derrida's ideas can acknowledge the diversity of meanings, languages, and learners in the classroom.

This kind of critique calls for more open and inclusive approaches to reading teaching, as we will see.

How the Science of Reading can fail the gestalt processor

From a deconstructionist and semiotic perspective, there are potential critiques about how the dominant views in and behind the SOR can fail GLP learners. First, the focus on bottom-up phonics and decoding rules does not align with the gestalt emphasis on grasping meaning holistically through pattern recognition. Second, the linear skill hierarchies presumed in the stage models as represented by the Reading Rope do not reflect the complex contextual processing of meaning in the gestalt processing mind. Next, the treatment of text as conveying stable meaning clashes with the semiotic and gestalt view of meaning as shifting and interpretative. Additionally, the goal of achieving automaticity through repeated subskills practice is at odds with the situational adaptiveness that is a strength of gestalt systems (Blanc et al., 2023).

Fundamentally, the conception of reading as extracting meaning imposed by the author contradicts the semiotic view of active meaning-making by the reader. The reductionist focus on mastering decoding skills overlooks how meaning emerges from broader pragmatics and usage events – another strength of gestalt systems. The emphasis on universal developmental trajectories and one-size-fits-all approaches, ignores the diversity of meanings constructed across contexts and cultures.

More pertinent to our central theme here, the SOR and its diagnostic testing regime atomize reading into discrete subskills rather than measuring **holistic language** use. In doing so, the SOR takes what should be a joyful experience and transforms it into drudgery.

Overall, deconstructionism and semiotics posit reading as a complex, inferential process grounded in social usage. In contrast, mainstream "reading science" often takes a technocratic, reductive view focused on skill accumulation. This diverges from the holistic, integrative nature of GLP (Robey, 1973; Sturrock, 2008), which is why it fails GLP learners like me so miserably.

Scarborough's Reading Rope – Language Comprehension

From this heavy introduction to the process, let's begin deconstructing the SOR with the reading comprehension aspects of the Reading Rope. In doing so, we'll see how GLP learners may struggle. We'll start with background knowledge.

When it comes to background knowledge, GLP learners tend to focus heavily on visual details and emotions in the words, while making logical inferences using prior understanding and reading "between the lines" feels less natural. Difficulties here can eventually inform a language processing disorder diagnosis, yet this assumes inference ability progresses via some standard trajectory, whereas in gestalt processing, as with cross-cultural contexts, meaning-making proves more subjective and context-dependent. Furthermore, background knowledge facilitates integrating and interpreting new information, but GLP learners often view texts more in isolation without recalling relevant connections, while divergent integration may actually stem from diverse backgrounds rather than some inherent neurological deficit; readings take shape per the reader's position and interests impacting integration. Likewise, tapping in to background knowledge helps readers anticipate upcoming content; however, tests indicate GLP learners predict less actively, as prediction gets construed as a skill driven solely by prior knowledge, whereas semiotics regards it as active meaning-making, not predetermined, with differences also stemming from varied interests and values across individuals. Additionally, entirely unfamiliar topics leave GLP leaners with scarce scaffolding to comprehend content, potentially overwhelming us and even causing meltdowns in autistic GLP learners, though confusion likewise arises from lacking awareness of norms and unwritten social rules; coping with unfamiliar topics thus involves learned practices and socialization, not just background knowledge. Finally, passage contradictions may go unnoticed or unreconciled by GLP learners due to more passive processing, while in autistic GLP learners, unresolved conflicts can spur hyper-focused attempts at resolution, often manifesting as "off-task behavior" and occasionally resulting in meltdowns. People also respond to inconsistencies differently based on attitudes toward establishment knowledge and conventions. Contradictions manifest from divergent expectations and values, not objectively. Uncritical acceptance of claims indicates socialization, not difficulty noticing contradictions per se (Bell, 1991; Finnegan and Accardo, 2018; Hoerricks, 2023a; Juul et al., 2014; Musiek, 1999; Noens and van Berckelaer-Onnes, 2005; Vulchanova and Vulchanov, 2022;).

Let's keep examining potential difficulties with language structures for GLP learners.

When it comes to language structures, GLP learners often focus more on overall meaning and may not fully process new grammar patterns, limiting understanding of complex sentences. Challenges arise when instruction overemphasizes abstract rules rather than meaning. Additionally, when focused on key words, GLP learners can overlook small but vital function words like articles, prepositions, and conjunctions that work pragmatically and semantically depending on context. Whether certain function words are needed depends on the surrounding text. Furthermore, the order and arrangement of words expresses meaning, yet GLP learners may miss nuanced subtleties due to more passive sentence processing. This happens when some syntactic structures get overemphasized. Pronoun confusion can also occur as connecting pronouns and antecedents requires analyzing sentence structure in ways that GLP learners may not grasp fully. Pronoun usage depends on understanding indexicality and how meaning depends on context, differences in which can stem from varied situational interpretations. Relative clauses starting with transition words like "that", "which", and "who" necessitate close syntactic attention that GLP learners often don't exhibit. Variations can manifest from diverse expectations, insights, and interests regarding linguistic sign possibilities, and this is especially prevalent in autistic GLP learners. Additionally, negation terminology can sometimes get overlooked during skimming, leading to meaning reversals, though inattention should not be automatically presumed given semiotic notions of selective attention influenced by interest, expectations, and values. Likewise, grasping how modifiers like adjectives and adverbs alter meaning relies on nuanced structure analysis that is less demonstrated by GLP learners, who process more holistically rather than through stepwise parsing. Finally, lengthy sentences featuring conjunctions, commas, and dependent clauses prove difficult for GLP learners to fully comprehend because, beyond syntax, multifaceted sentences also incorporate pragmatics, language use types, emotion, and idea synthesis. Ultimately, GLP learners' inclination to prioritize holistic meaning over meticulous language breakdown can engender comprehension gaps, chiefly with advanced syntax.

Intermission

Let's pause for a second. That was a lot of text to parse. To review, we examined potential reading comprehension difficulties for GLP learners through the lens of semiotics. We looked at how GLP learners may struggle with making inferences, integrating new information, predicting content, understanding unfamiliar topics, resolving contradictions, acquiring vocabulary, tracking pronouns, interpreting figurative language, using dictionaries, processing auditory language, forming word associations, managing memory load, learning grammar structures, noticing function words, recognizing syntax, comprehending pronouns and antecedents, analyzing relative clauses, processing negatives, understanding modifiers, and parsing complex sentences. It's important to note how these challenges arise not necessarily from cognitive deficits, but from differing socialization experiences, cultural orientations, modal affinities, and meaning-making practices compared to analytic processors. The use of semiotics in our analysis helps us to recognize reading as an active process of meaning-making relying on the reader's positionality, experiences, and interests. Ultimately, we find that a GLP learner's holistic processing can lead to comprehension gaps, especially with more complex language.

Continuing

Verbal reasoning, often tested through CLOZE reading exercises, significantly challenges GLP learners. CLOZE tasks require filling in missing words systematically deleted from a passage. Research shows GLP learners tend to struggle more on CLOZE tasks versus ALP peers.

Further analysis reveals factors contributing to GLP learners' CLOZE difficulties. First, CLOZE needs strong inference skills to determine contextually fitting words. GLP learners may falter if less experienced with nuanced inferencing. Additionally, CLOZE often omits function words like pronouns and prepositions. Sensitivity to these grammar connectors aids CLOZE success, but GLP learners' verbal strengths sometimes coincide with weaker grammar. Finally, CLOZE presents isolated words devoid of rich context. GLP learners' strong vocabularies don't help as much without ample contextual support. Thus, CLOZE challenges GLP learners by separating words from meaning, prioritizing grammar, and requiring tight inferential thinking. Addressing these areas may assist GLP learners in reaching their verbal potential (Trassi and Oliveira, 2019).

When it comes to additional verbal reasoning challenges, GLP learners tend to focus heavily on the explicit, while making inferences using logic, reason, and intuition proves less natural. Yet inference relies not just on reasoning but on assumed ideologies, backgrounds, values, affects, etc., highlighting the need for culturally relevant assessments. Similarly, interpreting figurative language like metaphors and idioms requires deducing non-literal meanings, whereas gestalt approaches interpret more concretely, even though figurative expressions depend on conceptual metaphors, cultural frames, shared affects, and ideological assumptions. Additionally, evaluating argument chains, evidence, and fallacies necessitates active analysis less demonstrated by GLP learners, while struggles occur when instruction presents language as purely logical and rule-based rather than fundamentally persuasive. Framing analysis as universally right versus subjective promotes certain analytical standards matching mainstream modes tied to specific ideologies and power structures. Grasping unstated ironic or sarcastic intent also relies on reading between the lines, with nuances often missed by GLP learners, as irony and sarcasm hinge on incongruity, framing, implicit attitudes, and cultural assumptions. Connecting ideas and rhetorical points requires reasoning skills to synthesize information, but gestalt processing focuses more narrowly. Presenting idea connections as factual rather than interpreted can cause challenges here as well. Making predictions also suffers as using logic and available information to anticipate upcoming text content proves diminished among GLP learners, with divergent expectations based on cultural models and values affecting predictive differences too. Likewise, reasoning chronologically about events and consequences seems harder for GLP learners, who concentrate less on order and connections, as perceived event order relies not just on chronology but on assumed frames of time, causation, and continuity. For autistic GLP learners especially, this relates heavily to the personal view of events versus the Quality World Picture, given autistic perceptions of time and temporality starkly differ from neurotypical perspectives (Hoerricks, 2023a).

The more passive gestalt processing style makes complex verbal analysis and reasoning tasks more difficult. GLP learners tend to focus narrowly on details rather than connections and inferences. Teaching methods promoting predictions, questions, summarizing, and personal connections provide a better way to build stronger inferential skills. Instruction solely focused on passive intake and memorization without thoughtful analysis diminishes higher-level comprehension, especially for GLP learners. Explicitly teaching reasoning strategies provides scaffolding to strengthen analytical and inferential capacities over time.

When it comes to literacy knowledge, GLP learners face certain challenges learning to read (Palincsar and Duke, 2004). Grasping concepts like print conveying meaning with left-to-right text flow and books having titles relies on explicit instruction less naturally absorbed by GLP learners, while conventions also differ cross-culturally (e.g., Japan). Acquiring alphabet knowledge—letter names, shapes, and order—needs focused study that is less intuitive for holistic processors. Sustained concentration also proves difficult due to limited attention spans, distractions, variable cognitive load, and interests, further hindered by additional factors like memory overload, task switching, and technology overstimulation that hamper single task or topic focus. Learning capitalization rules develops through print attention and is potentially overlooked by GLP learners as ubiquitous autocorrect now handles this function. Noticing and understanding punctuation purposes with periods, commas, etc. relies on print focus that is less prioritized by GLP learners, again with modern technology enabling lack of practice. Distinguishing features and purposes of various genres including stories, poems, and essays requires active teaching, while GLP learners' passive intake style risks genre confusion; recognizing genre itself often demands meta-awareness about content nature and intended purpose, which is less exhibited by passive processors. Discerning organizational structures like narrative stages, compare-contrast layouts, and problem-solution necessitates print focus, whereas gestalt approaches concentrate more narrowly on content, reducing cognitive load yet still risking overwhelm with excessive structural attention, especially in unfamiliar or complex texts. Graphic elements may also get overlooked as gestalt processors typically prioritize textual content for comprehension, while processing visuals exacts greater cognitive effort; attempting to decipher illustrations and diagrams alongside text biases linguistic emphasis, relegating graphics to secondary interpretive status.

We can often see struggling GLP learners using visual memory, guesswork, and grasping global meaning to navigate books. This can cause literacy knowledge gaps if essential print concepts aren't explicitly taught and internalized. A proactive, print-centric approach safeguards against deficit development by ensuring robust structural / foundational written language understanding, promoting comprehensive literacy.

Scarborough's Reading Rope – Word Recognition

Moving on to the other set of strands in the Reading Rope, it's important to remember that GLP learners tend to use a whole-word approach to language rather than analyzing component sounds and parts. We tend to rely more on sight recognition and guesswork rather than phonetic decoding when reading. As such, we may struggle with certain aspects of phonological awareness, which is the ability to detect and manipulate the sounds within words.

With this in mind, let's explore potential phonological awareness difficulties for GLP learners (Lindamood et al., 1992). When it comes to phoneme segmentation—breaking words into individual sounds like segmenting "cat" into /c/-/a/-/t/—favoring whole words means GLP learners may have trouble isolating and analyzing distinct sounds. Recognizing and distinguishing phonemes also requires precise auditory discrimination, which can be tough for some, especially in noisy or complex environments. Similarly, with phoneme blending—combining sounds to make words as in blending /p/-/e/-/n/ to say "pen"—GLP learners can struggle to assemble sounds together. Auditory issues also conspire against success here. Additionally, a general reliance on contextual guessing cues makes GLP learners less likely to focus on the isolated sounds within words needed for blending. Phoneme deletion poses other challenges – removing a sound, like saying "beach" without /b/ to make "each". Consciously dropping sounds is difficult for GLP learners. Phoneme deletion requires temporarily manipulating phonemic info in working memory, which is demanding for those with limited capacity or experiencing memory overload. Finally, phoneme manipulation involves substituting or reordering sounds to change words – like switching the /p/ in "pet" to /s/ to form "set". This requires breaking apart and rebuilding words in unfamiliar ways. Phoneme manipulation depends on focused attention to auditory distinctions between phonemes that some individuals cannot allocate sufficiently to perform the task effectively. Thus, GLP learners' natural inclination toward holistic language processing focused on meanings rather than individual phonemic components makes tasks like isolating, identifying, and manipulating phonemes within spoken language challenging. This is especially true if we have minimal phonics or phonemic awareness training or, like me, also cope with auditory processing issues.

When it comes to decoding, GLP learners may struggle in various areas (Alexander et al., 1991). As we rely more on visual memory, systematically linking letters to sounds proves difficult. Learning phonics rules and sound-letter patterns requires phonological word analysis. Moreover, visual data often takes priority in human perception, diverting attention from auditory aspects including precise sound-symbol relationships in text, posing particular challenges for those with learning disabilities like dyslexia. Blending unfamiliar words also relies on decoding individual sound-symbol correspondences together, a phonemic skill, whereas GLP learners tend to process words holistically rather than sound-by-sound. Additionally, unfamiliar or infrequent tasks rarely become automatic, while automaticity links to well-practiced, routine activities, so with limited phonics abilities, GLPs must visually memorize many words, vastly hindering automatic word recognition. Furthermore, high anxiety or stress impairs performing tasks automatically, so individuals in stressful situations like exams may struggle to shift from conscious to automatic processing. Longer multisyllabic words require decoding syllable by syllable, but GLP learners tend to guess words from partial visual cues instead of methodically decoding each part, and these words often convey complex concepts potentially less familiar to GLP learners. Nonsense words also lack meaningful context to infer pronunciation or meaning from existing patterns or vocabulary. Decoding made-up words like "frip" relies solely on phonics, not sight memory, proving extremely difficult. Moreover, assessments commonly deploy nonsense words, and test anxiety adds further challenges to already unfamiliar, non-meaningful terms. Homophones like "hair" and "hare" also confuse GLP learners who rely heavily on meaning cues, creating written and spoken ambiguity; hence if context remains unclear, we may fail to select the correct homophone fitting the sentence meaning. Finally, pig-Latin-style tasks manipulating sounds pose great difficulty for gestalt processors who struggle to segment and blend phonemes, with working memory and attention allocation frequently conspiring against success here, as throughout the Reading Rope framework. Essentially, GLP learners' visual and holistic language processing can hinder acquiring decoding skills rooted in phonics and phonemic awareness. Our strengths lie in meaning-focused reading rather than dissecting words into sounds. Consequently, while comprehending overall messages, we may encounter difficulties breaking words into phonemes and applying phonics rules to accurately decode new or complex terms.

Concluding our deconstruction of the Science of Reading, we finish with sight recognition of words. When it comes to sight word recognition, GLP learners may struggle in various areas (Aaron et al., 1999). As we rely on visually memorizing words, reading unfamiliar terms not in our limited sight vocabulary proves difficult, restricted by attention and working memory capacities that can increase with age, although requiring greater dependence on contextual cues to convey or understand meaning in the interim. Acquiring new words also takes repeated exposure before GLP learners commit them to memory, making building a substantial sight vocabulary gradual and effortful, as evidenced by my personal journey from functional illiteracy to achieved literacy in my thirties. Additionally, words with similar appearances like "was" and "saw" confuse GLP learners trying to distinguish them by sight alone, as subtle visual differences can blend per the gestalt principle of grouping like elements. GLP learners often unconsciously form mental shortcuts, assuming similar meanings or associations when words look alike, potentially causing confusion. Homophones and homographs also pose challenges, as identical sounds or spellings with different meanings make accurate sight reading difficult without phonics cues. Moreover, surrounding context influences specific interpretation, which GLP learners may overlook by prioritizing holistic context rather than scrutinizing individual words. Longer multi-syllabic terms also prove harder to memorize visually. Breaking them into recognizable chunks counters the gestalt approach. Irregular words like "yacht" with atypical letter-sound patterns require robust visual memory and repeated exposure; otherwise limited encounters hinder recognition. Gestalt processors may also reverse similar letters when relying on fallible visual recall rather than attend to fine details like letter orientation. Confusing left and right can extend to letter reversals between mirroring shapes. Finally, lacking decoding skills means individuals depend completely on memorization and word recognition. This impedes reading unfamiliar or complex words without a decoding system to supplement sight reading. In summary, GLP learners' visual memory dependence and holistic word recognition pose notable difficulties in developing flexible, proficient sight word reading, as expeditious whole-word recognition prevents readily and accurately reading new terms not committed to memory. Targeted instruction combining holistic and analytical word analysis strategies could help GLP learners become more adaptable, proficient sight word readers; we'll cover that later in the book.

Check for understanding

How are you doing? Were there any words or terms that you didn't understand? I'll bet there were quite a few. Pause a beat. Reflect. As before, go over your notes. Look up unknown words and add their definitions to your notes or in the margins.

This deep dive was necessary. Many slick marketing campaigns on the SOR bandwagon throw out the big, complex terms to confound and confuse. The previous sections were necessarily dense. It is my hope that in contextualizing these terms, you will have the tools to discern on your own when or if a particular intervention might be helpful for your students.

Nevertheless, did you notice any patterns or themes in the deconstruction? When I first began to dive into this subject, exploring why my system operates as it does, I discovered some common themes.

- Being a GLP learner requires an incredible amount of energy to maintain the memory space necessary to meaningfully engage with language. The less energy I have, the less "verbal" I can be.
- There is significant anxiety created in choosing the correct word or phrase to convey complex ideas. In tasks requiring long and complicated sentences and paragraphs, this anxiety is additive, often leading to meltdowns.
- We often rely upon echolalia to communicate when we are young. Transferring this bank of words and phrases to print takes considerable time and effort.
- When the sensory load is low, we can better concentrate on verbal tasks.

In my own studies, I chose to engage with semiotics to help me to understand the complexity of this issue. Did the inclusion of semiotic viewpoints within some of the elements of the deconstruction help you to clarify the issues surrounding the item under review? If so, how? If not, why not?

Hold on a minute!

"But, Dr Hoerricks," you might say, "I'm looking at a flyer from my favorite intervention vendor, and it clearly shows an 'ESSA Level 3' tag, which indicates that the intervention vendor has the evidence that it works. Surely the vendor can't just be part of the SOR bandwagon. Can it?"

Thus far, we've taken a logical look at the SOR. We've made arguments about how its approaches might leave entire populations of students behind. But you're right. Your eyes don't deceive you. There are vendors in the education marketplace that make claims, backed by studies and reports, that allow them to qualify their intervention for government funding in the US under the Elementary and Secondary Education Act (ESEA). A "Level 3" tag would indicate that the intervention meets the "Tier 3" evidence level under the Every Student Succeeds Act (ESSA), that of being supported by one or more well-designed and well-implemented correlational studies and containing statistical controls for selection bias. That's a very important condition, and one for which the implications are quite shocking when you consider them, as we did at the beginning of this chapter.

You see, as Ginsberg (2022) notes, the ESSA in the US aims to protect students from potential harm and wasted resources by requiring that educational agencies invest federal funds in interventions and practices supported by evidence of effectiveness. The ESSA stipulates that activities and programs funded by certain streams of federal education dollars must have at least one well-designed and well-implemented study (experimental, quasi-experimental, or correlational) demonstrating improvements in student outcomes. This evidentiary requirement is intended as a safeguard against implementing unproven or ineffective interventions that could potentially damage student learning, motivation, or wellbeing. The ESSA encourages reliance on objective evidence over subjective judgments or perceived merits in choosing activities to fund, increasing the likelihood that investments will benefit students as intended. While not mandating consideration of a full body of evidence, the tiered evidence definitions in ESSA (in our case, Tier 3) represent an attempt to steer spending toward vetted solutions and away from ineffective or even harmful options lacking an evidence base. Overall, the law aims to incentivize careful examination of supportive research and evaluative data before expending federal education funds on interventions, reflecting heightened policy attention to protecting student welfare.

But therein lies the problem. Again, most don't understand the implications of the ESSA tiers as they relate to studies conducted on human subjects. As we've seen, these human subjects are young children, Remember, interventions often target the grades TK-3.

Consider again that a well-designed experiment will contain a control group. The control group will not get the treatment under study. It will usually get nothing or some placebo. In educational research, the control group may maintain the status quo for their classroom while the treatment group gets the new, as yet untested intervention.

Now, remember what must happen for this research design to be ethically conducted. First, as most of these interventions begin with a single teacher's success with their students, and thus should be considered "action research", the research design should be presented to an independent IRB. The IRB would then review the design, checking for things like informed consent. Since children cannot provide informed consent in the US, their parents must have signed a consent form. To be compliant with the laws and regulations here in the US that govern the testing of human subjects, those born out of the atrocities of the Nazi camps, the risks of harm to the study's participants must be clearly stated.

At the risk of seeming repetitive, informed consent is a critical ethical and legal requirement in any human subject research designed to protect participants, especially vulnerable populations like children, from harm. For research involving children, researchers must obtain consent from the parents or legal guardians, who serve as gatekeepers for the children under their guardianship. Parents must be provided with a detailed consent form that explains all key aspects of the study in an understandable manner, including:

- The purpose and procedures of the research;
- Any reasonably foreseeable risks, harms, or discomforts;
- The potential benefits children may experience;
- How confidentiality will be maintained; and
- That participation is voluntary and can be halted at any time without penalty.

The consent form should clearly disclose the study design, procedures, time commitment, and any other expectations or consequences of participating. It should emphasize that parents can decline to enroll their child or withdraw at any time.

By explaining the study in plain language, including a translation when needed, consent forms enable parents to carefully consider the risks and benefits when deciding whether to grant permission for their child to participate. Researchers are obligated to adhere to any parameters outlined in the consent throughout the study. This empowers parents to be informed advocates who can safeguard children's welfare in human subject research (Grady, 2015).

Obtaining voluntary, informed parental consent protects children who cannot legally provide full consent themselves. It aims to minimize any risk of manipulated, coerced, or unknowing participation that could psychologically or physically harm a child. Researchers must be transparent and grant parental control over children's research involvement. Overall, consent requirements, with parents as gatekeepers, are a key human subject protection for minor populations (Albright and Harnett, 2022).

As a parent of six wonderful children, this means that I would have to consent to letting my child potentially participate in a placebo group, assigning them to a low or no growth trajectory. Clearly, those conducting the study (often so-called "evidence mills") intend to demonstrate the effectiveness of their treatment versus what the school is currently doing or against some competing product that the researchers believe to be inferior to the new treatment. An IRB must first sign off on a design that will consign half of the treatment group of young children to this low or no growth trajectory. Again, being the Chair of an independent IRB myself, there's no way that would happen at my IRB.

Teachers conduct small-scale participatory action research all the time. I've done it myself, with my students. But in such studies, everyone gets the treatment under study. No one is selected to be excluded from the treatment. In Chapter 4, I'll walk you through one such study that I conducted. For our purposes here, small-scale participatory action research refers to studies done by a researcher (a teacher or teachers) collaborating with a small group of students. Together they identify a problem to address. The group participates actively in designing and carrying out research to understand the problem and find solutions. This form of community-based research provides localized evidence while empowering people to make change. A hallmark is the democratic participation of all stakeholders in studying and acting on social or structural issues impacting their lives. Small groups might be engaged at a school, worksite, or neighborhood level to conduct participatory investigations and interventions relevant to their needs and context. The small scale allows close researcher-community partnership. This distinguishes participatory action research from typical academic studies done on, not with, communities (Hoerricks, 2023c).

When I began to work through the conundrum that is the SOR bandwagon, it was a lot to process. How could an entire industry be so cruel? As you consider what has just been presented, what feelings are coming up? How will you process them? Please pause a beat to reflect and engage in your go-to self-care routine.

Some things that might trip you up

Considering what we've just been through in this chapter, if your school is all-in on the SOR, what will you do with this new information? You will likely attend professional development sessions in the future facilitated by staff who are fully on the bandwagon that will preach the value of the Reading Rope. You may be provided with resources that may be appropriate for your ALP learners but will fail to help your GLP learners improve, no matter how faithfully you implement the solution. In the world of UDL), how can one scaffold when one truly does not know what the issues are with one's students? The facilitators might not have even heard that there are such people as GLP learners. You may search the vendors' websites for information about how their intervention supports GLP learners and find nothing, not even a mention of the word "gestalt". What will you do with your new knowledge?

As you worked through the deconstruction, you likely thought about the new information in relation to a student, friend, or family member's struggles. This "ah-ha" moment is to be expected. But facilitators really don't appreciate being derailed by distracting questions about the validity of their products or services for GLP learners. Their "evidence" for the efficacy of their "evidence-based" solutions will likely not include GLP students in their samples. Their evidence might have been obtained unethically from a so-called "evidence mill". Thus, you will likely choose to remain silent, preferring your career as a teacher to the uncertainty of advocacy.

I've made this choice for myself in my district. In my district, professional development is a monologue. As much as student-facing UDL is expected of us in our practice as teachers, not one thought is given to extending that into our own learning spaces. As a non-verbal autistic teacher (a GLP learner myself), most of the learning and development activity assumes that someone like me won't ever be present. The system doesn't imagine that a student with special needs (like me) would ever be considered a teaching peer (Hoerricks, 2023d).

This is where people often get tripped up. If your employer doesn't appreciate advocacy, don't do it. Inform your own practice. Change your own classroom. You'll discover, as I have, that when visitors arrive in your classroom, questions will abound. I am happy to answer questions about the "evidence" that my practice works for my learners. The "evidence", as you'll see, is in the increased skill set, confidence, and joy of your students. As for the administrators, they'll see the "evidence" when you switch from assessments **of** learning to assessments **for** learning. In case you are wondering about the difference between the two methodologies, here's a quick breakdown.

Assessment of learning:

- Focuses on summing up how much learning has occurred, usually at the end of a course or unit;
- Is designed to determine whether students have learned what was expected;
- Typically uses tests, exams, quizzes, projects, etc. that yield a score; and
- Results are often recorded as grades that are factored into the student's overall academic record.

Assessment for learning:

- Focuses on providing feedback to improve teaching and learning;
- Occurs frequently throughout instruction, often informally;
- Uses various methods (observations, discussions, quizzes, work samples, etc.) to gauge student understanding;
- Provides specific feedback students can use to improve as they are still gaining knowledge and skills; and
- Allows teachers to adjust lessons and techniques to better meet student needs.

Thus, assessment **of** learning aims to quantify learning, while assessment **for** learning aims to enhance the learning process. The first defines achievement, while the second guides progress towards it. Using both throughout education provides balance in gauging and supporting student growth. But, yes, outcomes necessarily improve when instruction is aligned with how students naturally acquire, learn, and use language.

Summary

In this chapter, we embarked on a journey to deconstruct the prevailing SOR and the often-referenced model of Scarborough's Reading Rope. Our exploration was fueled by the realization that these established approaches might not be well suited for guiding all learners toward literacy.

As we ventured deeper into this deconstruction, we encountered significant challenges within the existing "reading science" framework. We began to question whether the dominant theories truly account for the diverse learning styles and processing approaches of all students, particularly those who lean more toward the gestalt processing end of the spectrum.

Yes, it is a spectrum. I tend towards the far end of the gestalt side of the language processing spectrum. This is evidenced in my original autism diagnosis, that of having significant difficulty with functional language and needing significant support. Yet, over time and with a ton of work, I've been able to work in the world of ALP. In a sense, I've moved the needle a bit towards the ALP side of the spectrum.

Scarborough's Reading Rope, a model often regarded as comprehensive, was scrutinized from this new perspective. While the model provides valuable insights into the multiple components of reading, it became apparent that it might inadvertently neglect the **holistic** and intuitive nature of GLP learners. For these learners, reading isn't always a step-by-step assembly of isolated skills but a more integrated, intuitive, and context-driven process.

Deconstructing these conventional paradigms allowed us to glimpse the limitations in addressing the needs of GLP learners. We uncovered the potential bias of reading science towards analytic processing styles, which may not fully acknowledge the strengths and abilities of gestalt processors in understanding complex narratives and drawing connections intuitively.

Thus, our journey of deconstruction has revealed that the existing SOR may not be fully fit for purpose when it comes to bringing students of all ages and language processing types to literacy. This realization calls for a re-evaluation of our approaches to teaching and supporting these learners, recognizing their unique strengths, and creating a more inclusive and effective framework that truly accommodates their processing styles. It is an essential step towards nurturing the potential of all students, ensuring that no one is left behind in the pursuit of literacy and meaningful engagement with language.

3
Early childhood literacy

Learning objective

Students will be able to create a comprehensive literacy-rich environment that caters to and stimulates all learners in developing their early literacy skills.

> "Once you learn to read, you will be forever free." – Frederick Douglass

Rationale

The Common Core writing standard CCSS.ELA-LITERACY.W.11-12.7 provides an important framework and rationale for having students create comprehensive literacy-rich environments to develop early literacy skills. This standard requires students to conduct both short and more sustained research to answer a question or solve a problem. To successfully design literacy-rich environments, students would need to engage in an inquiry process involving research on topics like emergent literacy stages, key foundational skills, learner variability, evidence-based design strategies, developmentally appropriate materials and activities, and assessing environment efficacy. This research should involve synthesizing multiple sources to thoroughly understand these aspects of early literacy and environment design. Students may need to broaden or narrow their inquiry depending on the specific questions or problems related to creating an optimal literacy environment for a given learner population and setting. By engaging students in an iterative research process to deeply investigate key facets of designing effective literacy-rich spaces, this standard provides a methodology for students to develop the knowledge and skills needed to successfully create literacy environments that stimulate emerging reading and writing abilities in diverse young learners. The standard aligns closely to the learning goal's emphasis on synthesizing knowledge into a comprehensive environment design.

Introduction

How do humans gain literacy? Is it natural or normal? Literacy is not an innate human ability that develops naturally, but rather a complex skill that must be intentionally taught and learned. While humans are biologically equipped for spoken language acquisition, reading and writing must be deliberately taught through instruction and practice. For English, we presume this requires extensive instruction in areas like phonics, vocabulary, comprehension, and composition (Sakai, 2005).

Literacy as we now know it has a long history stretching back around 5,000 years to early writing systems such as those in Mesopotamia and Egypt. Those early scripts used pictograms and ideograms to represent concepts and objects holistically. This gestalt approach may have favored those who process language in a global, conceptual manner rather than as discrete parts.

However, a major development in literacy's history was the use of marks to represent the sounds and words of spoken language analytically, allowing many words to be represented by a small set of characters (Hannon, 2004). The origins of modern alphabetic systems like English can be traced back to the Phoenicians and then the Ancient Greeks and Romans, about 3,000 years ago. This atomistic, analytic approach likely favored those who process language in a part-by-part, sequential manner.

Throughout history, literacy has been limited to a small percentage of the population who received formal education. Mass literacy is a relatively recent phenomenon that arose through deliberate efforts to make education and literacy instruction widely available (Graff, 1994). With the spread of mass education, more individuals have been exposed to the analytical approach of encoding language into writing. Learning to read and write in English requires considerable time and effort, as the relationships between letters, sounds, and meanings must be analyzed and memorized. For example, English has an opaque orthography, meaning the relationships between letters and sounds are not always consistent or predictable. Compared to languages with more transparent orthographies, mastering written English likely requires more explicit phonics instruction and rote memorization of spellings, engaging analytic cognitive processes. Given its historical priority in formal schooling, analytic literacy has become entrenched in education systems, presenting challenges for more global, meaning-focused language processors like gestalt processors.

Yes, mastering literacy skills does take years of practice and guidance. Adults in the English-speaking world, like me, who for whatever reason did not have the opportunity for literacy education in childhood, can learn to read and write, but often struggle compared to those who learned as children (Scribner, 1984). Acquiring literacy as an adult demands great motivation and perseverance, as well as support from patient teachers or tutors. With commitment, adults can gain literacy and enjoy the enriching benefits of reading and writing, though it may not come as intuitively as it does to those educated in childhood.

Overall, literacy should not be viewed as an inevitable or natural part of human development. It is an acquired skill set that reflects specific and intentional educational and societal investments. Only relatively recently has universal literacy been an aspiration of so-called developed societies, rather than an inherent or automatic achievement of being human. Again, mass literacy arose from deliberate efforts to make education and literacy instruction widely available, not as an automatic by-product of economic development (Graff, 1994). Societies must actively foster literacy; it does not simply emerge. Although literacy facilitates intellectual achievements, it requires substantial efforts to spread through a population.

In the United States, federal programs like Head Start provide preschool education and early literacy support for low-income families. Many states also have their own early childhood education initiatives. Here, as we saw in the last chapter, there is a big emphasis on phonics instruction and reading readiness skills (Saracho, 2019). In Canada, most provinces have full-day kindergarten programs starting at age 4–5 that include literacy education. Popular approaches include balanced literacy and phonics (Nxumalo, 2019). In the United Kingdom, the government provides 15 hours per week of free preschool education for 3–4-year-olds, which includes early literacy. Phonics approaches like synthetic phonics are commonly used (Tembo, 2021).

In the European Union, similar efforts are under way to support early childhood literacy. In France, for example, nearly all 3–5-year-olds attend free preschool (*école maternelle*), which prepares them for primary school. The program focuses on language skills like vocabulary, speaking, and listening (Tobin, 2005). In Germany, kindergarten is available from ages 3–6 and emphasizes language and literacy readiness like rhyming and vocabulary. More formal reading instruction happens in primary school (Bloch et al., 2021). In Italy, preschool (*scuola dell'infanzia*) from age three covers early language and pre-literacy skills. Like Germany, explicit literacy instruction is part of the primary school curriculum (Musatti and Picchio, 2010). Finally, in Japan, kindergartens introduce literacy fundamentals like phonetics, but focus more on social development. Structured reading instruction begins there in first grade (Mulyadi, 2020).

There is a similar trend towards early childhood literacy development across the BRICS countries as well. In Brazil, the federal government provides some public preschools and literacy programs, but access and quality are uneven across regions. Individual states and municipalities run early childhood initiatives with varying approaches (Becker, 2007). In Russia, universal preschool education starts at age three with a literacy focus on reading, writing, counting, and social skills. The federal government oversees standards while regions provide funding and administration (Bodrova and Yudina, 2018). In India, the Integrated Child Development Services (ICDS) program provides health, nutrition, and preschool education for children under six. Literacy activities include storytelling, alphabet recognition, and environmental print awareness, though access and quality vary greatly (Reetu et al., 2017). In China, the central government has supported preschool expansion with a literacy focus on Chinese characters, phonetic awareness, and beginning math. However, funding and access are uneven between wealthy and poor regions (Li and Vandenbroeck, 2020). Finally, in South Africa, the preschool reception year (aka Grade R) provides a year-long program for 5–6-year-olds with some literacy fundamentals (Atmore, 2019).

Overall, literacy education in early childhood is seen as crucial for later academic success across diverse global contexts (Bai et al., 2020). While specific instructional approaches and access to preschool vary greatly, developing foundational language and literacy skills prior to formal primary schooling is widely regarded as beneficial. However, quality early childhood education requires adequate funding and resources, trained teachers, a developmentally appropriate curriculum, and a commitment to equity in access. Without sufficient investment, preschool alone cannot overcome literacy achievement gaps stemming from broader societal inequities (Hung et al., 2020). In promoting universal literacy, educators and policymakers must recognize both literacy's constructed nature and the vital role of early exposure and education.

Literacy and communication

My journey through Freemasonry hints back to the time when literacy was reserved for an elite few and the masses were left using only oral language. Indeed, Masonic tradition informs us that the masses of people throughout time were educated and informed via stories. In pre-literate societies, oral tradition was highly valued. Stories, legends, histories, and traditions were passed down this way through the generations. During our Masonic education sessions, we were told that an "instructive tongue" and an "attentive ear" are the keys to education and have played a vital role in preserving knowledge through the generations (Hoerricks, 2018). This emphasizes the significance of both clear verbal instruction and engaged listening in the learning process.

Before widespread literacy, knowledge and wisdom were imparted primarily through oral tradition – spoken stories, rituals, songs, and apprenticeship. Thus, the "instructive tongue" represents the effective communication of information from one person to another through speech. This requires the speaker to actively instruct in a clear, understandable manner tailored to the listener. It is a more active, interactive form of teaching than just reading texts.

Meanwhile, the "attentive ear" signifies focused listening and retention on the part of the learner. To truly absorb the knowledge being conveyed, the listener must pay close attention rather than letting the words go in one ear and out the other. They must remember and internalize what is being said.

Both clear speaking and attentive listening remain important even in today's education system. While literacy enables the preservation and transmission of knowledge via text, oral explanation and discussion are still key parts of teaching and learning. Lectures, seminars, presentations, and dialogue allow learners to build understanding, ask questions, and gain insights beyond the written word. An engaged, listening ear is vital for learning from these verbal interactions. So just as in ancient times, the instructive tongue and attentive ear continue to serve as essential conduits of education.

Along this line, Goody (1987) notes that the ways in which people communicate are tied to how they think and build their culture. When communication changes, it also changes how people interact. Language lets people connect and is crucial to culture and its dissemination of knowledge. Writing, however, takes it further. Writing shapes complicated societies and city life more directly. Writing doesn't just help trade and government work; it also changes how people process information and understand the world. In short, communication shapes both our outer social worlds and inner thinking. Where language builds cultures, writing transforms civilizations. Thus, how people communicate defines what it means to be human, as individuals and groups.

Taken further, the Sapir-Whorf hypothesis (Perlovsky, 2009) proposes that the language we use (speak / listen, read / write) influences how we think and perceive the world. It suggests that people who use different languages view reality in different ways. The structure of a language shapes how its speakers conceptualize their world and their behaviors. This hypothesis argues that language affects thought and culture. There has been much debate, however, about just how strong this influence of language on cognition really is.

As we are seeing today, developments in communication technology not only reflect but also transform cultures and worldviews. In our era, society is increasingly concerned about the influence of AI systems on language and communication. With their ability to generate human-like text, some fear AI could be used to manipulate opinion on a mass scale. Researchers warn that AI text generators may lack key attributes of human language like grounded meaning, complex reasoning, and social awareness (Dwivedi et al., 2023). If deployed carelessly, AI could flood digital spaces with synthesized content optimized to virally spread an agenda, rather than convey nuanced understanding. This raises important questions around the ethical development of advanced AI systems. How can we maximize the potential literacy benefits of AI technology for children while safeguarding developmentally appropriate learning, cognitive diversity, and human-centered pedagogy? Ongoing research and public dialogue are needed to responsibly guide the emerging role of AI in shaping language, culture, and society.

When cultures mix

Coming from outside of the dominant culture growing up and being an autistic GLP learner, I encountered many words and phrases from those around me that were not English (Hoerricks, 2023). When I would ask what the words meant, I was often told that there are no direct translations, or that the English explanation somehow cheapens the word. Words and expressions often do not translate neatly from one language or culture to another. Certain ideas and nuances can be tricky to convey accurately across linguistic and cultural boundaries. For example, the German idea of *schadenfreude*, meaning pleasure derived from another's misfortune, has no precise equivalent in English. The

French phrase *je ne sais quoi* tries to capture a quality that is hard to pinpoint or articulate directly in another language. Even for more concrete terms, exact translations may not exist – like *hygge*, the Danish concept of cozy contentment. These untranslatable words point to ideas, emotions, and perspectives unique to a cultural worldview. Full understanding requires immersion in the original cultural context. Translation can provide approximations, but some essence is inevitably lost. The gaps between languages remind us that different cultures shape distinct realities and meanings.

In my life, the first of these untranslatable words was given to me by my Scottish grandmother. When I would visit late in the afternoon, she would say that a *wee dram* of *uisge beatha* was in order, to celebrate my arrival. *Uisge beatha*, I was told, could be translated from Gaelic as "water of life". She noted that it had been Anglicized over the years as whisky (Scottish) and whiskey (Irish / American). To hear my grandmother tell it, the Gaelic people invented whisky. Sadly, I would later find out my grandmother was stretching the truth and that, in fact, Christian missionaries brought distillation technology to Scotland and Ireland, where it quickly integrated into the culture (Bathgate, 2003). Thus, in a historical sense, the Gaels attempted to wrap their language around the missionaries' *aqua vitae* – a distillation that is essentially aged and flavored ethanol (Rana et al., 2022).

In my classrooms, I hear a mix of accented English, Nahuatl, and Spanish. To my sensory system, Nahuatl sounds beautifully complex. I marvel at how speakers of the language can make the sounds necessary to make it make sense. Sadly, Rolstad (2001) argues that Nahuatl, the most widely spoken indigenous language in Mexico, is at risk of replacement by Spanish. Spanish, it is argued there, is the language of greater economic power, education, and social prestige. As with so many indigenous languages, the colonial language dominates then extinguishes the local languages unless something is specifically done to preserve them (Macedo, 2019). There, in losing language, we risk losing *Tlamictiliztli*, or "The Knowledge", meaning the deeper wisdom of elders and ancestors beyond just facts, including the emotional attachment to the information and the memories. [The root *tlamictia* in Nahuatl means "to know". Words ending in *-tilitztli* often refer to the action or process of something. The suffix *-iztli* in Nahuatl usually denotes an abstract concept or quality (Xocoyotzin, 1996).]

As a hyper-empathic autistic GLP learner, I find great joy in the aesthetic experience of hearing diverse languages spoken aloud. More than just comprehending literal meanings, I revel in the rhythms, intonations, and emotional resonances carried through vocal expression. Unfortunately, many indigenous and minority languages face endangerment in our globally interconnected world. When languages like Nahuatl decline or disappear, more is lost than just words and grammar. Entire worldviews, values, histories, and artistic sensibilities encoded within the language are forgotten. My mind delights in linguistic diversity, each language a unique window into our shared human capacities. But too often, political, and economic forces pressure assimilation to dominant tongues like English or Spanish. Though well intended, promoting literacy in these major languages often comes at the cost of oral heritage. More could be done to nurture multilingualism and give equitable status to indigenous modes of speaking, thinking, and connecting. As an educator, I wish to foster students' pride in their cultural fluency, not replace it with standardized language but nourish both. There are no easy answers, but valuing neurodiverse ways of processing language is perhaps a step toward healing and balance. The contours of each spoken word, after all, convey deep human experience.

Yet, happening first in schools in Mexico and now increasingly in US schools, we can see an educational movement towards a solution emerging – translanguaging. Translanguaging goes beyond just transitioning between separate "monolingual" languages. It recognizes language-minoritized students' ability to fluidly combine features of multiple languages to suit the context. For example, students may dynamically integrate words or structures from their home language and English within a single sentence or text to maximize expression. This flexible use of one's linguistic repertoire is an intrinsic quality of human language learning and development, and an asset for educators to build on, as students who speak different languages engage with each other. (Macedo, 2019).

Translanguaging aligns with my perspective as an autistic educator seeking balance. It pushes back against deficit views of bilingual students as possessing "two half languages". Instead, it honors their skills in accessing and integrating multiple language systems to convey meaning holistically. Just as I delight in the diverse contours of spoken words, translanguaging celebrates students' blending and shifting languacultures. This can empower meaningful communication and deep learning (Berryman et al., 2022).

Exploring translanguaging

Translanguaging is an approach that embraces the linguistic diversity found in many classrooms and allows students to fluidly utilize their full language arsenal for learning and expression. Rather than strictly separating languages, translanguaging recognizes students' ability to dynamically integrate features of multiple languages to convey meaning and enhance communication. For example, an emergent bilingual student may naturally combine words or structures from their home language and English within a single utterance or text to maximize comprehension and clarity.

Incorporating translanguaging strategies in early childhood education settings can foster inclusion, support learners who are still acquiring English, and validate the diverse home languages spoken by students and their families. The early childhood classroom provides a prime environment to implement translanguaging, as young children are still developing their language skills and have not yet been fully socialized into dominant monolingual ideologies prevalent in wider society. Taking a flexible translanguaging approach allows teachers to build upon children's existing linguistic strengths rather than viewing other languages as a deficit.

For students navigating multiple language worlds, like those in my classes who use English only at school, translanguaging can enhance self-expression, identity affirmation, and sense of belonging. It moves away from traditional "two solitudes" notions of bilingualism (Angelopoulou, 2020) towards an asset-based pedagogy that encourages learners to fully utilize their linguistic skills as an integrated system. Translanguaging opens more creative spaces for early literacy, storytelling, concept development, and peer interactions. When students' full language practices are welcomed into the classroom, learning can become more meaningful, equitable, and tailored to diverse needs.

By way of preview, there are many impactful ways teachers can adopt a translanguaging stance in their practice with their students. This includes allowing flexible language use during instruction, play, and projects, using multilingual materials, encouraging peer translations and explanations, welcoming home languages through family involvement, and normalizing cross-language connections as an everyday classroom occurrence.

In such a classroom, gestalt learners benefit from a flexible environment that allows them to harness all linguistic resources available to make meaning. Analytic processors are also empowered by translanguaging, as code-switching and translation allow them to gain deeper understanding and fully demonstrate competencies. The incorporation of translanguaging strategies acknowledges and affirms the rich tapestry of linguistic diversity present in classrooms. When teachers welcome the multitude of languages and language varieties children carry with them into the classroom, it sends a powerful message of belonging. Again, rather than demanding students leave aspects of their identities at the door, translanguaging values their full selves and sees their knowledge of home languages as resources to be leveraged in the learning process.

In creating translanguaging spaces, teachers can gain deeper insight into students' skills and knowledge. This comes when students and staff are free to communicate in their own voice, without being artificially constrained by expectations to separate their languages strictly. Translanguaging pedagogies empower students to integrate information and ideas seamlessly across the boundaries of named languages, developing a more holistic linguistic identity.

At its heart, translanguaging affirms that all students' ways with words deserve equal status and representation. It pushes back against biases that position some languages, language varieties, and language processing styles as inherently more valuable in academic spaces. By welcoming and celebrating the diversity of students' languaging practices, translanguaging fosters educational equity and inclusion. It makes clear that all students have a rightful place in our classrooms, regardless of ethnicity, culture, or home language background. When we as educators make room for the wealth of linguistic talents our multilingual learners possess, we build literacy communities where all can participate, engage, and thrive (Garcia et al., 2019).

Benefits of translanguaging

As educators, we often need to make the case to administrators when proposing new pedagogical approaches for our classrooms. With this in mind, as we look to make our early childhood settings more equitable and inclusive, I believe embracing translanguaging has immense benefits for supporting our multilingual pupils. Here's a quick list to get us started.

- Allowing children to freely use their entire linguistic capabilities during classroom activities and play. This means not policing children to only use the dominant school language or language processing style. Here, it's important to reinforce that all attempts at communication are valid and accepted.

- Displaying books, posters, labels, and signage in the multiple languages spoken by children in the classroom validates the diverse linguistic identities of all learners.
- Whenever possible, teachers can use words and phrases from children's home languages during instruction to aid comprehension and scaffold learning. For teachers without second language skills, connecting with families to build this knowledge base fosters inclusiveness and community.
- Encouraging code-switching and translation during peer interactions and play brings cohesion to the classroom. Begin the lessons, but let the children explain concepts to each other using their different languages and understandings. This helps children safely find their voice, beginning their self-advocacy journey early.
- Using translanguaging techniques during student assessments makes differentiation easier by enabling teachers to fully evaluate children's knowledge and skills when they can draw from their entire language abilities. Students can respond or explain in the way in which they feel most confident.
- As with the movement behind the community schools of my school district, having parents and family members participate in the classroom using their home languages not only shows that educators value linguistic diversity, but can work to raise the family's home language literacy level (Saunders et al., 2020).

Seen in this way, translanguaging is a way of fostering a learning environment where linguistic diversity and flexibility are the daily norm, not the exception. Again, this helps ease all learners into language learning in a way that is both fun and uplifting. Obviously, professional development for teachers on effective translanguaging strategies for instruction, communication, and inclusion would be necessary – beginning, of course, with this book. The key is to see children's existing linguistic resources as assets, to view language boundaries as permeable, to value flexibility, and to normalize translanguaging as an everyday practice. This provides an inclusive environment for all emergent language learners (Cenoz and Gorter, 2020).

Literacy beyond the school's walls

Translanguaging approaches in the early childhood classroom provide benefits beyond the school walls by lifting literacy practices in students' homes and communities. When teachers encourage students to engage in projects and assignments that involve interviewing family members in their home languages, for example, this promotes cross-generational learning. Parents and grandparents become valued literacy partners in the classroom community. Translanguaging fosters a welcoming environment where families feel respected for their linguistic knowledge. They can participate confidently using home languages. This engagement around translanguaging activities creates two-way learning between home and school. Literacy becomes a collaborative family experience grounded in linguistic diversity and flexible communication. Children also bring translanguaging practices into the home setting, normalizing code-switching, and multilingual expression in everyday interactions (Goodman and Tastanbek, 2021). In this way, embracing translanguaging in early childhood education strengthens literacy abilities across generations and empowers whole families with communicative resources.

Now certainly, teachers with no knowledge of the many home languages present in their classroom will need help creating the place and space necessary for their young learners to thrive. This is where the families can help. Here are some examples of how families can help support translanguaging practices in early childhood learning environments.

- Parents / caregivers can suggest items for classroom libraries to contain books in the home languages of students, not just in English. Books are displayed and labeled in multiple languages.
- Centers around the classroom have multilingual labels and materials. For example, the dramatic play area could have signs, menus, and props in different home languages.
- Families can lend their knowledge in helping to create word walls that display vocabulary words in English and children's home languages for key topics being covered.
- Teachers can foster community and student voice by displaying student artwork, writing, and projects around the room in whichever language was used to create them.
- Class-made charts, lists, and visual aids include translations contributed by students in their home languages.
- Teachers learn and use key words and phrases in children's home languages during the day, like greetings, expressions of praise, and daily instructions. These can be displayed on the word wall for added support.

- Multilingual and bilingual books are routinely used during read-alouds and literacy instruction. Engaging with stories in multiple languages exposes all students to different languages, building their vocabulary, and starts normalizing translanguaging in their lives.
- To support their natural language development, children are allowed to respond orally or in writing in their strongest language during instruction, with support for translation if needed.
- Play areas are created to promote translanguaging through diverse language roleplaying, multilingual puppets / toys, and open language mixing during pretend scenarios.
- Classroom centers have headphones, tablets, etc. to allow students to listen to stories and instruction in multiple languages.

The goal here is to visibly and auditorily surround children and their families with their languages to validate their linguistic identities and promote flexible translanguaging daily. When parents visit classrooms, they see translanguaging being used successfully, allowing them to bring the technique home to further support their children in their journey to literacy.

Who is in the classroom?

Seen in this way, translanguaging is a form of social learning. While social learning is often seen as just copying and trusting others, this view doesn't fully show the power of human social learning: where social information is often "curated" by helpful teachers (Gweon, 2021). I argue that both learning from others (social learning) and helping others learn (teaching) can be seen as making smart guesses guided by an intuitive understanding of how people think, plan, and act. This presupposes knowing who is in the classroom. This is where UDL can help.

The UDL framework provides critical guidance for implementing translanguaging opportunities in the classroom. UDL's emphasis on multiple means of representation encourages content delivery and materials in multiple languages to activate students' diverse linguistic strengths. Its focus on multiple means of action and expression validates the importance of letting students showcase comprehension through integrated language practices. Finally, UDL's validation of multiple means of engagement legitimizes translanguaging as a tool to enhance relevance, build background knowledge, and motivate emergent language learners. Overall, UDL requires educators to intentionally design learning in ways that leverage—not constrain—students' existing capabilities.

In line with the UDL framework's focus on multiple means of representation and expression, translanguaging in a social learning approach allows young children to make rich inferences from diverse linguistic evidence provided by others and generate informative evidence that helps everyone in the class learn. By studying social learning and teaching through an integrated theoretical lens, inferential social learning provides an account of how human cognition supports acquiring and communicating abstract knowledge across multiple languages (Gweon, 2021; Ellis, 2019).

Remember, language acquisition in early childhood education is a critical foundation for children's cognitive and social development (Gweon, 2021). Young learners come to school with varying skills and abilities shaped by their home languages and cultures. As we've seen, translanguaging is an approach that leverages children's full linguistic capabilities by allowing flexible use of multiple languages to make meaning and enhance learning. But that meaning-making and development look different to analytic and gestalt processors of language. Reminding us again that we must know who is in the room.

For analytic processors, who take a rules-based, bottom-up approach to language, translanguaging provides more examples of language use across different contexts. Seeing how grammatical structures and vocabulary flexibly adapt between languages helps them internalize patterns. Translanguaging also allows explicit bridging between languages to reinforce analytic understanding.

Gestalt processors, on the other hand, who take a whole-meaning approach to language acquisition, can use translanguaging structures to grasp deeper concepts and feelings without getting lost in language-specific details. Translanguaging allows holistic transfer of meaning across different linguistic forms, supporting big-picture learning for our GLP learners. Bringing in multiple languages also increases contextual cues that assist overall comprehension.

I saw this first-hand on my entry into teaching. While teaching my Special Day Class comprised of struggling fourth and fifth graders, I sought to support my students in English through the inclusion of translanguaging techniques. My students, many of them emerging bilinguals, had fallen far behind grade-level expectations. I recognized the analytical, explicit focus preferred by the ALP learners was insufficient for allowing the GLP learners to holistically acquire key skills.

On introducing past tense forms, for instance, I tried to provide direct translations between English and Spanish. Comparing placement of irregular verbs enabled rule-oriented ALP learners to systematically analyze parallel linguistic structures. Organizing vocabulary lists by themes with translations likewise built analytical comprehension.

For my GLP learners, however, structured grammatical study hinders intuitive acquisition. They thrive when flexibly encountering language in authentic discourse. Still, purposeful translanguaging can assist their whole-meaning approach. In reading a short story, I had the class read holistically first before focused textual analysis – allowing initial broad impressions to satisfy the GLP learners while still prompting the ALP learners' detailed examinations later. Similarly, video clips in Spanish and English established holistic meaning for gestalts before guided discussion targeted analytical comparisons.

Blending dual pathways thus empowers both learning orientations. Direct translation reinforces mental schemas for ALP learners; authentic multilingual exposure sharpens global intuition for the GLP learners. My lesson planning aimed to develop this repertoire further to promote contextual fluency for all. Thankfully, electronic translation tools like Google Translate provided pronunciations to help me sound out the Spanish words. Though my class was far behind at the beginning of school, these translanguaging techniques offered a path to English acquisition accessible to varying needs.

For teachers who incorporate translanguaging in their classroom, we see the benefits of not only increased skilled use of language but also in increased engagement and social interaction. Translanguaging validates all students' home language knowledge, empowering them to participate. For shy or struggling students, it lowers the affective filter and encourages contributions (Ryka, 2023). Peer teaching across languages gives analytic processors opportunities to explain concepts, while gestalt processors bring creative insights.

Ultimately translanguaging provides scaffolding for both **rule-based** and **meaning-based** language learners. ALP learners parse structure while GLP learners perceive whole concepts. By fluidly moving between languages, translanguaging allows all students to leverage their strengths. Both ALP and GLP approaches come together to mutually reinforce understanding from different perspectives.

So how does a teacher find out who's who in their classroom? The language differences are usually obvious. But the language processing differences aren't. Parents are often the ones who bring a student's language processing "problems" to a school's or teacher's attention. This may be before any formal evaluation has been completed on the student. With eligibility for special education services beginning at three years old in the US, this information may also be found in a student's IEP (if they have one). Teachers can also glean this information from simple observations of students, for example how do they talk and exchange information? There are screeners and tests that can be administered (Brannigan and Decker, 2006) but these are generally reserved for specialists like pathologists and doctors.

Speech pathologists note that kids who learn language in chunks (e.g., scripts or gestalts) can be hard to understand. This is because they might use phrases or scripts that don't make sense to the listener. For example, an upset student might say "walk it off" over and over. In talking to their parent, you find out they had been hit by a ball at baseball practice. Their coach told them to "walk it off" so they paired that phrase with feeling hurt. Now they say it when they are upset to communicate, "I'm hurt."

Unpacking gestalts

Remember, gestalt processors tend to comprehend language in holistic chunks rather than breaking things down into smaller components. When we hear or read a certain phrase or expression, it conjures up a complete idea or concept for us, with associated emotions and impressions attached. The meaning is embedded in the whole chunk of the language segment rather than being built up from an analysis of the individual words and grammar. For example, a common idiom like "it's raining cats and dogs" paints a vivid sensory image for the gestalt processor, while a more analytic learner would focus on the literal meanings of each word and find the phrase confusing or nonsensical. Indeed, as I put this phrase into writing, it triggers in the theater of my mind the musty smell of rain on the concrete playground.

This is the way I process the world around me. I know of no other way. I grasp the overall essence and impact of linguistic chunks all at once, rather than assembling meaning in a sequential, methodical manner in the way of the analytic processor.

Thus, with GLP learners, the teacher must investigate to figure out where their phrases come from and what they mean. It helps to work with parents since many of their scripts start at home. The goal is to collaborate and try to understand the meaning behind their language. Additionally, with a multilingual classroom, the gestalts might not be in English. Thus, it's helpful to keep a chart of phrases to meanings for each child as you get to know them and their families.

Some other signs that your young learner might be a GLP learner (Mott, 2023):

- Use of immediate / delayed echolalia;
- Use of incoherent strings of language (it may sound like language, but you can't understand it);
- Use of single words without progression of adding words together;
- Demonstrates rich intonation (may sound melodic or "singsong");
- Repeated use of specific phrases;
- May repeat scripted language, possibly from songs or media;
- Watches / replays the same video or section of video on repeat; and
- Is very drawn to music.

Stages of literacy development

With our classroom roster finalized and student information gathered, we progress to examining stages of literacy development in human populations. It was essential that we first explored the challenges and complexities of today's classroom to establish an inclusive and comprehensive teaching approach right from the start. Rather than plunging ahead with instruction and only later discovering gaps in our methodology after disheartening student assessments, we have built a strong foundation by thoroughly investigating the diversity of learning needs and experiences students bring. Armed with this understanding, we are positioned to craft instructional strategies that provide scaffolded support, leverage strengths, and enable each child to gain literacy skills. This proactive, student-centered outlook, rooted in research, sets us on the path toward positive outcomes as students' reading, writing, listening, and speaking abilities blossom over the school year.

The literacy stages of ALP learners

The development of literacy skills in young children should mark an exciting cognitive and educational journey. As children grow from infancy to the early school years, they advance through identifiable stages of literacy learning. For the ALP learner, these include the pre-literacy stage from birth to age 6, where oral language foundations are established; the emergent literacy stage from ages 4–6, when awareness of print concepts and letter-sound relationships develops; the beginning literacy stage from ages 6–8, as basic decoding and encoding skills are acquired; and finally the fluent literacy stage around age 8 and beyond, when reading fluency, writing cohesion, and higher-level analytic skills mature. Tracking and understanding these literacy stages provides insight into children's growing ability to process and unlock meaning from increasingly complex language and texts. The stages reflect the development from early oral language to basic decoding, to fluent and automatic literacy skills using sophisticated analysis (Gleason and Ratner, 2022).

- Pre-literacy (birth to 6 years): In these early years, ALP children are developing oral language skills through listening and speaking. Important pre-literacy skills include phonological awareness, vocabulary development, understanding of story, and print concepts.
- Emergent literacy (ages 4–6 years): Children start recognizing letters and symbols, understanding that print carries meaning. They are learning that words are made up of sounds and letters. Early reading and writing behaviors emerge.
- Beginning literacy (ages 6–8 years): Children develop more fluency in decoding and encoding words. They expand their sight word knowledge and use of context clues. Writing becomes more conventional. Sentences and stories become more complex.
- Fluent literacy (ages 8+ years): Children become fluent, automatic readers. They can comprehend and analyze increasingly complex language and texts. Writing is more cohesive and organized. Higher-level literacy skills like inference making continue to develop.

Some key milestones for ALP learners:

- Around age 5: knowledge of alphabet and letter-sound relationships;
- Ages 6–7: decoding simple words and sentences;

- Ages 7–8: reading independently with accuracy and comprehension; and
- Ages 9+: use of morphemic and contextual analysis in literacy tasks.

In summary, ALP learners generally progress from pre-literacy skills to decoding to fluent reading and writing using increasingly sophisticated language analysis skills. This allows them to unlock meaning from more complex texts. The above mirrors what can be found in any teacher preparation class, echoing the so-called SOR. As we've discovered previously, it's valid for about 60 per cent of the human population. But what about the other 40 or so percent? What about our gestalt processors?

The literacy stages of GLP learners

In a general sense, the development of every child's language ability involves elements of both analytic and gestalt processing skills. Gestalt processing refers to the mind's hard-wired preference for understanding language as a whole unit, not just individual words, or rules. This develops through identifiable stages in early childhood. From birth to around 18 months, infants are in an observing stage, absorbing language as holistic auditory input. From 18 months to 3 years, the experimenting stage emerges, as toddlers begin to use predictable language patterns like repetitive phrases or short sentences, often called either immediate or delayed echolalia depending upon when the phrases are heard and repeated. Around ages 3–5, the integrating stage occurs, where children start combining words in novel ways to express more complex ideas. Finally, around age five and beyond, children should hopefully reach the flexibility stage, using language creatively and understanding implied meaning or metaphors. Tracking the progression through these stages highlights how children who are gestalt processors gradually process larger language units for comprehension, not just individual words, or analytic rules. Their holistic language skills allow them to derive and convey meaning from broader linguistic contexts (Blanc, 2012).

But these progressions aren't always evident. Children rarely are typical in their progressions. Often, and especially in autism, when the child doesn't follow the usual progression, the child is referred to specialized staff, such as a speech therapist, for help with language. (An important aside – speech therapists / speech and language pathologists do not teach literacy skills as such. They don't teach people to read. More on this in Chapter 4.) Rather than segregate the child from the learning environment, it's preferable for teachers to be informed as to the stages of language development in GLP learners so they can identify where the learner is on their path, then proceed accordingly in incorporating and supporting them in the classroom.

- Stage 1 – Gestalts in their original form: These can be as short as one word or as long as a movie script. The echolalia here is delayed and scripted.
- Stage 2 – Mitigations of gestalts: These are mixed and matched chunks of words, shortened versions of favorite gestalts, or the changing out of single words from previously successful scripts.
- Stage 3 – Isolation of single words, plus two-word combinations: This builds the foundation for generative grammar in the next stage.

- Stage 4 – Beginning grammar: For the first time, students can create fully novel, self-generated utterances by combining isolated words from stage 3.
- Stages 5 and 6 – More advanced grammar.

With all of this in mind, imagine being a college student stuck between stages 3 and 4, away from home for the first time. I was very nervous about starting college and being away from my supportive friends. I knew it would be different from high school. I struggled a lot with talking to people and expressing my thoughts using full sentences. When I tried to explain things, I would get stuck on certain words or phrases I had memorized because it was hard for me to come up with new ways to say things on the spot. Reading the textbooks was next to impossible for me since my language wasn't very advanced yet. I wasn't great at writing essays or papers either. The good news was that, as I was a football player, my classes weren't that rigorous. The hard part was doing presentations in front of the class and participating in group discussions. That was quite uncomfortable for me, relying as much as I did on echolalia to communicate.

In his early work on language acquisition in autistic children, Prizant (1982; 1983) along with colleagues (Prizant and Duchan, 1981; Prizant and Rydell, 1984) observed that immediate and delayed echolalia are linguistic phenomena frequently exhibited by young autistic learners. They found that many autistic children tend to use echolalia extensively as they are acquiring language and communication skills.

For example, an autistic child may immediately imitate a sentence their parent just spoke, or repeat a phrase they heard on a

TV show hours or days later. Some key findings were that immediate echolalia serves a functional role for autistic children to process unfamiliar language input. Delayed echolalia reflects a more mature linguistic processing ability, with children drawing on stored phrases to serve communicative functions like affirmation or turn-taking.

Overall, the research indicated that echolalia provides an important scaffolding for autistic language development and should not be discouraged. Many autistic individuals, like me, rely heavily on repetitive language like echolalia to learn how to converse before developing more creative, flexible communication abilities. Echolalia reflects a neurodiverse way of acquiring language – taking in linguistic input, practicing through repetition, and gradually gaining competence. With support and understanding of echolalia's role, autistic gestalt processors can learn to communicate effectively using this process. These seminal studies led to greater awareness of the learning strategies autistic GLP learners use to make sense of the complex social phenomenon of language.

Yet literacy development for autistic people varies greatly depending on the presence, impairment, or absence of functional language abilities. For me, a level 2 autistic (no cognitive impairment / impairment of functional language), I could learn to decode text and recognize sight words with explicit instruction – relying upon my memory of the sound of the reader and how I felt when learning to encode the information, yet I struggled with phonics. Reading comprehension and higher literacy skills like inference making were not possible when I was young.

Unfortunately, the challenges faced by GLP learners in educational settings have only recently been recognized in the research world. Westerveld and Paynter's 2021 study shows that more research is still needed to understand these issues. This gap in the research explains my own struggles with literacy when I left college in the 1980s, before there was much awareness of gestalt learning needs. Even today, Harris et al. (2021) are still working to validate screening tools, and only now including assessments for language learners. This demonstrates that supporting gestalt processors in the general education classroom is an ongoing process. More resources are clearly needed to provide guidance to teachers.

But hold on. Before you work on building out your own program, you may be tempted to simply buy something off the shelf. After all, designing and validating a new instructional program can be lengthy and difficult. This is especially true if you have no experience with instructional design. It may seem easy to purchase something off the shelf, but how can you trust what's being provided?

The What Works Clearinghouse

The What Works Clearinghouse (WWC) is an important resource for educators looking to select "research-backed" interventions and programs, especially for special populations of learners. Operated by the US Department of Education's Institute of Education Sciences, the WWC works to assess the existing research on different educational practices and tools. Their goal is to provide teachers with trustworthy information on "evidence-based" programs that have been proven to positively impact student outcomes. Whether searching for a new literacy curriculum, behavioral intervention, or program for English language learners (ELLs) / emergent bilinguals (EBs), the WWC can help streamline the selection process through its ratings, reviews, and search functions. Teachers can feel confident choosing an intervention vetted by the WWC to meet their students' unique needs.

The WWC can help teachers select and screen literacy interventions for special learner populations in a few important ways.

- Evidence ratings – The WWC reviews and rates the quality and effectiveness of research evidence for educational interventions and practices. This includes reviewing studies on literacy programs and assigning ratings to indicate if there are positive, potentially positive, mixed, no discernible, or negative effects based on the research. These ratings can help teachers narrow down effective options. Yet, beware. Some of the work of "evidence mills" manages to filter into the WWC. Remember, in the previous chapter, I provided a few things to look for when evaluating the evidence rating.
- Specific populations – The WWC often looks at research on how interventions affect specific populations like ELLs, EBs, or students with disabilities. Teachers can find interventions tailored and tested for the populations they work with.
- Topic areas – The WWC organizes interventions into topic areas like literacy, math, or behavior. Teachers can easily zero in on literacy-focused programs that may help their students.
- Descriptions and key findings – The WWC provides descriptions of interventions and summarizes key findings from effectiveness studies. This helps give teachers insight into how the programs work and what outcomes they might expect.

- Cost-effectiveness – Some WWC intervention reports analyze and rate the costs versus benefits of programs. This helps teachers weigh if certain literacy curriculums are worth the investment for their budgets and needs.
- Search filters – The WWC has search filters so teachers can narrow results by criteria like grade level or learning format (in person, online, blended). This makes finding relevant literacy interventions easier.

In a nutshell, the WWC is a centralized source teachers can use to make evidence-based decisions on selecting literacy interventions for special populations of students. The evidence ratings, summaries, and search functions help streamline the screening process.

Check for understanding

At this point, we want to ensure we fully grasp the information covered so far, before moving on. We're about to explore some activities and exercises that can be set up separately for ALP and GLP learners, before blending them together with translanguaging to demonstrate what a fully supportive classroom environment might look like. Put the book down for a minute, reflect on what you've learned, and process this moment. Then, when you're ready, return to the text.

Some things that might trip you up

So far, I've presented a lot of information. You may be new to language instruction, or a veteran teacher. Your school may have unlimited resources, or, like mine, quite limited … well …

everything. You may be a parent of a child struggling with language, looking for answers. I won't make assumptions. Rather, I'll explicitly outline below the various evidence-based activities that can support each language processing type, beginning with the developmental stages for ALP learners and ways we can assist them in the classroom.

Language instruction can be challenging for many reasons. You may feel overwhelmed with all the new information if you're just starting out. Even experienced teachers may struggle with limited resources. Parents may find it difficult to support a child struggling with language. There are many potential obstacles, regardless of one's background and circumstances. The key is to take it step-by-step, utilizing proven techniques tailored to each student's needs. With patience and the right guidance, progress can be made. I aim to provide practical support so you can feel empowered, not discouraged, by the language learning process.

Exercises and activities for analytic language processors

The following are some highly recommended exercises and activities to help children develop oral language skills through listening and speaking (pre-literacy) (Duke et al., 2006; Parsons and Ward, 2011).

- Read aloud to children daily and have them retell key details or events from the story. Asking questions about the story boosts comprehension.
- Sing songs and recite nursery rhymes to help children hear the rhythms and patterns of language. This builds phonological awareness.

- Play sound and word games that focus on identifying rhymes, syllables, initial sounds, and phonemes. I-spy, sound sorting games, and oral blending games are great for this.
- Engage in real conversations with children throughout the day. Model good listening skills and build vocabulary by rephrasing what they say and introducing new words.
- Give children time for dramatic imaginative play, which helps them practice conversational skills and use language in context. Provide props like dress-up clothes or puppets.
- Do show and tell activities where children describe an object or picture using complete sentences. Have them present to the whole class.
- When reading, point out print concepts like spaces between words, directionality of text, differences between letters and words.
- Limit screen time and make language-rich activities and listening games a daily habit. Model good speech and grammar.

The key in the pre-literacy stage is lots of interactive, fun activities that get kids listening, speaking, and thinking about language. Developing these oral abilities builds a foundation for literacy.

Now for some emergent literacy activities (Duke et al., 2006; Parsons and Ward, 2011).

- Provide magnetic letters, letter stamps, letter beads, sand trays, etc. so students can practice forming letters and experiment with print.
- Do name activities like making name puzzles or tracing name cards. Help students recognize the letters in their own name.

- Read alphabet books and point out letters and their sounds. Go on letter hunts in books or the environment.
- Sing the alphabet song and work on alphabet order with puzzles or by playing alphabet flashcard games.
- Teach phonological awareness with songs that focus on rhyme, syllables, and alliteration. Do clapping games to break down word parts.
- Help students notice words all around them – point out signs, labels, captions. Show how words are separated by spaces.
- Do interactive writing activities where an adult models writing a word and the child attempts to copy it.
- Provide writing implements and paper for scribbling, pretend writing, and invented spelling. Praise all attempts.
- Read books with predictable patterns and encourage students to chant or fill in missing words. This helps build the concept of a word.
- Do sound dictation by saying simple words slowly and having kids try to write the sounds they hear.
- Ask children to tell you a short story and scribble it down as they talk. Then "read back" this emergent writing.

The key in the emergent literacy stage is to provide multisensory activities that make print fun and begin linking sounds to letters. Support all early writing and reading attempts to build confidence and skills.

Now let's move on to activities that support beginning literacy skills (Duke et al., 2006; Parsons and Ward, 2011).

- Provide plenty of culturally relevant books at their reading level. Alternatively, let them select books of interest to build motivation and fluency.

- Do shared reading and think-alouds to model using context clues, picture cues, sounding out words, etc. to unlock meaning.
- Practice sight words through games like sight word bingo. Use flashcards to drill common tricky words.
- Do word families and word pattern activities, sorting words that end in "-ight" or "-ake", for example. This reinforces decoding skills.
- Play games like word or sentence scramble that require decoding and reassembling words.
- Work on word building and word manipulation with magnetic letters to change beginning / ending sounds, compound words, and contractions.
- Write silly stories together using target vocabulary words they are learning. Help sound out spelling when needed.
- Have them dictate stories you scribble down. Then have them read back their own stories to build confidence.
- Ask them to summarize texts they read and explain vocabulary in their own words to check comprehension.
- Make writing a daily habit. Provide journals, notebooks, and story paper. Guide creative writing, but let them choose the topics.
- Celebrate all attempts at reading and writing. Gently correct only a few errors at a time during this stage.

The focus at this stage is on providing meaningful print interactions, decoding practice, and chances to build reading stamina and writing skills. Be patient and encouraging as skills develop.

Moving forward, here are some activities to build fluent literacy skills (Duke et al., 2006; Parsons and Ward, 2011).

- Have students read silently for 20+ minutes a day and log minutes read. Guide them to books that are "just right" for their reading level. Many assessment instruments provide Lexile levels in their results, as well as a suggested ZPD for growth.
- Do book talks where they share about a book they have read. Have them describe characters, setting, plot, and personal connections.
- Read a high-quality text together. Stop and ask inference questions – "Why do you think the character did that?" This builds comprehension.
- After reading, have them recount key details and the sequence of events. Ask them to summarize the main idea.
- Explore figurative language and literary devices in texts – identify metaphors, alliteration, and onomatopoeia. Discuss how they impact meaning.
- Compare / contrast two books with similar themes. How are the characters and plots alike and different? Fill in a Venn diagram.
- Do "reader's theater" by having them act out a scripted scene from a book [my absolute favorite].
- Guide them through the writing process – plan, draft, revise, edit. Teach revising skills like adding descriptive details.
- Explore different text types – reports, persuasive essays, stories. Study an author's craft in developing that genre.
- Provide authentic writing opportunities like letters, book reviews, and blogs. Publish their work to make reading meaningful.

The focus as students progress into full literacy is applying higher-level comprehension strategies, analyzing texts, sharing interpretations, and purposeful writing.

Exercises and activities for gestalt language processors

Shifting focus now to supporting GLP learners in the classroom, creating an inclusive environment conducive to their learning style is key for their language development. Remember, GLP learners take a more holistic approach to processing language, integrating information across modalities. As such, targeted strategies are needed to nurture their global, big-picture perspective.

Rather than breaking language down into discrete parts, look at ways to immerse GLP learners in rich sensory-based language experiences. Find opportunities for them to actively engage with language using multiple senses. Prioritize meaning over structure, providing language input that emphasizes real-world context and practical usage. Leverage their visual-spatial strengths, draw connections to their existing knowledge, and tap into their creativity.

GLP learners learn best when language is embodied and experienced, not just explained. Allow plenty of time for dramatic play, storytelling, and hands-on activities that bring language to life. Be open to movement and improvisation as conduits for language learning. Foster their imagination, validate their non-linear thinking, and encourage novel self-expression. Meet them where they are developmentally.

In short, the following strategies, tailored to the gestalt processing preference at stage 1, can unlock GLP learners' potential in the classroom. An inclusive, multisensory approach builds on their strengths, while giving them tools to develop language skills holistically (Bell, 2007; Blanc, 2012).

- Model short scripts for common situations like greetings, asking for help, or expressing needs. Use visuals and consistent language they can echo.
- Sing simple songs with repetition and gestures they can imitate, like *The Wheels on the Bus*, *If You're Happy and You Know It*, or a simple song recommended by the student's family in their home language.
- Read predictable, patterned books and pause so they can fill in the repeating word or phrase, like in *Brown Bear, Brown Bear, What Do You See?*.
- Use props and toys that inspire scripted play, like puppets, pretend play sets, or trains. Model simple play scripts.
- Point out environmental print like exit signs, logos, or labels. Read them aloud consistently when encountered.
- Provide sensory materials like shaving cream or rice and model tracing letters or numbers while saying the shapes.
- Use their individual interests to motivate learning scripts – recite facts about trains, numbers in Pi, or dinosaur names.
- Make scripted cards for daily routines like hand washing or tooth brushing steps that can be posted visibly.
- Set up sorting or matching activities focused on categories students enjoy like vehicle types or animal classes. Model noun labels.

The key at this stage in their development is to meet them at their stage and use repetition, visuals, sensory input, and their unique interests to provide language exposure. With support, their scripts can build into spontaneous phrases over time.

Now, some activities to support GLP learners at Stage 2 as they start to modify and combine scripts (Bell, 2007; Blanc, 2012).

- Read books with predictable patterns, but substitute in new vocabulary words – "Brown bear, brown bear, what do you hear?".
- Sing familiar songs but change out words – "The wheels on the bus go swish, swish, swish".
- Model taking two short scripts and combining them. "Want more" + "please" becomes "Want more, please."
- Play with scripts socially. Read a short, scripted line from a book and have them fill in the response.
- Use scripts verbally, but leave a blank at the end. Encourage them to fill it in – "I like to eat … ".
- Make scripted cards with two options so they can swap in a different word – "I want _____" with pictures for eat / drink, etc.
- Make slight mistakes in familiar scripts. See if they correct you – recite numbers in the wrong order.
- Add gestures, visuals, and tactile elements to scripts. Feel textures as you count, hold up finger puppets for social scripts.
- Model using the same script in different scenarios – "excuse me" when wanting to get by someone or interrupting.
- Provide factual scripts related to special interests they can recite and add to – planet names, stats for trains, etc.

The goal here is to provide scaffolding for script experimentation through prompt fading, substitution, and expansion, meeting them at their developmental stage while building flexibility.

Moving on, let's peek at some activities to support a GLP learner at Stage 3 as they isolate words and combine two-word phrases (Bell, 2007; Blanc, 2012).

- Read simple, repetitive books and emphasize target words by pausing and repeating them.
- Sing songs that isolate words. Pause after singing a word for them to repeat it back.
- Play sorting games focused on particular words. Sort transport images into cars versus trucks. Label the categories.
- Model and prompt two-word combinations in daily activities – "more milk", "go out", "my turn".
- Set up request opportunities where they must combine a verb + noun – "get ball", "open door".
- Model expansion from one word to two during play – Child: "Dump." Adult: "Dump truck."
- Intentionally pause between two words said sequentially to highlight word separation.
- Emphasize word pairs that commonly occur together – "big dog", "blue car", "cold ice".
- Use visual supports like icons on cards that can be combined into phrases – noun + verb cards.
- Provide blank fill-in cards or books – "I see a ____" and they select a picture card of the item seen.
- Reinforce all two-word attempts verbally and physically – expand to a phrase if needed.

The goals at stage 3 are to highlight individual meaningful words and model combining them into simple phrases. This builds a vocabulary foundation for the next stage of their grammar development.

An important aside must be made here. I've deliberately not tied the stages to age ranges. Every GLP learner progresses at their own pace. For me, movement through stage 3 to stage 4 happened in my teens through to my thirties. I used delayed echolalia and my superior recall skills to mask my difficulties with language. I wasn't really creating much original language in school.

Nevertheless, let's consider some activities to encourage beginning grammar skills for GLP learners at Stage 4 (Bell, 2007; Blanc, 2012).

- Model using simple sentence starters like "I see ... ", "I want ... ", "It's a ... ", and have them fill in the last word.
- Ask open-ended questions that require a verb + noun – "What do you see?" "What are you eating?".
- Have them use new word combinations to make requests – "I want apple" versus just saying "apple".
- Expand utterances to model grammar – Child: "Big dog." Adult: "The dog is big."
- Provide sequence cards for stories – first, next, last. Have them combine these into sentences.
- Play with toys and narrate actions – "The boy is jumping." "The girl is singing." Encourage them to copy.
- Read predictable books, but pause before rhyming words. See if they can fill in with the grammar pattern.
- Label emotions you observe – "You look happy." Expressive language is motivating.
- Write short phrases they say and read them back to highlight grammar growth.
- Maintain patience with grammatical errors and simply model correct forms.

The goals at stage 4 are to provide consistent models of grammar structures and encourage attempts through expansion, CLOZE sentences, questions, and interactive play. Meet them at their stage while introducing new linguistic patterns.

Finally, we consider some activities to continue building more advanced grammar skills for a GLP learner at stages 5 and 6 (Bell, 2007; Blanc, 2012).

- Model using conjunctions like "and", "but", "because" to combine ideas into sentences. The *Conjunction Junction* videos on YouTube are a fun way to do this.
- Demonstrate forming sentences with prepositional phrases – "The dog is under the table."
- Read books with dialogue and act out conversations. Highlight use of pronouns for back-and-forth speech.
- Expand sentences to add descriptive details – "The cat is black" becomes "The cat is small and black."
- Ask WH questions that need more complex responses – who, what, when, where, why, and how questions. Drill down or explore responses by engaging in the Five Whys technique (Kohfeldt and Langhout, 2012).
- Work on the use of irregular past tense verbs – "I sang", "He swam", "They ran".
- Practice forming negative / affirmative sentences – "The sky is not blue. It is grey."
- Model using comparatives like "-er" and superlatives like "-est".
- Demonstrate strategies for dealing with sentence errors or word-finding problems.

- Encourage journal or story writing through modeling, scribing, and sentence starters.
- Continue expanding elaborate, creative sentences students produce. Add details or vocabulary if needed.

The goals at this stage are providing models of diverse sentence types and advanced grammatical forms while encouraging spontaneous usage through play, reading, and guided conversation. Meet their skills while stretching language complexity.

Putting it all together

Now, let's put this all together. First, let's see what it might look like in a translanguaging environment containing stage 1 GLP learners and pre-literate students.

- Storytelling with props – Have children retell a familiar story using props, costumes, or puppets. Allow them to use words, gestures, drawings, or objects to get ideas across. This builds narrative skills through multiple means of representation.
- Picture book making – After a shared experience like a field trip, have kids make a class book with drawings / photos about it. Let them dictate or write captions in their strongest language. Bind the pages to create a multilingual book.
- Sound and action games – Play games where kids connect sounds and gestures, like snapping for letter sounds or clapping a syllabic rhythm. This helps build phonological awareness across languages.
- Listen and draw – Read a story aloud and have kids draw a picture capturing the main idea. Allow opportunities to clarify meaning in multiple languages. Share drawings afterward.

- Scavenger hunt – Provide a list of items in both languages and have kids search to find the matching objects. They can work in pairs and utilize both languages as resources. Celebrate what they find.

The main goals at this level are to tap into diverse language strengths, encourage collaborative meaning-making, and spark interest in literacy through interactive, multisensory activities that lower barriers to participation.

Moving on to emerging literacy / stage 2, we find more fun ideas for our classrooms and shared spaces.

- Sound scavenger hunt – Provide a list of letter sounds in multiple languages and have kids search books and the environment for words starting with those sounds.
- Tactile letter tracing – Use shaving cream, sand, or another texture to finger trace letters while saying letter names / sounds in English and the many home languages.
- Drawing story dictation – Scribe a short story as kids draw pictures to match. Allow them to clarify meaning using any language. Display the translations together.
- Alphabet movement – Assign gestures or dance moves for each letter sound. Have kids perform their "letter dance" as you sing the alphabet song.
- Shared pen pal letters – Have each student dictate a letter to a fictional pen pal. Share and translate the letters as a class. Send replies.

The main goals of these activities are to promote letter and sound recognition, build phonological awareness, make print fun and meaningful, develop pre-writing skills, introduce early concepts of print, encourage language and listening abilities, and help students make connections between speaking, reading, and writing.

Now for some beginning literacy / stage 3 activities.

- Bilingual book club – Partner students to read a high-interest book together. Have discussions and activities in students' choice of language(s).
- Word art – Make pictures and designs using cut-out sight words in different colors and languages. Label the artwork in all represented languages.
- Dictated story writing – Students dictate stories you scribe in their dominant language. Translate together and illustrate the stories.
- Front load vocabulary – Preview new vocabulary words in reading texts by highlighting them in students' home languages. Make a word wall.
- Literacy centers – Set up literacy stations focused on different skills (decoding, writing, word play) with multisensory options at each. Rotate through.
- Partner reading – Pair students up to read a dialogic text (two voices) in two languages. Switch parts and languages on repeat reads.
- Word sorts – Sort vocabulary words from texts by language, letter / sound features, parts of speech, meanings. Reinforce patterns.
- Language experience stories – Take turns recounting shared class experiences. Scribe these first-hand stories told in students' choice of language(s).
- Translation game – Students translate teacher-created sentences into their home language to reinforce grammar structures. Peer check.

- Multilingual word games – Adapt word games by allowing students to brainstorm target words in multiple languages for peers to guess.

These activities aim to support emergent language learners as they develop more conventional literacy skills like decoding, fluency, comprehension, and writing. The activities take an interactive, multisensory approach designed to leverage students' developing home language abilities and background knowledge while introducing grade-level literacy concepts and texts.

Specifically, these activities seek to promote collaboration, tap into multiple learning strengths like speaking and listening, make connections between oral language and literacy, teach key academic vocabulary within meaningful contexts, reinforce specific decoding and grammar skills, provide differentiated support through centers, and validate students' diverse linguistic assets through activities like translated stories and multilingual word play.

Finally, we have fun learning activities for fluent readers / stages 4+.

- Reader's theater – Act out scenes from books in two languages. Assign parts so students play roles in both languages and work together to translate. Be careful, however, as GLP learners with good word recognition and prosody can often mask their lack of comprehension in such exercises (as I did). Be sure to check for understanding frequently as you get to know students.
- Language experience stories – Students take turns sharing personal stories orally in their dominant language. Scribe and translate them together. Illustrate and publish.

- Compare / contrast texts – Students find examples of figurative language techniques used in texts from two different cultures / languages. Compare their impacts.
- Multilingual writing – Provide a writing prompt and encourage students to pre-write in their strongest language. Peer edit with a multilingual partner.
- Author's chair – Students share a piece of original writing in their chosen language. Ask questions and give feedback as a class. Display the work in the class.
- Mixed language collages – Students make a collage about a topic, incorporating text, words, and images from multiple languages to convey ideas.
- Multimedia biographies – Research a historical figure and make a digital presentation including text, audio, and visuals in multiple languages.
- Translation game – Give students bilingual texts with blanks. Partners work together to translate missing words from one language to fill the gaps.
- Vocabulary charades – Students act out vocabulary words found in their texts for peers to guess in either language. Extend by using the words in sentences.

These multilingual literacy activities aim to leverage older students' developing language abilities for continued reading comprehension and writing skill growth. The activities take an interactive approach that validates children's diverse cultural and linguistic assets through collaborative peer work, choice of languages, and opportunities to showcase multilingual creations. Specifically, the activities seek to build confidence using multiple languages flexibly, reinforce understanding of texts by discussing and translating concepts across languages, motivate through multicultural literature and personalized writing topics, teach key vocabulary within multilingual contexts, provide scaffolds like translanguaging and visuals to support comprehension, allow creative expression in students' strongest languages, and encourage purposeful bilingual writing through drafting, feedback, and publishing. The emphasis is on utilizing students' growing biliteracy and metalinguistic skills for richer literary analysis, deeper conceptual connections, and producing original multilingual work. The translanguaging techniques used at this stage promote fluency in navigating back and forth across languages. The goal is to nurture enthusiastic, confident readers, writers, and communicators who see their multilingualism as an asset and use it effectively to interpret texts, share ideas, and create meaning.

These multilingual literacy activities offer numerous benefits to monolingual students in such a linguistically diverse environment. Through collaborative group work and open sharing of ideas in multiple languages, monolingual pupils have rich exposure to different languages and cultures. They also gain an appreciation for their classmates' bilingual skills. The interactive discussions, translations, and visual supports aid comprehension of texts and concepts for all students. Monolinguals can learn key vocabulary words as they hear them used in various languages. The emphasis on validating students' cultural backgrounds motivates engagement. Allowing creative works in students' strongest tongues gives monolinguals insight into the value of fluency in more than one language. Overall, these techniques create an inclusive classroom where monolingual students can develop respect for multilingualism and leverage their peers' knowledge to supplement their own learning.

Summary

Through our rather detailed exploration of early literacy, it has become evident that literacy is not an innate or natural human ability, but rather a complex set of skills that must be intentionally taught and learned. Typically developing analytical processors progress through predictable stages from pre-literacy foundations to decoding ability to fluent, automatic reading and writing. Typically developing gestalt processors, on the other hand, comprehend language more holistically, benefiting from activities that validate their scripts and ability to grasp meaning from broader contexts. By understanding these diverse developmental pathways, we as educators are better equipped to meet all students at their current stage and provide the appropriate scaffolds to continue their growth.

The research-based activities shared here target the needs of both processing tendencies at different levels. Additionally, incorporating translanguaging techniques and UDL principles allows us to create classrooms that flexibly leverage students' full set of skills. The result is an inclusive literacy environment that nurtures reading and writing skills in all students, regardless of learning differences, language background, or developmental trajectory. When we honor the multitude of ways students come to unlock meaning from text, we can ensure that all emerge with tools to actively participate in an increasingly interconnected world.

4
Young adult literacy

Learning objective
Students will be able to evaluate research-based literacy instruction and interventions to improve reading, writing, and language skills among young adults with a range of skills and abilities.

> "The beautiful thing about learning is nobody can take it away from you." – B. B. King, American blues musician

Rationale
Our learning goal centers on utilizing academic research and robust evidence to design and evaluate effective literacy instruction and interventions for young adults with diverse needs. This aligns seamlessly to several key Common Core standards (e.g., CCSS.ELA-Lit.RL.11-12.1, CCSS.ELA-Literacy.W.11-12.7, and CCSS.ELA-Literacy.SL.11-12.1.A). Students must closely analyze texts to cite textual evidence and justify reasoned inferences – the bedrock of appraising research to inform literacy program design and differentiation, allowing learners to fulfill the goal. Additionally, standards promoting real-world research inquiry to solve problems relate directly to investigating and synthesizing multiple sources on literacy pedagogy to create materials. Coherent writing production standards equally apply when generating

written plans and resources as stipulated. Finally, academic discussion standards covering evidence-based preparation connect strongly to collaborative literacy program development through thoughtful, reasoned exchange of opinions. Thus, the central research, communication, application, and differentiation themes running through these standards neatly mirror the substantive skills and knowledge required to achieve the learning goal. The standards therefore provide an apposite framework to facilitate student progress towards the goal.

Introduction

Before we begin, it should be noted that many of the reading, writing, speaking, and listening activities and exercises presented in the previous chapter would make wonderful additions to an inclusive and vibrant secondary classroom. They need only be updated with grade-level materials that are culturally and linguistically relevant to the students therein.

Beginning of year (BOY) is never a fun time for teachers or students. It's filled with anxiety and stress. When the school year starts, secondary students often know the frustration and boredom they'll face during the upcoming weeks of standardized testing. But we teachers understand the real value in assessing where students are with their reading, writing, and communicating. Checking their ability levels helps us map out a teaching plan to help them progress. Besides, it is quite common for students moving from primary up to secondary school to show up at their new school ahead of their student files being transferred. This means the new teachers haven't received the students' full background records containing all the important details on academic history and progress, such as their abilities and needs, SEND support requirements (e.g., IEP / 504 plan), attainment and assessment data, behavior notes, and target objectives.

Essentially, while the teachers know they have new students coming, without having that cumulative file for each of them, the new students are unfamiliar in terms of their capabilities, strengths, challenges, or what extra provisions they require. This lack of insight poses issues for teachers looking to tailor lesson plans and responsively shape learning experiences. Without the BOY assessments, teachers may launch courses missing key context around these new additions to the cohort, hampering efforts to enable adaptive planning fitted to each student's needs.

So, in this transition period before the files come across, teachers face greater difficulty personalizing learning for the benefit of their incoming youngsters. It's an unhelpful gap requiring bridging to ensure new students don't have their induction undermined but instead feel truly seen, valued, and set up to progress on day one.

By uncovering students' baseline abilities, favored languages, and processing tendencies early on, we can help our learners use familiar cultural tools to build skills in comfortable ways. The goal is to turn these BOY assessments into a positive tool, so students feel seen and set up for a year where their unique needs are understood, and learning is tailored specially for them.

Upon receiving the results, these assessments may inform you that many of your students are well below grade level. After all, reading achievement among US high school students suggests many are behind grade level, with only 37 per cent of 12th graders nationally scoring proficient or above in standardized assessments. Additionally, large gaps persist between white students and students of color, with just 23 per cent of Black and 35 per cent of Hispanic students reaching proficiency. Compared to the 1990s, average reading scores have declined over the past decade for high school seniors (NEAP, 2023). Based on international assessments, US students score around average in reading compared to other so-called developed nations. While precise grade-level deficiencies are difficult to determine, it is clear that a significant percentage of American high schoolers lack proficient literacy skills, with substantial variation between demographic groups and geographic locations. Overall, the data indicate reading instruction and literacy remain pressing issues for many US secondary schools.

But, by the time one becomes a teenager, it's assumed by the educational system that one has age-appropriate literacy skills in one's primary language. By now, you know that this wasn't true for me. You likely also know that a great many students make their way out of elementary school in need of serious help. The challenge for educators, administrators, policymakers, and parents is what to do with this cohort.

I'll use my current school as an example. I teach at a magnet school. Magnet schools generally have a special focus. Mine is the arts and sciences. We have an amazing theater program and one of only two working farms in the second largest school district in the US. We attract students from all over the region. Also, we don't discriminate against students with learning challenges. If a student's family applies for them to attend our school, they're largely admitted.

Looking at the state's dashboard of standardized testing data, one can easily see that students in the greater Los Angeles area are reading and comprehending many grade levels below where they should be for their age. We talked about what to do about this in the primary school grades in the previous chapter. Here, we'll discuss what can be done in the secondary school grades.

Framing the discussions in this chapter will be some of my own research, conducted at my school site just a few years ago. The research design was informed not only by my own lived experiences, previously discussed, but also by my more recent experiences as a classroom teacher. Let's begin there.

Becoming an autistic public school teacher

When I was finished with my Teach for America (TFA) induction boot camp in the summer of 2020, at the height of the global pandemic, I began to interview with principals for my first teaching placement. The TFA staff were incredible in handling all the set-up, finding out where teachers were needed and organizing the interviews. In my first interview, I was asked about what sort of skills and abilities I would bring to the school's Special Day Class, or SDC. I disclosed that I am autistic, alexithymic, and have a ton of sensory issues. For myself, I shared, I seek to create calm and balance in the classrooms I inhabit. Understanding that alexithymia is present in most of the neurodivergent population as I do (Hoerricks, 2023), I wanted to leverage that sensory ability to the class's advantage.

The questions that followed lead me to believe that the principal had already chosen a candidate, and that I was a likely add-on so that he could check the box indicating that he had interviewed several people for the position and that the process was competitive. This is something that happens all the time in American civil service. I had experienced a lot of this in my work with the City of Los Angeles in my previous career. Thus, I didn't take it personally when I didn't get the job.

My next interview lasted over an hour. The principal had an open mind and a truly open position for an SDC teacher, the SDC discussed in the previous chapter. She asked many of the same questions as the previous principal but was intrigued by my responses. We dove so deeply into the conversation, it felt more like an autistic infodump than a job interview. She explained that she had fourth and fifth graders with a range of eligibilities, some with 1:1 behavioral intervention, and most with complex trauma. All were with or at risk for emotional / behavioral disorders (EBDs). An hour after we ended the call, I was offered the position. Having been fully "out" as my autistic self in the interview, and it having been essentially an infodump, it was an incredibly joyful moment to be seen, heard, and validated like that.

When school began, I met the kids of what the staff had unironically dubbed "fight club". The kids had hair triggers, and behaviors were off the charts. But, within a few weeks of patience, routine, and not reacting to their provocations, things calmed way down. With things calmed down, we began to learn.

Because I was a new teacher, an intern, I was observed by my administrator quite frequently. I could sense that she was baffled by my style, but she saw the results. As noted in the previous chapter, my students were learning and growing. Not to spend too much time on recollection here, I will say that the average growth on standardized tests of literacy (e.g., DIBELS) for the students in my class that year was over 25 per cent. Plus, the students' behavioral problems diminished greatly. So great was their improvement, the assistant principal in charge of discipline noted to me his delight that fights in my class went from three per day before I arrived to less than three per week. My results there fueled my rapid progress through my internship, and I was able to complete it in just that one year.

The following year, there were many changes at my school. The welcoming and amazing principal had been promoted and a new one assigned. The school's assistant principals had all been promoted as well. There was a new regime, one that I didn't know and that didn't know me. Plus, many of the local parents chose to keep their students at home and take advantage of the district's distance learning options. The pandemic was still present, but students had returned to classrooms late into my internship. Parents, evaluating their feelings on campus life during a pandemic, decided in large numbers to continue to keep their kids home. Enrolment at my school dropped by almost a quarter. In the US, the enrolment at a school dictates the number of teachers needed for the various classes and programs. Clearly, not all teachers would keep their placements. As a new probational teacher with only one year of experience, I was the first to be let go.

I received the news on "Norm Day". I came to school as normal and was met at the gate by the principal. I was to clear the classroom of my personal things without delay and without interacting with students. I was to turn in my key and leave as soon as possible. Someone from the regional office would contact me, the new principal said rather abruptly and impersonally. That call came three weeks later.

When the regional office finally called, I was told that I was going to be assigned to a magnet school within the region as a Resource Specialist Program (RSP) Teacher. The school, a full inclusion school, had grades spanning from 6 to 12. I would be supporting ninth grade English classes as a co-teacher. I was told to report to the school's principal the following day, prepared to work in the classroom.

On day one, I was introduced to the classes and the staff. At first, I just sat, listened, and felt the energy and vibe of the rooms (Hoerricks, 2022a). Although these English classes weren't part of a SDC, they had all the same emotions and energies. Students were struggling. Students were bored. Students were disengaged. Students, if given a choice, would likely walk out and just hang out with their friends.

There, in those English classes, I saw myself as a struggling teenager. I saw all the same systemic problems. I saw and felt all the emotional problems. I saw and felt the trauma responses. I saw, also, that I had the lived experience of overcoming the things they were facing.

I conferenced with my co-teacher and shared my insights. A wonderful and caring woman, she empathized with me but noted that much of what happens in the classroom from an instructional standpoint is governed by the Educational Code, the Common Core State Standards, and such. She realized that most of the class was well below grade level, but she was required to present her instruction at grade level. Scaffolds and supports, she offered, were the job of the RSP teacher – me.

I reached out to the instructional support team. I was familiar with the Multi-Tiered System of Supports (MTSS) and its constituent Response to Intervention (RtI) from my teacher prep program. I asked if the school had a formal RtI program. I was told that the school's leadership considered RtI to be an elementary school concept, not fit for purpose in the upper grades … so no, no RtI. I reached out to the Developmental Reading teacher, another RSP, for help. I thought of, perhaps, looping some of the struggling kids into his class. He told me that, unfortunately, students must be assigned to his Developmental Reading class through their IEP, that he couldn't just pull kids out of their English class for help.

With official resources unavailable, I again sat down with my co-teacher to plot out what could be done given the constraints of the system. We'll explore that later in the chapter. First, I want to dive in a bit to MTSS to discover why it wasn't available at my school, and if it could possibly have helped my group of struggling learners.

Multi-Tiered System of Supports

MTSS, again, stands for Multi-Tiered System of Supports. It is a framework used in many schools around the world to provide targeted academic and behavioral interventions to students based on their individual needs. There are some key points about MTSS in schools. It involves providing instruction, interventions, and supports at increasing levels of intensity based on each student's needs (Fien et al., 2021). There are typically three tiers:

- Tier 1 – high-quality core instruction for all students in the general education classroom;
- Tier 2 – targeted small group interventions for students who need more support in addition to tier 1; and
- Tier 3 – intensive individual interventions for students with the greatest needs who do not respond sufficiently to tiers 1 and 2.

In MTSS, data-based decision making is used to identify students in need of support and monitor their progress. Universal screening and progress monitoring data inform what interventions students receive and whether those supports should be adjusted over time. It aims to provide the right level of instruction and interventions efficiently, and early on before issues worsen and students require other, more intensive services (De Bruin, 2021).

The goal is to prevent long-term academic failure. MTSS involves collaboration between general education teachers, special education teachers, specialists, administrators, and families to wrap a slew of services and supports around struggling students. It's not a specific program, per se. It's more of a team-based approach that is used to problem-solve and make decisions about student support.

The MTSS umbrella includes space for both academic and behavioral support. Under MTSS, the behavioral supports are called Positive Behavior Interventions and Supports (PBIS) with RtI covering the academic side (Khan, 2020). Some examples of MTSS interventions include small reading groups, social skills instruction, check-in / check-out mentoring, and counseling.

In general, MTSS is a multi-tiered early intervention and prevention framework that schools can utilize to help all students succeed academically and behaviorally. The intensity of instruction and support is adjusted based on real-time data monitoring.

Response to Intervention

RtI) is closely related to and often used interchangeably with MTSS when discussing this topic, but there are some key differences. RtI more narrowly focuses on academic interventions, while MTSS expands support to behavior / social-emotional issues through PBIS. RtI is often used to identify learning disabilities and determine eligibility for special education, while MTSS has a broader goal of providing support to all students. Where MTSS emphasizes a school / district-wide approach and systems change, RtI can be implemented in individual classrooms. Thus, RtI can be viewed as the academic and identification piece within the larger MTSS framework that also incorporates behavioral and social-emotional support for all students school wide (De Bruin, 2021; De Bruin et al., 2023).

The key components of RtI within MTSS include:

- Universal screening – All students are screened and benchmarked 3–4 times per year to identify students who may have or be at risk for academic or behavioral problems;
- Progress monitoring – Student progress is monitored frequently (weekly or bi-weekly) to see if interventions are working and identify students needing more support;

- Tiered intervention – Students receive differing levels of support based on their level of need. Again, tier 1 is high-quality instruction for all students. Tier 2 is targeted small group interventions. Tier 3 is intensive, individualized interventions;
- Data-based decision making – Data are used to determine which students need additional support, match interventions to student need, and evaluate if interventions are working;
- Fidelity of implementation – Evidence-based interventions are implemented consistently and with fidelity; and
- Collaboration – There is collaboration between teachers, interventionists, and families throughout the RtI process.

Again, the goals of RtI are to provide "research-based" interventions matched to student needs and closely monitor student progress to make data-driven decisions about instruction and intervention effectiveness. Within an MTSS framework, RtI is supposed to provide a preventive, differentiated model to close achievement gaps and help all students succeed.

MTSS around the world

MTSS and RtI aren't just American concepts. The frameworks are also being adopted and implemented in other countries around the world.

- Canada – Many provinces and territories including Ontario, Alberta, and Nova Scotia are implementing MTSS in their school systems (Whitley and Hollweck, 2020).
- Australia – MTSS aligns with the nationwide RtI approach and is being promoted by education agencies in various territories (De Bruin, 2021; De Bruin et al., 2023).

- New Zealand – MTSS principles are integrated into New Zealand's educational approach, particularly the Learning Support system (Gillon, 2023).
- United Kingdom – Some MTSS elements are being incorporated into programs like Achievement for All, which promotes structured interventions. It is not as formalized as in the US (EEF, 2023).
- The Netherlands – The Netherlands is trialing MTSS approaches in select regions and schools, often under labels like Multi-Tiered Prevention System (Hingstman, 2021).
- South Africa – Pilot projects are exploring MTSS to support inclusive education and improve outcomes (Gagnon et al., 2021).
- Denmark – Denmark is trialing MTSS as part of efforts to support students at risk of academic failure (Sandhaug et al., 2022).
- Sweden – MTSS aligns with Sweden's three-tiered model of support and is gaining attention (Lundqvist, 2023; Roos et al., 2023).
- Ireland – Ireland is in the early stages of promoting MTSS through pilot programs and academic research (Banks, 2021).

So, while MTSS originated in the US, many other countries are recognizing its benefits and gradually implementing adaptations suitable to their educational contexts. Some early results indicate that it is helping schools around the world better support all students' needs.

A path forward

Getting back to the meetings between my co-teacher and me, it's important to remember that as attractive as MTSS and RtI are

/ were, it wasn't an option at my school. It required systems and resources that weren't available. In our discussions, we quickly determined a few key things:

a) Whatever was to be done would have to be done by me, the RSP teacher;

b) Whatever needed to be acquired in terms of instructional materials would have to be furnished by me. There were no school resources; and

c) Whatever was to be done couldn't take too much instructional time away from the general education curriculum. My co-teacher had her approved syllabus and pacing plan for the year and did not want it altered significantly.

I thought back to my first placement. I scoured the research, the bulk of which can be found in the references for this chapter. I assembled an overall idea. Then a unit plan. Then individual lessons. I found data tracking tools. I put things together and made my formal pitch. I wanted to do a series of 20-minute "workshops", taking over the low-stakes "warmup" exercise time at the beginning of the class period. I also wanted to conduct the exercise like a small-scale action research study and publish my findings, thus I needed a bunch of permissions.

Challenging behaviors in the classroom

Consider that when one enters high school unable to adequately read and comprehend, this will present a problem to one's social and emotional growth. It should go without saying that reading is a fundamental skill necessary for success in school and life.

However, many students with or at risk for EBDs struggle with reading skills that fail to improve over time (Alexander et al., 1997; Alexander, 1997; Anderson et al., 2001; Bal, 2018; Brunzell et al., 2019). These reading difficulties can have profound impacts on a student's social, emotional, and academic growth, especially as they transition to high school (Burke et al., 2015; Coleman and Vaughn, 2000). Students entering high school with inadequate reading and comprehension abilities face significant challenges across all subject areas. Without strong literacy skills, students struggle to access content knowledge and complete assignments. As the achievement gap widens, these students may experience feelings of frustration, anxiety, and low self-esteem (Hinshaw, 1992).

Reading challenges make it difficult for students having or at risk for EBDs to actively participate in class discussions or collaborative work. They may avoid participating due to embarrassment or act out due to frustration. Social interactions with peers may also suffer if the student feels ashamed or isolated. Inadequate reading skills prevent students from fully engaging with curriculum and peers, limiting their social-emotional growth (Levy and Chard, 2001). As students progress through high school, lack of reading proficiency increasingly hampers their ability to gain content knowledge, develop analytical skills, and communicate ideas effectively. As my lived experience shows, this can have long-term consequences, reducing opportunities for higher education and career prospects (Benner et al., 2010).

The research shows that interventions targeting reading skills are critical for students with or at risk for EBDs (Benner et al., 2010;

Costello et al., 1999; Costello et al., 2003). Again, reading proficiency affects all areas of development – academic, social, and emotional. And again, students without adequate literacy abilities struggle to access the grade-level curriculum, participate in class, interact with peers, and gain independence (Vaughn et al., 2002).

And then there are our GLP learners. Remember that our GLP students rely heavily on absorbing the full meaning and context from written texts and social interactions. For these learners, weak reading proficiency is particularly detrimental to their academic, social, and emotional development. Without strong literacy skills, GLP learners will struggle to comprehend curriculum content, follow classroom discussions, interpret peer contributions, and grasp subtle social cues (Mesibov et al., 2004). This deprives them of the holistic understanding and big-picture context they need to learn new material, collaborate effectively, build social relationships, think critically, and communicate ideas. GLP learners with poor reading skills at this age are at a disadvantage in making inferences, connections, and interpretations. This affects their class participation, peer engagement, self-confidence, and sense of belonging.

It's important to note here that the students I was facing in my new placement did not have the advantage of previously being in an inclusive translanguaging classroom, like the ones we saw in the previous chapter. Yet, as teachers, we must teach and support everyone in the class. This is where I was beginning.

Diving into the research

As I dove into the research to create my study, I found that it showed that teachers could increase the reading and comprehension scores of students with or at risk for EBDs (Sanders et al., 2019; Sanders, Jolivette, et al. 2021; Sanders, Rollins et al., 2021, 2022). However, most of the studies took place in what we might call ideal or controlled settings. When I was investigating this, no study had examined these issues in an urban or US Title I school setting. My small-scale action research study would feature a cohort of ninth grade public school students (n=117) with well below baseline English language skills as determined by state-wide standardized testing who had or were at risk for EBDs.

My student population contained a mix of students with an OHI, AUT, or SLD eligibility for special education services where an EBD was or may have also been present (n=18). It also included a mix of general education students (n=99) without IEPs, but where an EBD may also have been present. My analysis of the available behavioral data showed that parents, teachers, and school psychologists were all concerned about the behavioral challenges and study habits of these ninth grade students.

Given that the studied population, the kids in our class, had many years of experience with the school district's PBIS strategies, the assumption was that the students should not still present challenging behaviors and learning deficits. Yet, the data show that each year, the students fell further behind in reading skills and comprehension, and their behaviors became more of an issue in their classes.

I thought back to my dissertation (Hoerricks, 2018) and William Glasser's work on student success (1998a, 1998b, 1998c, 2001, 2003, 2008). Choice Theory seemed a good theoretical construct on which to base my study. Where PBIS is heavily flavored with behaviorism, Choice Theory seemed a better fit for developing the self-regulation that students were lacking.

You see, B. F. Skinner's theories of operant conditioning and reinforcement have significantly influenced modern classroom management strategies (Schlinger, 2021). His work promoted providing students with immediate feedback, praise, and rewards to reinforce desired behaviors. This concept has influenced many school behavior management programs that used token economies (Kazdin, 1982) as a system of rewards. Importantly, Skinner's theories have helped form the basis for applied behavior analysis (ABA) and functional behavioral assessment (FBA), widely used interventions in special education settings (Callahan et al., 2023; Kestner et al., 2019). ABA applies principles of operant conditioning to shape behaviors, while FBA aims to identify the functions maintaining problem behaviors.

However, Skinner's reward / punishment-based techniques have faced criticism, especially from neurodivergent communities. Many see his approaches as overly rigid and failing to account for student dignity, autonomy, and self-determination. Some even liken ABA to "dog training", arguing it can ignore the emotional needs of autistic and other neurodivergent children. The neurodiversity movement generally advocates for more inclusive, identity-affirming practices over behaviorist tactics rooted in Skinner's theories of reinforcement and conditioning. Though his methods are still widely used, Skinner's legacy remains contentious among modern disability advocates seeking alternative classroom management strategies.

To be fair, not all ABA approaches and uses are problematic. For example, ABA has its proponents among parents and caregivers of level 3 autistics, where safety issues are frequently a concern. Many level 3 autistic individuals experience "pica", an eating disorder entailing ingestion of non-nutritive substances like dirt, paint, or batteries. This can obviously pose serious health risks. Techniques based in ABA, such as differential reinforcement, can train alternative actions to replace pica and similar dangerous behaviors. When a child engages frequently in unsafe behaviors like bolting into traffic or self-harm without warning, ABA supporters view these interventions, when properly overseen, as some of the only methods to build essential safety skills (Fields et al., 2021). So, for the most impacted families struggling with critical safety issues, ABA's capacity to modify behaviors can provide an indispensable lifeline, albeit one still requiring judicious and compassionate implementation. But students with support needs this high won't typically be seen in full inclusion settings, like the classes at my school.

Nevertheless, while behaviorist approaches have their proponents, other schools of thought offer alternative perspectives on classroom ecology. Notably, Dr William Glasser's Choice Theory instead emphasizes building intrinsic motivation and self-directed learning. This humanist approach focuses first on fulfilling core psychological needs for belonging, autonomy, and competence. Satisfying these needs cultivates the classroom relationships and climate for student engagement in the learning process itself (Sullo, 2011).

Choice Theory advocates personalized, collaborative models like multi-age classrooms where peer mentoring allows students to take active responsibility for their education. Students self-evaluate mastery of concepts, becoming accountable to their own learning rather than the judgment of rewards or consequences. The teacher facilitates this autonomous regulation through feedback and support rather than top-down discipline. While perhaps less direct, addressing the underlying deficit of essential psychological needs to promote organic self-regulation may better honor student dignity. Where safety permits, avoiding the imposition of conditioned compliance has been shown to empower students' capacity for self-actualization. This facilitative posture contrasts sharply with Skinner's therapist-led stimulus-response manipulation.

Unfortunately, classroom behavior programmes like PBIS bringing tokens and incentives into school culture further enmesh external reward systems. While understandable to overtaxed educators like my co-teacher, such quick fixes inadvertently undermine the belonging, competence, and intrinsic motivation students need to truly own their education. Creating space for supportive teacher-student relationships and student autonomy proves more conducive to long-term solutions.

Self-Regulation Strategy Development

The Quality School's emphasis on self-direction does not negate the need for direct, explicit instruction. Teachers are vital to not only provide instruction but also to model appropriate behaviors (Hoerricks, 2022a; Hoerricks, 2022b). One of the most important behaviors that teachers model in a Quality School is self-regulation. Like all other topics presented in the classroom, self-regulation strategies must be explicitly taught and modeled if the students are to learn the concepts and begin to develop strategies on their own.

Self-Regulation Strategy Development (SRSD) is an evidence-based instructional approach that supports the self-regulated use of academic strategies by combining direct explicit instruction of an academic strategy with self-regulation skills (e.g., goal setting, self-reinforcement, self-monitoring, and self-statements) (Scruggs and Mastropieri, 2007). SRSD has been an effective instructional method for improving reading comprehension deficits (Mason, 2013; Sanders et al., 2019) for students diagnosed with various disabilities, including those having or at risk for EBDs, spanning grades 4 through 12.

The components of SRSD make it an apt instructional approach for students having or at risk for EBDs. Firstly, SRSD expressly accounts for metacognitive skill and engrained learning behaviors (Harris and Graham, 1999) – both frequent challenges among said cohort. Many wrestle with inefficient learning tendencies (e.g., off-tasking, noncompliance) plus substantive impairment in self-direction across planning, progress monitoring, and completion of academic work (Mastropieri and Scruggs, 2014). So, SRSD directly teaches self-management tactics integrable when learning, strengthened as appropriate per individual need (Sanders et al., 2021). Moreover, the staged framework inherently scaffolds EBD students (Ennis and Jolivette, 2014) as skills strengthen. Thus, SRSD deliberately targets the self-regulatory and counterproductive habits often afflicting those having EBD by systematically fostering positive disciplinary behaviors to remove barriers to achievement. The emphasis on meta-strategies for succeeding at complex tasks makes it well matched to transforming the capability beliefs and academic codes of behavior within this group.

To accomplish its goals, SRSD uses multiple recursive stages to teach an academic strategy to mastery. These stages can be combined, reordered, or repeated as necessary (Harris et al., 2002). Teachers can manipulate these stages based on the individual needs of their students. These stages are (1) develop and activate background knowledge, (2) discuss it, (3) model it, (4) memorize it, (5) support it, and (6) independent practice (Sanders et al., 2021). More on these later in the chapter.

A summary of "the problem" in our classes

When a student is lagging in all areas of literacy, in reading, writing, speaking, and listening skills, it's important to take a strategic approach to remediation. Most programs recommend focusing first on building fundamental reading abilities. Reading provides the basis for strengths in other literacy domains, as we'll see in Chapter 6. However, motivation is key. Teachers must make remediation engaging for the student while mitigating negative feelings, especially as students get older. We can start with alphabet basics if needed, coordinate efforts with parents and other support staff, set realistic goals, and praise progress.

Remediating literacy gaps requires patience and persistence. But, with concerted effort across settings on foundational skills, students can gain competence over time. When working to improve the literacy skills of a struggling student, our goal should be to strengthen the fundamental abilities that serve as the foundation for reading, writing, speaking, and listening. By providing targeted instruction that is customized to the student's needs and interests, as well as feedback that motivates and encourages the student's efforts, we can help shore up their foundational literacy blocks and set them on the path to competence across all domains.

With this in mind, my students were all well below their grade-level benchmark in reading and comprehension. According to their standardized test data, many were at least three grade levels below the benchmark. This severely impacted their ability to access the curriculum in any meaningful way. Additionally, many had behavioral challenges, including aggressive tendencies that had interfered with previous attempts at interventions.

The intertwined academic and behavior deficits, often referred to as the failure cycle, of students having or at risk for EBDs negatively impacts learning and skill acquisition. Again, reading comprehension is one academic area where students having or at risk for EBDs often display significant deficits. The SRSD instructional approach is one method that accounts for these students' behaviors, making it a promising approach (Sanders et al., 2021).

SRSD, I found, helps improve literacy for all students in several important ways.

- Explicitly teaching reading strategies like summarizing, making inferences, and monitoring comprehension directly builds students' literacy skills, regardless of processing style or native language.

- Self-regulation techniques help students reflect on their learning, set reading goals, self-monitor their progress, and reinforce their growth. This metacognitive approach benefits both analytic and gestalt processors.
- For analytic processors, the structured strategy instruction allows them to break down reading into discrete steps they can methodically apply. Self-regulation helps them stay focused on each phase.
- Gestalt processors are aided by seeing the "big-picture" purpose of each reading strategy. Self-regulation allows them to monitor their overall comprehension.
- SRSD's emphasis on making strategies flexible and self-driven helps students adapt techniques to their own learning needs and texts.
- The SRSD principles of scaffolded instruction, individualized feedback, and gradual release of responsibility provide differentiated support for all learners.
- Using SRSD consistently develops self-regulated readers who proactively apply strategies. This creates independent, motivated readers with improved literacy.

In sum, SRSD's blended approach of explicit strategy instruction and metacognitive self-regulation benefits diverse learners with varying skills and processing styles. Implemented effectively, I believed, it could enhance reading proficiency for both general education and special education students.

The solution

After researching many successful small-scale action research studies that featured SRSD, I determined it could be just the thing to help my struggling students.

It wasn't some new fad or flash in the pan. The SRSD approach has been around for 40 years – it was created by Karen Harris and Steve Graham to improve writing skills for kids with special needs. But the studies that I found show it works all over – with individuals, small groups, and entire classrooms. Plus, it seems to work for students from primary through high school.

Better still, it's not a set of pre-made lesson plans or even a commercial product. It's more like a fully customizable framework. Indeed, SRSD gives students the tools to manage their own learning goals. They learn step-by-step strategies to complete different tasks, organize their thoughts, reflect on progress, ask for help, all those wonderful self-direction skills we wish they had. Thus, it helps unlock their potential by empowering them to track and achieve their own success.

And that's what really sold me on SRSD. It isn't just teaching content, it's nurturing deep personal capabilities – help with planning, motivation, handling frustrations, and so on. Plus, it lets kids take the driver's seat. And the research shows that kind of self-efficacy lifts achievement in the long run.

Again, the more I conducted my autistic deep dive on the subject, the more I became convinced that these strategies could be life-changing for students like mine. SRSD taps into social-emotional needs, not just academics.

With that introduction and fanfare out of the way, here is the overall structure of SRSD. It is comprised of six interconnected and iterative stages (Harris, et al., 2008).

- Develop and activate background knowledge: Build on students' existing knowledge and experiences relevant to the

strategies being taught. Get them thinking about what they already know about the topic and the process.
- Discuss skill and strategies: Explain and discuss the specific strategies students will learn, so they understand what the strategies are and how they can help improve their skills.
- Model skill and strategies: Demonstrate the strategies in action, showing students examples of how to apply the strategies properly.
- Memorize strategies: Have students memorize the steps of the key writing strategies through mnemonics, visuals, or other memory techniques. This helps internalize the strategies.
- Guided practice of skill and strategies: Provide opportunities for students to practice applying the strategies with support and feedback. Slowly remove supports to aid independence.
- Independent practice: Let students independently apply the strategies to new tasks to cement their understanding and transfer of the skills. Check for sustained strategy use.

The What Works Clearinghouse (2017) reviewed nine studies that met the methodological parameters like the study I was about to conduct. Most of the experiments showed positive results, while none of the included studies yielded negative results.

While the WWC review is useful, it does not fully encompass the breadth of research that has been conducted on the effects of SRSD. The research shows that SRSD has been used with general education students, autistic students, students with learning disabilities, and students with or at risk for EBDs (Asaro-Saddler, 2016; Garwood, 2018; Graham et al., 2012; Losinski et al., 2014). Further, SRSD has been used to improve students' written expression, reading comprehension, math fractional skills, and self-advocacy (Cuenca-Carlino et al., 2016; Cuenca-Carlino et al., 2018; Garwood, 2018; Mason, 2004; Mason, 2013; Mason et al., 2013; Mason et al., 2006; Sanders et al., 2018).

In keeping with the framework versus product concept, I found a whole community of teachers using SRSD in their classes as well as websites that freely offer SRSD resources. One such site, ThinkSRSD.com, offers a host of resources for anyone seeking to implement SRSD in their classrooms. For example, ThinkSRSD.com offers pre-constructed assessments, graphic organizers, mnemonics, graphs, self-regulatory strategies, and plans that may be implemented or used as exemplars for instructor-constructed materials.

Thus, the plan was set. I would begin with a data analysis, examining the students' BOY scores on their assessments, conduct the SRSD intervention in the weeks before the middle of the year assessments to prepare the students for success, then analyze the results.

What follows is a breakdown of the different steps of the SRSD intervention I conducted, with accompanying explanations. SRSD prepares students for success by following the gradual release of responsibility model (Fisher and Frey, 2013). This begins with direct instruction and modeling, which research shows are essential for effective literacy instruction (Spear-Swerling, 2019). Students with disabilities as well as those from culturally and linguistically diverse backgrounds, who may be accustomed to different communication and writing styles, can especially benefit from this explicit form of teaching. Seeing clear models of both the process and expected products, along with direct explanations of what to do and how to do it, supports students' learning.

Pre-intervention data analysis

Before implementing any academic intervention, it is crucial to first conduct a thorough data analysis to identify student needs, determine appropriate targets for instruction, and establish a baseline for measuring progress. Collecting and analyzing relevant student data lays the groundwork for designing and delivering effective interventions tailored to address specific learning gaps. For students significantly below grade-level benchmarks, data analysis is especially important to gain insight into the root causes and magnitude of the literacy deficits to map out an instructional plan. Pre-intervention data such as diagnostic assessments, standardized test scores, grades, and observational notes can illuminate exactly which foundational skills require remediation and reveal how far behind students are relative to grade-level expectations. A data-driven understanding of student abilities and challenges allows teachers to set realistic goals, monitor ongoing progress toward benchmarks, and quantify intervention outcomes. The time invested in meticulous data analysis prior to intervention pays dividends by ensuring instruction is differentiated to student needs. A data-informed remediation approach has the greatest potential to shore up fundamental literacy blocks and put struggling students on track to curriculum access and academic success.

In my case, I didn't need a deep dive into the data or to perform a regression discontinuity analysis to select students who would receive the intervention. All my students' scores were below the mean. All had significant issues across a variety of domains. Thus, all would be included.

The intervention

During the intervention, I switched roles with my general education co-teacher. I became the primary teacher, modeling the strategies and guiding the students. Below is a brief outline of the intervention I designed and used.

Lesson 1 – Develop and activate background knowledge. In my case, I introduced the POW (for organizing writings) and TRAP (for supporting readings) mnemonics illustrating ways in which students can thoughtfully engage with their texts.

POW stands for:

- **P**ick my idea(s) – Select a topic and outline key points to cover;
- **O**rganize my notes – Structure identified ideas and content; and
- **W**rite and say more – Produce an initial draft, then build detail and description.

TRAP stands for:

- **T**hink about the text. Predict what it will contain;
- **R**ead it. Take your time;
- **A**sk yourself about the main idea and the supporting details; and
- **P**araphrase: put it into your own words.

These memorable devices encode the overarching process students follow when approaching reading and writing tasks. I then proceeded to model their use with a text the students were already using. Their lesson had them reading the text (TRAP) and writing a response (POW) based on a teacher-provided prompt. In small table groups, the students practiced filling in their organizers based upon what they had observed.

Lesson 2 – Discuss skill and strategies. This step involves the teacher modeling how to analyze an exemplar text to identify key features of its genre or subject. In my case, I presented students with a new graphic organizer that enabled them to collect vital information to assist them in identifying the main idea of a text. The organizer included spaces to collect:

- who
- what
- where
- when
- why
- how.

I projected a short story while handing it out for them to annotate. Here's the story:

> *This was not how Jordan wanted to spend his Saturday morning! He finally told his mom about a toothache that had been bothering him all week. His tooth was really hurting now. His mom made an emergency appointment for him to see a dentist at the Super Smiles Dental Clinic. Jordan knew he needed to do a better job brushing and flossing his teeth. He had a feeling the dentist didn't have good news, and he was right. Unfortunately, Jordan had a cavity that needed to be filled. He promised the dentist (and his mom) that he would brush and floss better from now on!*

Together, we found details in the text and put them in the correct boxes in our organizers:

- Who – Jordan, Mom, and the dentist;
- What – Jordan has a toothache;
- Where – at the emergency dental clinic;
- When – Saturday morning;
- Why – Jordan didn't do a good job brushing his teeth; and
- How – Jordan's mom drove him to the clinic.

With this information gathered, we had a lively discussion about the main idea of the text. Students built upon each other's responses. Eventually, we came to a consensus that the text is about the importance of proper dental hygiene.

Lesson 3 – Model skill and strategies. After analyzing a strong example in lesson 2, the process repeats in lesson 3 with a weaker text to illustrate absent or incorrect elements.

First, I revisited the TRAP mnemonic and graphic organizer. Students shared with their elbow partner about what they recalled from the previous lesson. I then moved to a flawed case, missing certain elements that were highlighted previously.

Here, I used an ambiguous text from a 1970s edition of a standardized test. Bransford and Johnson (1972) noted that this specific text was too problematic for use in testing scenarios. Essentially, its effectiveness in measuring the intended skills was suspect. As an interesting aside, I've included the paragraph in my collection of examples to test the effectiveness of using various AI tools to assist in the classroom. Most chatbots, including ChatGPT 3.5, failed to correctly identify the procedure that the paragraph describes.

Nevertheless, here's the text. Can you identify the procedure that it's describing?

> *The procedure is actually quite simple. First you arrange things into different groups. Of course, one pile may be sufficient depending on how much there is to do. If you have to go somewhere else due to lack of facilities that is the next step, otherwise you are pretty well set. It is important not to overdo things. That is, it is better to do too few things at once than too many. In the short run this may not seem important, but complications can easily arise. A mistake can be expensive as well. At first the whole procedure will seem complicated. Soon, however, it will become just another facet of life. It is difficult to foresee any end to the necessity for this task in the immediate future, but then one never can tell. After the procedure is completed, one arranges the materials into different groups again. Then they can be put into their appropriate places. Eventually they will be used once more and the whole cycle will then have to be repeated. However, that is part of life.*

(Bransford and Johnson, 1972)

Guiding students to identify ambiguity allows experience scrutinizing errors and omissions. In the example text, did you identify the procedure? What are they describing? Here, context is missing.

I modeled my thinking as I worked through it, positing first that it seemed like a recipe for baking bread. But that thesis broke down when the procedure called for breaking down the components into different groups. Clearly, once bread is baked, the baker can't break it down into flour, salt, yeast, and water again.

So that was out. When I finally revealed the answer, that this text is describing doing laundry and putting the clean clothes away, many students admitted that they've never washed their own clothes. Thus, they had no context for unlocking the text.

Here's the overall script for modeling how I came to the conclusion that the text described a procedure for doing laundry.

- Arranging things into different groups – sorting clothes into separate piles by color, fabric type, etc.
- Going somewhere else due to lack of facilities – needing to go to a launderette if you don't have a washer / dryer at home.
- It's important not to overdo things – overloading the washer or dryer.
- The procedure seeming complicated at first but becoming routine – laundry being a chore that seems complex when you first do it yourself but becomes a regular routine.
- After the procedure, arranging materials into groups again – folding and sorting clean clothes back into separate piles.
- The clothes will be used again and the cycle repeats – wearing the clothes again before needing to wash them.

To my mind, however, the feedback from my students revealed a common flaw in our testing, that of cultural bias. Many standardized tests present texts or concepts that students fail to connect with because they lack cultural knowledge that the test assumes they possess.

Lesson 4 – Memorize strategies. Here, I modeled the entire process from start to finish. Students need to see and hear what happens from identifying key information in a text, making notes, reading, writing, and then checking and revising their work. I did a "think aloud" while modeling. This allows students to understand what they are supposed to be thinking about and what questions they can ask themselves during the reading / writing process. These think-alouds should also include teachers modeling self-statements of what they do when they make a mistake or get stuck so that students can learn to internalize these to support their persistence through academic tasks. Students should follow along with the teacher and complete all the same tasks (e.g., analyzing the topic, taking notes) so that they are already comfortable with the process as the teacher begins to release some of the responsibility to them. Here, the goal was to use the graphic organizers to assemble information relative to the questions being asked of a text, using this information to select the appropriate answer from each question's answer pool.

In this case, we engaged with a text about the Wright Brothers and the birth of flight. We collected information in our organizers. Then, I presented them with four multiple-choice questions on the text. I modeled how to use the information in the organizers to support their choices for the correct answers. I illustrated how to discern the main idea from the supporting details, as well as how the supporting details provide the support of the main idea. Doing this, drilling this, helps students memorize the process, making it more automatic for them.

Lesson 5 – Guided practice of skill and strategies. Here I guided students to work collaboratively. I prompted the students through each stage of the process, but I supported the students as they supplied the information and produced most of the work product. I lead the process (all the steps from lesson 4) with the students helping to supply the information throughout. Also, I reviewed self-statements to support persistence and success, as well as encouraging students to create their own content while reminding them to complete their work. In this lesson, the students were instructed in the basics of the writing process, using this information to deconstruct the reading to find where in the sample paragraphs answers to comprehension questions may be discovered. For example, if we know that thesis statements are generally found in the first few sentences, and that supporting details are often found in the middle of body paragraphs, then how might we use this information about writing paragraphs to discover where this information resides within a reading selection?

Lesson 6 – Independent practice. Here, I supported students to work collaboratively but with more independence. I led the students in the steps of the process (again, all the steps from Lesson 4), and monitored and supported them to work collaboratively to:

- Take notes from the source;
- Turn the notes into sentences;
- Paraphrase what they had read;
- Check their own use of their graphic organizers; and
- Support each other to use self-statements.

This time, I pushed them a bit. The text I chose was a poem from Scottish poet Charles Mackay. I let them know that often, on standardized tests, they'll encounter such dreary poetry as Mackay's. Normally, they'd react negatively to such a reading prompt. In this case, to self-regulate our emotions, I demonstrated how the students could collect information from the text, seeking to link specific words in the question pool to words in the sample text, without having to read the complete (long) poem and keep it in working memory. This direct correlation of answer text to source text supports the goal of citing evidence from the source text in providing answers to questions. The "beginning with the end in mind" aspect of using the question pool to select only relevant portions of the text for examination supports their emotional regulation.

Lesson 7 – Support independent work if the students are ready. In the final lesson of our intervention, I supported students to generalize and use the strategies in other subject areas as well as to write independently. I presented them with a sample text about the baobab tree and a mix of constructed response and multiple-choice questions. They were able to choose the strategy that worked best for them for each of the presented questions. This served a two-fold purpose of assessing their proficiency in the use of the presented strategies as well as attempting to control for prompt dependence (Hoerricks, 2022b). At the end of the exercise, we held a class discussion about the choices students made regarding strategies, and which strategies seemed most appropriate for certain question types.

Summary of "the solution"

To review, I conducted my intervention at a Title I public school in urban Los Angeles, California with the intention of building on existing literature regarding the use of SRSD among students having or at risk for EBDs.

Pre-intervention data analysis revealed that my population of students were well below their grade-level benchmark in reading and comprehension. According to their norm-referenced standardized test data, many were at least three grade levels below their nationwide peers. This continued to impact their ability to access the curriculum in meaningful ways. Additionally, many had behavioral challenges, including aggressive tendencies that interfere with interventions.

As my work demonstrated (Hoerricks, 2022c), the SRSD intervention given before the assessment battery improved student scores on their norm-referenced standardized test. The ninth grade students who actively participated in the intervention increased their scale score by an average of 120 points from the previous year's administration. Fully supported with new skills and strategies, to my amazement, the students with IEPs outperformed general education peers by an average of 29 points. One student, an autistic GLP learner, outperformed the entire ninth grade, placing third overall at the school.

The students demonstrated that they could apply the lessons learned to not only overcome the emotions of test day, but to achieve significant growth from the test's previous administration. Their ability to perform well on the test indicated that they were clearly learning and growing. With their newly gained skills and strategies, they were better able to demonstrate that growth as reflected in their test scores.

Educational implications

The literature review conducted prior to carrying out my research study revealed that SRSD could not yet be considered an "evidence-based practice" for a reading intervention. No studies were found where SRSD approaches were used on a population of special education students or students with or at risk for EBDs in a US Title I setting. Yet, my study attempted to ascertain if this promising approach could improve outcomes for such a population, thus adding the results of my small-scale participatory action research study to the literature. The study's results showed that students with IEPs and students with or at risk for EBDs could, when properly supported, perform as well as or better than their peers in their general education classrooms.

It was hoped that the results of this study would inform the wider education community as to the need to fully support students' needs, both academic and emotional. The results speak to the intertwined nature of such supports. For example, my school site lacks a fully implemented MTSS program. It has a mature PBIS program but lacks the RtI component. In this case, the intervention served as an RtI intervention for the school's ninth grade students. As an efficacy study, it worked. The results indicated that the students who participated in the intervention achieved meaningful growth. As such, the results make the case for using this approach as a whole-class method in schools, even those that practice full inclusion of their special education students in general education classrooms.

What this all means

This chapter brings to light several critical issues regarding supporting secondary students who face intertwined reading challenges and behavioral difficulties. As many students enter high school lacking adequate literacy skills, their struggles to access the curriculum and achieve academic success have resounding impacts on their social-emotional growth. Research points to the need for intensive, differentiated reading interventions, yet systemic supports are often lacking, even when student deficits are clear. While comprehensive frameworks like MTSS are recommended, targeted approaches like SRSD also show promise for building essential reading strategies and self-direction. The success of the SRSD intervention, even though it was small-scale participatory action research, indicates the academic and behavioral benefits of providing explicit literacy instruction coupled with metacognitive techniques, despite limited resources.

Ultimately, the experiences that I've related in this chapter emphasize that reading interventions alone are not enough to fully support struggling secondary students. While addressing literacy gaps is crucial for access and academic success, schools must also prioritize providing social-emotional supports to nurture engagement and wellbeing. As we've seen, students with reading challenges often experience frustration, anxiety, isolation, and diminished self-confidence. Left unaddressed in primary school, these issues can manifest in problematic behaviors that further hamper learning. Comprehensive interventions must build students' emotional coping skills alongside reading strategies. By creating a supportive classroom climate and fostering caring teacher-student relationships, as we covered in the previous chapter, and explicitly teaching self-regulation techniques, schools and teachers can help students overcome behavioral roadblocks. Social-emotional development is intertwined with academic growth. An integrated approach that targets reading proficiency while also providing emotional backing develops the whole child. Prioritizing both literacy skills and socio-emotional health is key to ensuring secondary students reconnect, reengage, and reach their full potential.

Check for understanding

As you take in and synthesize the information presented in this chapter, did you notice any motifs or concepts taking shape regarding your emotional state or perspective? Maybe certain passages sparked a memory or personal anecdote that could relate to the topic at hand. It's valuable to document these connections and revelations as they arise. Our lived experiences offer insight that can profoundly deepen our understanding. Take a moment to collect and record any of these personal reflections or reactions you had while reading through the chapter. Integrating your own stories and emotions with the hard facts being presented will lead to more meaningful takeaways and a richer relationship with the knowledge.

Some things that might trip you up

I've presented a lot of information thus far. Terms like MTSS, RtI, and SRSD might be new to you. Or you might be a veteran teacher and thus familiar with these strategies. You might be in an amazing school with unlimited resources. You might be, like me, at a Title I school with limited resources. I won't presume.

There are some potential challenges a teacher may face in implementing SRSD with a diverse high school classroom featuring varying needs. Let's look at some of the issues that came up when I was planning and implementing my intervention.

- If you don't have a co-teacher, finding time to provide explicit SRSD instruction alongside required curriculum and pacing plans can present a significant challenge. Thus, you will need to balance integration and small group approaches.
- Differentiating to meet the needs of ALP and GLP learners. In the absence of a co-teacher, analytic students may get overwhelmed by too much big-picture context. Gestalt students may struggle with breaking down strategies.
- Scaffolding appropriately for students at vastly different reading levels takes time. During the work in class, advanced students may get bored while lower-level students get lost.
- Managing behaviors if students with or at risk for EBDs act out due to frustration with challenging strategies.
- Providing enough repetition and practice opportunities to solidify self-regulation techniques. Often, there isn't enough time in the calendar to re-teach content.
- Coordinating with other staff to reinforce SRSD concepts.
- Ensuring instruction aligns with students' IEP goals and accommodations.
- Monitoring student progress and adapting strategies based on ongoing informal assessment.
- Finding culturally relevant texts that enable translanguaging techniques and strategy practice.
- Gradually releasing responsibility as students gain independence – avoiding over-modeling or prompting.
- Encouraging peer collaboration and modeling within small groups without letting activities get off-track.
- Balancing the fidelity of the SRSD implementation with flexibility to meet classroom needs.

It was a lot of work. There were two of us in the classroom, the general education English teacher and me, the SpEd RSP. With thoughtful planning, differentiation, scaffolding, progress monitoring, collaboration, culturally responsive instruction, and data-driven adaptations, we were able to implement SRSD successfully. It requires intention and problem-solving to meet each learner's needs.

Ultimately, a teacher's relationship with students is critical to the success of SRSD implementation. When there is a strong, positive teacher-student relationship built on trust and respect, a feature of Glasser's Quality School, students will be more receptive to SRSD instruction. They will feel comfortable taking risks in practicing new strategies, asking questions, and collaborating with peers. A caring teacher who shows interest in students' perspectives and progress will motivate students to persist through challenges. Struggling students need empathy and encouragement to face difficult literacy tasks. Without a nurturing relationship as a foundation, students may shut down or act out when lessons become demanding. They need to know the teacher understands their frustrations and believes in their potential. Teachers who develop rapport through mutual understanding, humor, and cultural responsiveness will find students more willing to buy into the intensive scaffolding needed in the modern inclusive secondary classroom. Building community and utilizing the power of relationships is key to helping students engage meaningfully with the curriculum. A strong teacher-student connection provides the emotional safety net students need to take on substantial academic challenges.

Supporting yourself through it all

As an autistic person with alexithymia, I can attest to the importance of checking in with oneself during stressful situations. Believe me when I say that it is vital that teachers remain composed when modeling within SRSD. As teachers guide students through an intensive reading intervention, it's critical they monitor their own emotional wellbeing. Supporting struggling learners through a challenging literacy curriculum can be mentally and emotionally draining. Practicing regular self-care—including breathing exercises, mindfulness, connecting with colleagues, exercising, unplugging, and other therapeutic activities—allows teachers to replenish their energy and patience. By proactively caring for your own mental health, you can remain emotionally available to empathize with and motivate students. Modeling healthy self-regulation also positively influences classroom climate and relationships, as I was able to accomplish in my first posting. Prioritizing self-care isn't selfish – it's an essential part of sustainable, effective teaching.

Summary

In this chapter, we discussed strategies to help secondary students who are struggling with literacy. Building on the work from previous chapters, here we focused on building reading and comprehension skills. We found that reading difficulties and behavior issues often go hand in hand. Many students these days lack strong literacy skills. This makes it hard for them to understand what's going on and do well in their classes. Students can get frustrated and act out, which leads to more problems.

We discussed the different systems schools can use, like RtI) and MTSS). These give struggling students extra help, targeted on their specific needs. However, many schools don't have the resources to implement these programs.

I shared my experience as a special education teacher at an urban high school. Many ninth graders at my school are below expected reading level and act out in class. My school does not use RtI or the full MTSS suite of services and supports. So, I shared what works for me in my classes, an instructional method called SRSD. This method, or platform, teaches students specific strategies like summarizing and making inferences. It also teaches students to monitor their own learning and progress, taking ownership of their educational journey.

The strategies embedded in SRSD help students with or at risk for behavior issues to improve their literacy skills. Learning self-regulation techniques helps manage behavior and learning. The study that I shared shows that approaches like SRSD can help struggling high school students. The basic structure was provided so that others can have the benefits of implementing it in their classrooms.

5
Adult literacy

Learning objective

Explain the extent of adult illiteracy both in your local area and nationwide, and analyze potential strategies to improve adult literacy rates in your local area.

> "Literacy is a bridge from misery to hope. It is a tool for daily life in modern society. It is a bulwark against poverty, and a building block of development, an essential complement to investments in roads, dams, clinics, and factories ..." – Kofi Annan, former UN Secretary General, on the power of literacy to change lives, communities, and nations.

Rationale

A substantive rationale linking research into authentic social issues with civic responsibility features strongly across the Common Core ELA standards. CCSS.ELA-Literacy.RI.11-12.7, for example, expects integration and evaluation of sources when solving problems – directly mirroring requirements in examining adult literacy barriers and sculpting access improvements. Analytic immersion builds situated understanding – evaluating statistical prevalence, economic consequences, and social inequity impacts of education marginalization regionally and nationally. This grounding contextualizes issues in a genuine community advancing moral purpose.

Adjacent standards echo interpreting complex arguments and appraising reasoning behind catalytic texts that awakened consciousness historically around injustice. Insight gleaned informs strategic direction to uplift communities through equitable literacy programs suiting underserved needs. Communication standards further reflect the duty to transmit conclusions to key decision-makers via persuasive writing or advocacy platforms.

Ultimately the standards coalesce around discovery of truth within injustice through reasoned research, and responsible presentation of restorative solutions optimizing community potential. The learning goal fosters this same cycle of insight, empathy, and activism driven by civic integrity. Propelling students to tackle literacy inequities with academic diligence fosters real-world breakthrough while affirming the interleaving of knowledge and moral purpose at education's heart. Thus, the learning goal and supportive standards champion conscientious scholarship and clear communication guiding public policy for collective advancement.

Introduction

At this point in our discussion of literacy, I hope that I've made the case for high-quality inclusive language instruction in primary and secondary schools. As we've covered, literacy refers to the ability to read, write, speak, listen, and communicate effectively. For students, strong literacy skills are essential for academic success across subjects and for full participation in their education (Le et al., 2019). However, as we've seen, literacy instruction in many schools fails to provide adequate support, especially for groups such as ELLs, students with disabilities, and those from disadvantaged backgrounds. This leads to persistent achievement gaps and missed opportunities.

While improving literacy instruction for students is crucial, we must also consider literacy skills among the adult population. As students graduate from high school and enter the workforce or pursue higher education, their ability to effectively communicate and comprehend information remains vital. Periodic national assessments allow us to track trends in adult literacy over time. The results reveal demographic disparities and guide efforts to meet the diverse learning needs of adults. Just as gaps in K-12 student achievement persist, data show segments of the adult population continue to lack basic literacy proficiencies. To promote an educated, skilled workforce and engaged citizenry, it is essential that we provide high-quality literacy instruction and support across the lifespan (Cushing at al., 2019; Foster, 2020, Krenzke et al., 2020).

Differing from childhood and young adult literacy, adult literacy refers to the ability of adults aged 16 and older to utilize and comprehend written text, perform quantitative and mathematical calculations, and use technology and digital media. Strong literacy proficiencies allow adults to effectively participate in the workforce, engage in continuing education, and carry out tasks required for daily life. In the United States, the literacy skills and competencies of the adult population are assessed through periodic national surveys sponsored by the National Center for Education Statistics (NCES) (Krenzke et al., 2020).

These surveys, such as the Program for the International Assessment of Adult Competencies (PIAAC), utilize probability sampling to select and interview a representative sample of US adults. Respondents complete standardized tests that evaluate proficiencies in literacy, numeracy, and problem-solving in technology-rich environments. The tests are designed to measure skills ranging from basic vocabulary and computation to advanced reading comprehension and mathematical reasoning. By analyzing results from the sample, researchers can generate national estimates of adult literacy rates and educational functioning levels. The data allow for comparisons of proficiencies across geographic areas. Overall, the surveys reveal literacy rates in the American adult population have improved slightly over recent decades, though segments of the population continue to lack basic proficiencies. Certain demographic groups, including racial / ethnic minorities and adults without a high school diploma, consistently demonstrate lower than average proficiency.

In a best-case scenario, outcomes from these periodic surveys inform the allocation of government resources towards adult education and workforce development initiatives (Cushing et al., 2019). The results, it is said, help target programming to geographic regions and subpopulations with the greatest literacy needs. It is hoped that educators will utilize the data to guide curriculum development aimed at advancing the skills of adult learners. Repeating the surveys allows measurement of trends over time, and evaluation of whether literacy rates are improving.

Ultimately, national adult literacy surveys aim to promote a highly skilled workforce and more civically engaged populace. In the real world, we know that illiteracy continues to be a problem that defies solutions (Bulajić et al., 2019; Chall et al., 1987; Rigg and Kasemek, 1983). Thanks to our work thus far, we have a good idea as to why.

Illiteracy is not just a problem in the United States. Illiteracy and functional illiteracy are significant issues affecting populations around the world. In 1978, UNESCO provided important definitions surrounding literacy at its 20th session. Illiteracy there was defined as the inability to understand, read, and write simple statements about everyday life. This represents a complete lack of basic literacy skills. Functional illiteracy, they noted, refers to lacking the literacy skills needed to fully function and participate in society and one's community. While a functionally illiterate person may have basic reading and writing skills, they lack the ability to apply these skills effectively in daily life. That was me, until my mid-30s.

The implications of illiteracy and functional illiteracy are far-reaching. Illiterate adults face considerable barriers to obtaining employment, accessing healthcare information, participating politically, and more. This can lead to poverty, poor health outcomes, and social exclusion. For communities, high illiteracy rates perpetuate cycles of disadvantage. Functional illiteracy also reduces an individual's ability to reach their full potential and contribute meaningfully to society. Despite global progress, literacy challenges persist. Various estimates show that there are still at least 773 million illiterate adults worldwide (Harman, 1970; OECD, 2021; Sticht, 2022).

Back here in the United States, adult illiteracy is an issue that impacts millions of adults. According to statistics from the US Department of Education, around 43 million adults lack basic literacy skills. This equates to approximately 14 per cent of the total adult population. Illiteracy does not impact all demographics equally, however. Minority groups, low-income communities, immigrants, and older adults are disproportionately likely to have low literacy skills (Barron, 2022).

There are several factors that contribute to illiteracy among adults. Many adults did not have access to consistent, high-quality education as children that was matched to their language acquisition style, and thus never developed strong literacy abilities (Harman, 1970). Specific learning disabilities like dyslexia also play a role, making it harder for some people to learn to read well (Vágvölgyi et al., 2021). Poverty and cultural / language barriers in immigrant populations are other key causes. There are also normal declines in literacy skills as people age without keeping up regular practice (Barrett and Cocq, 2019). Then, again, there are the problems we have been trying to prevent in the previous chapters of this book, the lack of acknowledgement of the way humans acquire and learn language (Hoerricks, 2023).

In sum, widespread illiteracy among adults causes individual and societal problems. Adults with low literacy skills are much more likely to face unemployment, get stuck in low paying jobs, develop health problems, get scammed or taken advantage of, or become incarcerated (Keefe and Copeland, 2011). This creates cycles of poverty that reduce quality of life. On a broader scale, illiteracy reduces economic productivity and global competitiveness for a country's workforce (Lewis, 1997). Clearly, adult illiteracy is a major concern with far-reaching impacts that requires coordinated efforts to address.

Why are so many adults struggling with literacy?

With all of this in mind, we are faced with an obvious question, given all the money thrown at literacy programs and schools: why are there still at least 773 million illiterate adults worldwide? Why does 14 per cent of the US population lack basic literacy skills? More personally, why did I graduate from a decent public school in suburban Los Angeles functionally illiterate? With all the money spent, with all the special programs, with all the teacher trainings, with all the standardized tests, I somehow managed to earn a high school diploma … and I couldn't comprehend what was put in front of me. Why? It turns out there are quite a few reasons.

First, adults who did not complete high school or only attained lower levels of education often did not receive comprehensive literacy instruction during key developmental stages in childhood and adolescence. Reading and writing abilities build cumulatively over time, scaffolded on top of foundational skills established in early grades. Without this solid base, adults may lack grade-level proficiencies and struggle with basic reading comprehension, vocabulary, writing coherently, and performing mathematical calculations (Carlson, 2010).

Not finishing high school, for whatever reason, deprives students of essential literacy instruction needed to progress skills to an advanced level. Curricula in late high school focus on honing sophisticated analysis, writing, and communication abilities that prepare students for college and careers. Adults deprived of these opportunities often read well below a 12th grade level and have underdeveloped writing skills. Those who lack strong basic reading and writing skills will struggle to gain more advanced literacy abilities. It's hard, after all, to develop higher-level skills if the basics are not solid (Singh et al., 2020).

Regional disparities in school quality also contribute to literacy struggles (Aikens and Barbarin, 2008; Kapur, 2014; Stantcheva, 2022). Adults who attended lower-resourced, underperforming schools as children are less likely to have received rigorous literacy education supporting skill building. For adults lacking a strong educational foundation, it requires substantial, sustained instruction to overcome core reading, writing, document use, and quantitative difficulties. Don't worry, however. I've got a plan for this.

Then there is trauma and poverty. The all-consuming cognitive load of poverty impedes the bandwidth needed for learning (Sanchez, 2021). Struggling to meet basic needs causes constant anxiety and reduces the mental capacity available for complex skill development. Living paycheck to paycheck leaves little time or energy for literacy education. Research shows poverty-related stress cognitively taxes the brain (Mani et al., 2013).

Trauma also changes brain structure and function in ways that undermine learning. Exposure to violence, abuse, discrimination, loss, and other trauma triggers continual stress responses. This impairs memory, attention, and higher-order thinking critical for literacy (Hertel and Johnson, 2013).

Those dealing with both poverty and trauma face cumulative cognitive burdens. The chronic stress of trying to survive day-to-day while also coping with trauma's after-effects depletes mental reserves, making sustained focus difficult. Remediating skill deficits requires mental energy these adults lack (Johnson, 2019). Additionally, those struggling economically have less access to resources supporting enrichment and skill development. Limited time, transportation, childcare, books, and technologies impose barriers. Fewer educational opportunities exist in disadvantaged communities.

A path forward

What can be done for adults struggling with the lack of literacy skills necessary to participate in their communities?

Circling back on my language learning journey, and my journey through Freemasonry, the next big breakthrough occurred for me within the Scottish Rite. About a year after receiving the Third Degree in my Lodge, I petitioned to join the Ancient and Accepted Scottish Rite, an appendant body within Freemasonry that is considered by many to be its "university".

The Scottish Rite is a Masonic body that supplements the first three degrees of Freemasonry. It consists of 29 additional degrees divided into four groups. The Lodge of Perfection confers degrees 4–14, covering lessons on duty, truth, justice, and toleration. The Chapter of Rose Croix confers degrees 15–18, reflecting on historical settings and figures. The Council of Kadosh confers degrees 19–30, emphasizing faith, hope, and divine love. The Consistory confers degrees 31 and 32, teaching about true allegiance to country and lawful authority. Thus, within the Scottish Rite, the lessons of the first three degrees of freemasonry are elaborated upon through additional ritual degrees and moral lessons (Hoerricks, 2019b).

Unlike the degree work in the first three degrees, where the ritual cast often wears tuxedos or dark business suits, the degrees of the Scottish Rite are exemplified on stage in full dramatic form. The members of the ritual cast often wear elaborate costumes and make-up. Pasadena, where I call home, is known around the Masonic world for excellence in the performance of the ritual and its century-old cathedral. There, the members pride themselves on using the old "Pike scripts", with their long and complicated monologues written in Victorian English that harken back to the days before radio. The problem with these scripts, however, is that the ritual cast must memorize volumes of lines for the often three-hour-long ritual performances. Some monologues occupy several pages in the script. It's simply not possible for most adults to memorize that much text and recite it perfectly, especially those for whom English is not their primary language. The solution to this problem is where we pick up on our journey.

Having become a full member of the Scottish Rite, I now had full access to its programs. I joined its Knights of St Andrew internal service organization and soon found myself volunteering to assist in a variety of ways. I helped in the kitchen at mealtime. I helped at fundraisers. I organized a Burns Supper, the annual homage to Scotland's Bard (McGinn, 2011). These were all amazingly helpful in my language journey as I gained access to new situations and scenarios, and thus new gestalts. But the real eureka event happened when I was asked to assist Stage Craft as the backstage prompter.

A vital part of the backstage prompter's work involves sitting discreetly in the wings, attentively following along with the script of the Degree as each scene unfolds onstage. From an unseen vantage point, the prompter remains actively engaged throughout the entirety of the performance, ready to subtly feed the actors their lines as needed. Requiring a laser focus, the prompter listens for any missed or flubbed lines, poised to quickly whisper the correct wording to the ritual cast, seamlessly enabling them to get back on track. The prompter must maintain complete concentration in case their prompting services are required. Their subtle assistance from offstage allows the show to carry on smoothly and continuously without interrupting the experience for the audience (Egan and Gurr, 2002). Thus, the prompter's behind-the-scenes support provides a valuable safety net for the actors during each production. In essence, I had my own private "readers' theater" of sorts.

Readers' theater

Readers' theater can be a fun and engaging way to build literacy skills, which involves staging dramatic readings in class. Participants are assigned roles in a script that has been adapted from a story, poem, or other text. Rather than memorizing lines, readers practice delivering their parts by reading aloud expressively. The focus is on oral presentation, not elaborate costuming or staging. Readers use only minimal movement and props to act out their roles. The emphasis is on practicing fluent, dramatic reading using vocal expression, tone, and pacing to bring the story to life. Readers' theater provides an entertaining approach to building skills like reading comprehension, vocabulary, and fluency (Young et al., 2019; Young and Rasinski, 2009).

Following along with a script, but not themselves reading it aloud, can provide meaningful benefits for adults with limited literacy skills, even without actively reading every word. Hearing fluent oral reading promotes phonological awareness as the learner listens to the sounds and rhythms of fluent reading. Tracking the script from left to right and top to bottom reinforces print concepts and word boundaries (Malo and Bullard, 2000; Samuelson et al., 2018).

Seeing the printed words supports making connections between spoken vocabulary and written forms. Looking at the text also provides exposure to new vocabulary words in context. Having a visual reference facilitates comprehension of the story while listening. Concepts like capitalization, punctuation, and paragraph structure that support reading comprehension can also be absorbed through observation.

The fluent, expressive reading of others serves as a model to emulate, which is especially helpful for GLP learners. Following along builds self-confidence and motivation to participate more actively in the future by demonstrating to the learner that they can follow with guidance. Being part of the social experience makes literacy feel more accessible.

Thus, while learners are not actively reading, the multisensory experience of viewing the script, listening to expressive reading, and absorbing meaning provides scaffolding that can incrementally build literacy skills and engagement. The combination of modeled reading, print exposure, and comprehension support meets adults at their level while nurturing development (Rupley et al., 2020).

Indeed, looking back on my time as a backstage prompter brings back vivid memories and countless gestalts encoded deeply in my mind. I can still conjure the voices of those incredible actors as if it were yesterday. Their impassioned delivery and emotional range left an indelible mark. Though many years have passed, I can replay entire scenes in my head, hearing the iconic lines delivered in the signature styles of my now-departed brethren.

Indeed, when I pass by the soaring stone walls of Pasadena's Scottish Rite cathedral, I am transported back in time in the theater of my mind. Though almost two decades have passed since my years as prompter, this hallowed hall still stands active in my mind in its ceremonial purpose. I can vividly recall the palpable excitement building backstage before the opening of each Degree. As I fed the missing lines of the scripts to my learned brethren, their sonorous voices seemed to project to the very rafters of the temple, encouraged by the building's amazing acoustics. Though the theatrical trappings are put away between the Rite's gatherings, I can still hear the resonant voices of those esteemed performers bringing the allegorical teachings of Freemasonry to life. Their moving recitations echo through my memories, transporting me back to those moments at the crossroads of theater and tradition.

My time as a prompter showed me first-hand how storytelling and performance can engage learners. Those experiences shaped my later work in the forensic sciences, as well as in adult literacy programs. Just as our Lodge drew on timeless stories, tapping into cultural storytelling traditions can make a variety of endeavors entirely more relevant and captivating. The skills built through oral story exchanges, like active listening, comprehension, and vocabulary, are the foundations for literacy.

My prompting days taught me the power of voice, performance, and tradition to engage an audience. First, I used these new skills to support myself in writing scientific reports and delivering expert testimony in trials. Now I apply those lessons to help a new generation of learners gain literacy through the magical art of storytelling.

Before time was time

My time as prompter also reminds me of when I was very young, sitting at my grandmother's house, listening to stories on her old record player. She would tell me that we Scots have a grand tradition of storytelling. The old Scottish storytellers, the *seanachaidhs* (pronounced SHAN-a-hees), were the gifted poets, reciters, and oral historians who acted as the living repositories of ancient tales, myths, and folklore in medieval Gaelic culture. Often attached to royal courts as privileged advisors and entertainers, the hereditary *seanachaidhs* memorized immense amounts of verse and stories going back generations. Their prodigious memories allowed them to creatively recite epic poems, origin myths, genealogies, and legendary narratives during gatherings, sometimes accompanying themselves with music. As highly respected bearers of ancient tradition and lore, the *seanachaidhs* were essential to preserving Scottish identity and unity at times of cultural transformation prior to widespread literacy. Their time-honored storytelling skills connected ages past to the present through the power of the spoken word (Allison, 2011; Byrne, 1983; MacLean, 2009; Ross, 2000; Szasz, 2007; Wright, 2007).

The Gaelic title *seanachaidh* has no exact equivalent in English. A *seanachaidh* was a professional custodian of *seanchas* (pronounced SHAN-ahas): the "lore" or the communal memory, history, and experience of a people, often in the form of literature and song-poetry. This storied heritage was deeply woven into the fabric of Gaelic society (Newton, 2015). Nearly every *cenél* (meaning kinship, pronounced SEN-el) or clan in the Scottish Highlands at one time had their own hereditary *seanachaidh*. This learned person could recite the precise descent and lineage of that family group, placing it within the broader interconnected web of *cenél*, clan, and noble houses. Again, the *seanachaidh* served as a living archive of ancestral lore, bloodlines, and deeds stretching back centuries (Macpherson, 1966).

Through their mastery of language, rhyme, and rhetoric, the *seanachaidhs* animated tales of the past with poetic grace. At gatherings, their spellbinding voices transported listeners across time, linking current generations to legends of Gaelic antiquity through the ancient arts of memory and narration. The *seanachaidh* ensured the threads of heritage, kinship, and cultural identity remained interlaced between past and present, even amid ages of strife and change. For medieval Gaels, the continuity of memory inherited from bard to bard connected the ages.

Thinking back now, with all that I've learned along the way, and understanding language processing styles as heritable, I've often wondered if the ancient *seanachaidhs* were GLP learners. As it turns out, these oral traditions align well with the capabilities of GLP learners in a variety of ways.

- The emphasis on holistic narrative absorption through listening plays to a GLP learner's strengths at extracting higher-level meaning and patterns from speech.
- The incremental, dialogic nature of oral storytelling allows contextual learning and progressive concept development ideal for GLP learners.
- The use of allegory and symbolism mirrors how gestalt processing can rapidly interpret and link conceptual metaphors and analogies, especially in autistics.
- Memorization and transmission of folk knowledge mirrors the autistic GLP learner's capacity for recalling volumes of interconnected information.

Indeed, as I sat behind the stage as the prompter those many years ago, my gestalt processing mind was absorbing the massive volumes of cultural information that the scripts contained, and the actors delivered. It was encoding them with the tone, tenor, and emotional content that was present in the delivery. As someone who relies upon delayed echolalia, and who now had this volume of cultural information to draw upon, this experience would serve me well in the other areas of my adult life that were beginning to take off.

Soon, I would demonstrate my new knowledge in a series of presentations in front of some very influential Masons. One of these men, Pasadena's Classroom Director, would invite me to replace him when he aged out of the position. As the Classroom Director, I was responsible for "filling in the blanks" for new members of the Scottish Rite as they progressed through the Degrees. Each Degree had its own script, of course. But each also had liturgy, legenda, and, separately, commentary found in Albert Pike's magnum opus *The Morals and Dogma of the Ancient and Accepted Scottish Rite of Freemasonry*.

With my newfound literacy skills, I devoured these texts. My script-making mind integrated what I learned into my script repertoire. My decades of experience in improvisation with delayed echolalia meant that I could quickly and easily answer even the most obscure or esoteric question students had. During those years, I met and instructed many of the area's best and brightest … me … that functionally illiterate autistic GLP learner …. me. It was an incredible experience. Being in these spaces, speaking extemporaneously about topics of interest with mature adults, and holding my own in doing so, was (and remains) a very proud moment for me.

But what I discovered in that place and space was that so much of what my autistic GLP brain had done naturally in digesting the old texts does not come naturally to most. Part of my popularity as an instructor and presenter in Masonic circles was in making these old texts accessible to ordinary folks. Brothers who believed themselves to be quite educated could not penetrate the lengthy Victorian prose. Me, with my gestalt processing, cultural background, and lived experiences, was able to do so with ease. Finally, it seemed, my autistic brain had found its place. However, even as I felt the immense joy at finally finding community, the lack of literacy skills in my professionally successful Brothers confused me.

Literacy in professional spaces

I think of my time in service to the House of MacFarlane as career number one. Then, I had lots of odd jobs and such, in addition to my role as ghillie to Michael, that I strung together to support myself. In helping the family's enterprises, I was also working as a commercial artist and designer. I created advertisements for a variety of outlets, websites, stationery, and such. Eventually, I would work an almost full-time job at a bespoke computer company running their art department. This experience led me to work in partnership with creative software maker Adobe, and to the massive trade show Showbiz Expo.

I was working for the computer company, now long since shuttered, using whatever computers they had lying about. It was slow and frustrating to work, wait, work, wait, in those early computing days. The company was known for making great storage servers for the Hollywood studios. My naturally curious mind wondered what might happen if I wandered into the engineering and production spaces and sort of helped myself to some parts. Without asking permission, I did just that. I found what I needed to create what became a massively powerful workstation and video editing bay. When my bosses found out what I had done, they were quite upset … at first. Once they realized that they could generate more profits from workstations than storage servers, they were more forgiving of my transgressions.

It was this experience, along with my leisure time activities as a champion caber tosser at the Scottish Highland Games, that led to career number two. It was at an event in Huntington Beach, in sunny Southern California, that I met the man who would later get me hired into civil service. There, practicing my emerging conversational and storytelling skills, I proudly told him what I had done for my company and how successful it was. I had no idea that he was looking to hire someone with my skill set, not just the art and engineering but the "fixer" stuff as well.

Less than a year after that fateful meeting, I was working for the City of Los Angeles as a Police Surveillance Specialist 1 (PSS1). A PSS1 is kind of like a communications or low-power electrician who occasionally gets shot at. In the days before digital telephone and mobile phones, it involved climbing telephone poles, setting up surveillance cameras, tapping phones, and all the "Q Section" stuff you find in Bond movies. It was quite a unique position, one that didn't require a lot of reading and writing … at first.

Things changed forever for PSS1s with the advent of the mobile phone and the digital video recorder. Because we were experts in our disciplines, we were tasked to come up with ways to handle these new types of evidence. No more analogue VHS or cassette tapes. Now, the evidence was all digital. Digital / multimedia evidence and digital / multimedia forensics were born. With them came the quickening of my literacy skills. I now had to write detailed reports, skim countless hundreds of pages of expert reports, and speak extemporaneously at trials about all things technical. Oh my …

What about writing?

It was also around this time that the new leadership at the city wanted to upgrade everyone's education. To be promoted in the future, they said, everyone needed a college degree. I examined their new scheme and quickly panicked. To make more money than I was currently making with overtime included, I would need at least a master's degree to be promoted to such a base-salary level. Remember, at the time all I had was an associate degree in political science that I managed to string together before quitting school in the early 1990s.

Thankfully, the county's Sheriff had negotiated with the local colleges to create evening cohorts of civil servants. I wouldn't have to take four or five classes at a time. I would be able to take one short class at a time and get a bachelor's in just three years. So back to school, I went.

Support for disabilities had come a long way since the 1990s. Teachers understood learning disabilities and had begun to use things like sentence starters and paragraph frames. One professor I met in the program suggested a form of "occupational therapy": blogging. He suggested I find source materials related to my job, my tools and tech, and the types of cases I was working. He further suggested a paraphrasing strategy that had me reading and summarizing these "mentor texts" that I found. Blogging thus was a way of creating and packaging longer gestalts for later use. It's a practice that I've employed to this day to support me in my work.

You're probably thinking, why are we just now getting into the writing portion of literacy? That's a very good question to ask at this point. I'll say that it's been intentional. Writing is one of the last skills to develop in gestalt processors, especially autistic GLP learners. Thus, the work we're about to do here has the appropriate timing, working on it as an adult. Plus, for those of your learners who get to writing proficiently earlier, you can take what you learn in this chapter and apply it to them at the appropriate time.

There are a few potential reasons why writing skills may be delayed in some people, especially those who tend to process information more holistically like our GLP learners.

- Difficulty with fine motor skills: Some people struggle with fine motor coordination, which can make handwriting and typing more challenging. This can cause delays in developing fluent writing skills (Chandler et al., 2021).
- Challenges with planning and organization: GLP learners tend to absorb details as a whole before separating out parts. This can make the organizational demands of writing more difficult, like structuring paragraphs, and sequencing ideas. This is where graphic organizers, sentence starters, and other such supports can help (Zajic et al., 2020).
- Prosody differences: GLP learners absorb the prosody, or the rhythm and intonation of language, along with content knowledge. This can impact written expression, making it harder to translate thoughts into writing that flows well (Chafe, 1988; Diehl and Paul, 2012).
- Executive functioning issues: Many GLP learners have challenges with executive functions like working memory, impulse control, and planning (especially true in autism / ADHD). These issues can make it harder to keep track of details, sequence ideas, and stay focused when writing (Hilvert et al., 2019; Soto et al., 2021).
- Perfectionism: Some people, particularly those with ADHD, strive for perfection in their writing, which can slow the

process as they obsess over minor details. This can inhibit developing writing fluency (NoackLeSage et al., 2019).
- Anxiety: Writing tasks that are open-ended or vague in expectations can provoke anxiety in autistics, especially GLP learners, who do better with clear structures / guidelines. This anxiety can disrupt writing development (Ozdowska et al., 2021).

Thus, motor, organizational, prosodic, executive functioning, perfectionistic, and anxiety-related factors may converge to make writing skills slower to develop for some learners, especially GLP learners. This is why I've waited until this chapter to focus our attention on writing. Along the same lines, my dissertation research uncovered some interesting findings regarding autistic college students. One notable result was that the optimal age for an autistic person to enroll in college and finish their degree without withdrawing was 45 years old (Hoerricks, 2018a). Given the writing load in college, it's no wonder.

Modeling and "mentor texts"

The Common Core State Standards emphasize the importance of students studying and analyzing quality mentor texts to enhance their own writing skills. This is highlighted in the anchor standards for writing in grades 6–12, which establish the practice of examining varied mentor texts as fundamental for developing strong language and writing abilities. These anchor standards explicitly state that students should develop and strengthen writing through the emulation of models of writing (CCSSI, 2023). This indicates the essential role that mentor texts play in building students' knowledge of language conventions, effective style, and vocabulary. By reading and analyzing canonical literature, seminal historical texts, contemporary writing, and even the works of their peers, students are exposed to exemplary samples of writing.

Gallagher (2023) notes that these texts serve as virtual mentors to student writers. Through close study of the techniques, structures, word choice, and rhetorical strategies used by accomplished authors, students gain insights they can apply to their own self-expression in writing. They can try on the moves of these mentor writers in their own compositions. The diversity in the styles, genres, and formats of mentor texts gives students an expanded toolkit of skills to develop.

Exposure to quality mentor texts also provides authentic glimpses into how language functions in the real world for a myriad of audiences and purposes. Students get to witness language used skillfully in the hands of masters. The vocabulary, style, and conventions they observe in excellent mentors become a part of their internal bank of knowledge to tap into and emulate. Guiding students to thoughtfully analyze the writing of others lays the foundation for their own effective use of language.

If a mentor text is a piece of writing that can be studied and analyzed by a writer to provide examples and inspiration for their own writing, then I had been exposed to an entire library of mentor texts at this point in my life. I had access to the wealth of information available at the Scottish Rite. I had access to informational texts in my role as a forensic scientist. As I was finding books and articles to paraphrase and expand upon for my blog, I had even more mentor texts. Plus, I was reading at least one fiction book per week, usually science fiction. The fact that they were all relevant to me, in some aspect of my life, made the learning stick. Remember, mentor texts:

- Are exemplary samples of writing in a particular genre, format, or style. Mentor texts demonstrate excellent craft, technique, and form;
- Are selected purposefully to teach specific writing skills or techniques. For example, a personal narrative could mentor effective character development;
- Are not templates, but guides. Mentor texts should inspire writers, not confine them. The skills are emulated, not copied;
- Can be excerpts or full texts, both fiction and nonfiction. Variety is best to expose writers to diverse techniques;
- Are revisited and studied closely. Writers examine the mentor text multiple times to really understand the moves the writer made;
- Are springboards for writing. Study of mentor texts segues into the writer's own original composition; and
- Build a writer's toolbox. The skills learned from varied mentor texts become part of a writer's repertoire.

One of the key benefits of using mentor texts is that they provide excellent examples for writers to model their own work after. Studying high-caliber mentor texts in a genre gives writers a much richer sense of the conventions and techniques that strong writing in that genre entails. Adult writers who are struggling to learn writing conventions get to see sophisticated sentence structure, impactful vocabulary, logical organization, compelling voice, and other attributes embodied within these texts. This crystallizes what optimal writing looks like so the writer can emulate those features (Culham, 2023; Gallagher, 2023). For instance, a forensic science report mentors technical writing skills like clear organization, precise language, and accurate documentation that the writer can integrate into their own lab reports. Studying an exemplary forensic report shows the writer how to logically structure the background, methods, results, and analysis sections (Hoerricks, 2018b). The writer also notes how the report objectively describes the scientific process and findings using exact terminology and measurements. Careful citation of sources throughout the report demonstrates how to substantiate claims. The writer can model these conventions of precise organization, objective tone, and accurate documentation in their own forensic science reports. Having this shared example brings the standards of technical scientific writing to life so writers can emulate and improve their own lab report writing. Unlike abstract rules, mentor texts give concrete illustrations of effective writing embedded within an authentic piece. Writers actively learn by example, using the mentor text as a guide to improve their own self-expression. The shared model of examining the same mentor provides a common language and reference point for writers as they strengthen their literary skills.

Product-based and process-based approaches to teaching writing

The approaches teachers use to teach writing have a significant impact on students' development as writers. When planning writing instruction, teachers must decide how to approach the task based upon several factors. As far as our work is concerned, we'll concentrate on the product-based and process-based approaches. The choice of approach depends entirely upon the teacher's goal.

The main difference between product-based and process-based approaches to teaching writing is the focus. In a product-based approach, the primary focus is on the result or final written product. Students are given mentor texts to analyze and then encouraged to mimic those texts in their own writing. The emphasis is on grammatical correctness, appropriate use of vocabulary, and producing a similar organizational structure and style; like in our forensic science report example. In contrast, process-based approaches focus more on the actual process of writing. Students are taught strategies for brainstorming, drafting, revising, and editing, like in our POW example for struggling high schoolers. The goal is to develop strong writing skills through the recursive writing process rather than perfectly mimicking a model text. Process approaches stress creativity, content development, revision, and peer feedback over replicating structure and style. While product approaches value accuracy and form, process approaches prioritize the ongoing development of writing strategies and skills (Selvaraj and Aziz, 2019).

Check for understanding

Having reviewed the key concepts around adult literacy rates and impacts, let's pause and ensure you have grasped some of the main points.

Consider the various stats and factors we discussed regarding adult literacy levels around the world. Can you recall some of the primary data points covered around issues like overall rates, disparities between groups, and changes over recent decades? Make sure you understand the scale and implications of different adult literacy proficiency bands.

We also explored connections between literacy skills and life outcomes. Do you understand how literacy rates correlate to other core measures in your context? Check that you recollect some of the main associations highlighted around lower literacy, vulnerability, and societal challenges.

Furthermore, in terms of initiatives, can you describe some major government and charity programs targeted at improving adult literacy and their general aims or methods in your area? Have you noted any remaining gaps where more interventions may be beneficial?

Spend some time reflecting on how complete your comprehension is around the key concepts and discussion points covered regarding adult literacy. Note down any areas where you feel less clear on the facts, links, or response efforts described so you can review.

Some things that might trip you up

We took our time getting here. There was a lot of information presented. I want to make sure that we're on solid ground before proceeding to our activity. Let's look at places where both teachers and students might get tripped up.

Students who struggle with language may get tripped up when using a product-based approach to writing:

- Trying to mimic complex vocabulary or sentence structures from a model text that are beyond their current proficiency level. This can lead to errors or awkward phrasing;
- Focusing too much on reproducing the organization and style of a model text rather than developing their own voice and style. This limits creativity;
- Getting confused by advanced grammatical structures in a model text, leading to incorrect grammar usage in their own writing as they try to copy it;
- Having trouble analyzing the linguistic features of a model text (vocabulary, tone, grammar patterns, etc.) if their language skills are weak;
- Struggling to apply feedback on grammar and language usage errors due to limited language proficiency;
- Having minimal development of their own pre-writing and editing strategies due to over-reliance on mimicking the model; and
- Feeling frustrated or demotivated when unable to successfully reproduce features of sophisticated model texts.

The emphasis on accuracy in product approaches can overlook the current language limitations of struggling students. Focusing too much on the end product rather than supporting the process can compound their difficulties.

Students who struggle with language may also get tripped up when using a process-based approach to writing:

- Having difficulty generating and organizing ideas due to limited vocabulary and language skills;
- Struggling to produce coherent drafts that effectively communicate their thoughts (especially true for GLP learners);

- Making multiple grammar, spelling, punctuation, and word choice errors due to weak language proficiency;
- Having trouble providing meaningful feedback on peers' writing or incorporating peer feedback into revisions;
- Finding revision challenging because they don't have the language skills to reword or refine their drafts;
- Feeling overwhelmed or aimless without clear models to guide the writing process;
- Submitting final drafts that still contain many language errors without targeted grammar instruction;
- Receiving feedback focused more on ideas over grammar issues, so language errors persist;
- Having underdeveloped self-editing skills to polish drafts due to language gaps; and
- Lacking language proficiency to implement stylistic suggestions or develop voice.

While process approaches develop crucial writing strategies, students with limited language abilities may need more structured guidance to improve language accuracy in their writing.

Teachers, too, may struggle. Here are some ways teachers may get tripped up when presenting lessons on product-based or process-based approaches.

Product-based approach:

- Providing model texts that are too advanced for the students' current proficiency level;
- Focusing too narrowly on mimicking text features rather than encouraging creativity;

- Assuming students can analyze model texts independently without sufficient guidance;
- Providing inadequate explanations about key linguistic features of model texts;
- Giving feedback that is overly focused on accuracy over content;
- Moving students into independent writing before they can successfully emulate models; and
- Assessing writing only on how closely it matches the model text.

Process-based approach:

- Assuming students have sufficient language skills to implement the strategies;
- Providing too little guidance on developing ideas, structure, and language;
- Giving feedback focused solely on content, ignoring language errors;
- Having unrealistic expectations of what students can achieve independently;
- Skipping scaffolding steps students need to successfully use the strategies;
- Moving through the writing process too quickly for students to implement feedback;
- Lacking strategies to address persistent student grammar and vocabulary issues; and
- Letting major errors remain unaddressed in final drafts.

Teachers need strong preparation to appropriately scaffold either approach for their students' proficiency levels, which is a foundational element of UDL.

How might we fix it?

When using a product-based approach, teachers must provide appropriate model texts. Selecting culturally relevant samples that align with students' current proficiency allows for more independent analysis and heightened interest. As skills improve, teachers can incorporate progressively more complex models. Rather than expecting students to immediately mimic models, scaffold the process. Think-alouds and discussions help students identify key features before writing. Explain unfamiliar language in models and allow creativity within the framework. Outlines and sentence frames support structured practice opportunities. Shift feedback to ideas and message clarity rather than demanding identical mimicry. Have patience as students work to incorporate new vocabulary and structures correctly.

With process-based approaches, teachers must build the foundational language abilities each phase requires. Generating ideas independently may be challenging for students with limited skills. Provide sentence starters, word banks, and graphic organizers as scaffolds. Conferencing individually during drafting can target problem areas. Peer editing is essential to catch grammar, language, and convention errors. Mini lessons that address recurring errors equip students with tools for self-editing later. Students need sufficient time between drafts to implement feedback. Model strategies like highlighting issues that need improvement. Guide students through each step at first with clear instructions and examples. Meet students at their level and bridge gaps in proficiency.

In either approach, to assist GLP learners, provide overview diagrams of your lessons. Use color coding and annotations to illustrate connections between stages. Share strong and weak examples of student writing under each approach. Gestalt learners may benefit from seeing the big-picture flow before diving into the details. Allow opportunities to brainstorm and mind map to activate their global thinking skills. Visual scaffolds like storyboards and plot graphs can help gestalt processors develop ideas holistically. Emphasize key patterns and relationships between ideas and language structures to support their intuitive learning style. Be patient and allow time for immersion before expecting structured output.

The key to any approach used is to intentionally support students' current abilities while developing the language and strategies needed for progress. With appropriate scaffolds that are gradually removed, students can avoid pitfalls and experience writing success.

Don't panic

Large language model (LLM) artificial intelligence assistants have powerful natural language generation capabilities that can help teachers quickly produce customized materials to support just about every element of their practice, including product and process writing approaches. Teachers can describe the proficiency levels, needs, and challenges of their students and let the AI generate appropriate model texts, think-aloud scripts, outlines, sentence frames, word banks, graphic organizers, mini lessons, rubrics, and any other materials. The AI can tailor these resources to the teacher's instructions, with the level of complexity and scaffolding determined by the teacher. This allows educators to instantly access an abundance of differentiated instructional materials optimized for their students' needs. Rather than the teacher having to build these from scratch, the AI becomes their invaluable collaborator that creates materials customized for each writing approach and student. This saves teachers time while providing each student with targeted support. Together, the educator's expertise and the AI's unparalleled language generation ability and speed can facilitate engaging, effective writing instruction for all learners.

Don't believe me? No experience with AI LLMs? No worries. Here are a few prompts that will help get you started, regardless of your chosen tool.

- Generate a model essay for a fifth grade class on the topic of recycling. The students are ELLs with basic proficiency. Provide an introduction, three body paragraphs, and a conclusion. Use simple vocabulary and sentence structure.
- Create a think-aloud script modeling literary analysis of the short story *The Gift of the Magi* by O. Henry for a tenth grade English class reading at grade level. Include references to plot, character development, and theme.
- Build a five-day lesson plan for a second grade class introducing narrative writing. Include outlines for mini lessons on brainstorming ideas, story structure, drafting opening sentences, adding dialogue, and revising. Create accompanying student handouts.
- Produce a rubric for assessing eighth grade science fair projects. Include four levels of criteria for research quality, display board content, oral presentation skills, and responses to judges' questions.

- Design a vocabulary graphic organizer for ELL high school students reading *The Great Gatsby*. Include 10 Tier 2 academic words and definitions in context, synonyms, antonyms, and sample sentences.
- Generate three model paragraphs analyzing the symbolism in Chapter 7 of *The Scarlet Letter*. Include topic sentences, evidence from the text, commentary, and closing sentences. Target a 12th grade Advanced Placement (AP) literature class.

Here are a few more, tailored specifically to adult learners.

- Generate a lesson plan for an adult education reading group focused on improving comprehension of newspaper articles. Include pre-reading questions to build background knowledge, vocabulary exercises for five difficult words, and post-reading discussion prompts tied to real-world connections. Target adults reading at a fifth grade level.
- Create an outline for a 30-minute small group session for adults preparing to take the General Educational Development (GED) writing test. Focus on developing a five-paragraph persuasive essay. Include brainstorming, thesis statement writing, topic sentence, and transition sentence frames. Reference the published GED essay scoring rubric requirements.
- Design two model paragraphs comparing and contrasting two workplace policies or procedures manuals. Include Venn diagrams noting similarities and differences and transitional phrases like "in contrast" and "similarly". This is for entry-level service workers reading around a seventh grade level to practice critical thinking literacy skills.

Summary

For neurodiverse educators who process language through a gestalt cognitive style, like me, storytelling can become a powerful pedagogical tool. Drawing from one's own cultural background provides a reservoir of relatable tales. Tying reading passages to students' own communities makes the material more meaningful. Personal stories also model narrative structures, inspiring lesson plans on memoir writing.

But an instructor's life experiences alone are not sufficient. The skills of the *seanachaidh*—active listening, rhetorical technique, audience adaptation—are key. Each student arrives with their own story. Skillful dialogue elicits their goals and interests. Only once their narrative is appreciated can the teacher's tale be tailored to expand their vision.

In this chapter, I shared how my natural gift for absorbing interconnected details without losing sight of the whole both supports and enhances my teaching practice. Through metaphors that resonate, learners see fresh connections. Here, past and present coalesce to illuminate the future. And so, the ancient heritage of teaching through stories is reborn, evolving into new cultural expressions. For in every student's voice, the possibility of a new chapter waits to unfold.

The aim of integrating narrative storytelling methods into modern instruction is not just formulaic transmission of rote literary skills. Rather, it is the collaborative emergence of deeper meaning through contextualization and creative engagement. In this process of finding one's authentic voice, the act of crafting stories that speak to one's lived experience can feel truly empowering.

Educators who thoughtfully adapt enduring techniques—metaphor, cultural resonance, co-constructed story building—make space for more transformative learning. By valuing the diverse narratives learners already hold, instruction can become less top-down and more collaborative. Adaptability also matters – just as ancient bards tailored recitals, so too can faculty dynamically apply narrative elements their students relate to. Remember, in this effort, LLM AI assistants can be your friend.

In this way, the timeless tradition of sharing wisdom through stories is revitalized and amplified rather than replicated. Students transition from passive listeners to empowered authors crafting living narratives. Thus, the storytelling circle ever widens, as new voices join who see their own tales reflected. This emergent process of finding one's authentic voice and sharing it may be one of the most profound lessons of all.

6
Cross-curricular literacy

Learning objective

Students will be able to articulate the benefits of integrating literacy instruction across subjects and utilizing project-based learning. After reviewing research, learners will synthesize information on how cross-curricular literacy approaches and project-based learning can enhance student learning, rather than compartmentalizing literacy to a single subject.

Rationale

The learning goal for students to assess literacy integration and craft arguments for improving school-wide collaboration is well aligned to several Common Core standards. Specifically, the emphasis on teamwork and presenting perspectives orally links to CCSS.ELA-Literacy.SL.11-12.1 on effectively participating in collaborative discussions and CCSS.ELA-Literacy.SL.11-12.4 on conveying distinct viewpoints to others. The need to construct evidence-based claims connects to CCSS.ELA-Literacy.W.11-12.1 on creating cogent arguments. Analyzing multiple viewpoints and conducting research to propose recommendations utilizes

CCSS.ELA-Literacy.W.11-12.7 on synthesizing sources to investigate a complex problem. Additionally, evaluating cross-curricular connections draws on complementary literacy standards from humanities and technical courses. Thus, the multifaceted critical thinking and communication embedded in the goal applies appropriate benchmarks as well as subject-specific literacy skills to enable students to thoroughly research an issue.

Introduction

By the time students reach my classes, there are many assumptions about their knowledge level and skills. At a minimum, high schoolers are expected to be able to read and comprehend grade-level content in each of their classes. In my experience, few do. Teachers at my school are encouraged to erect structures in their classrooms to support students in their learning journeys. As a result, posters of sentence starters and word walls adorn most classes.

I think about the geometry classes that I support as a co-teacher. Geometry is usually taken by 10th graders, yet a few 9th and 11th graders are present each year. The 9th graders are seen as farther along by the counseling staff. The 11th graders are likely taking the class over after not passing the first time. There is a high concentration of ELLs / EBs in our classes given the demographics of the area. Thankfully, my co-teacher is from the neighborhood and speaks fluent academic Spanish. Between the two of us, we're able to navigate the language needs of our students quite well.

My co-teaching partner, as the "roster-carrying" teacher, spends a lot of time over the summer making "his room" an inviting and stimulating place for students. It includes the requisite word wall and the posters of sentence starters. It's gorgeous, and he takes great pride in its presentation. The room is packed with students each class period. So much so that it's often hard for us teachers to move about the classroom to check for understanding.

The curriculum guide has us setting quite a fast pace. We are advised by our instructional coaches to teach two full lessons, along with the initial warmup, and a cooldown or exit ticket exercise at the end that checks for understanding in our 90-minute class periods. When students struggle, we try to slow things down and do a bit of re-teaching. Sometimes, especially on short days, we do some station-rotation to really drill home fundamental skills.

My school emphasizes annotation strategies in all subjects. In math classes, the acronym CUBES guides students to circle, underline, and box important information of various types before evaluating and solving the problem. We give them a minute or two to do this step before checking for completeness; then moving ahead with the lesson.

Every so often, I'll see a student staring off into space and I'll check in with them. The usual cause of their inattention is a lack of comprehension. They simply lack the skills to decode and the knowledge of the content vocabulary to understand what's being asked. Thus, they do a minimal amount of annotation. Never once, in my almost two years supporting geometry with my co-teaching partner, have I seen a student get up and look at the amazing word wall. Not once have they asked a clarifying question about vocabulary. This, my friends, is a serious problem.

This is why we're dedicating a whole chapter to cross-curricular literacy.

Identifying knowledge gaps

A major obstacle for many students is this lack of grade-level vocabulary knowledge. When students are missing a substantial number of key words, they face severe challenges making sense of textbooks, lectures, tests, and other academic materials aligned to grade competencies. Information is presented using technical terms and sophisticated words they do not understand. This creates an ever-expanding knowledge gap between the language used to teach advanced concepts and the limited vocabulary students have mastered.

Without the vocabulary to fully grasp lesson content, students quickly fall behind. Material becomes incomprehensible when basic foundational terms are unfamiliar. For example, a geometry lesson on rigid transformations like reflections, rotations, and translations will be confusing if students are unfamiliar with terms and phrases like "axis of reflection", "center of rotation", "degree of rotation", or "directed line segment". Without grasping this content-specific vocabulary, students cannot construct the meaningful mental models necessary to complete their work. Key connections and relationships go undetected. Students may miss questions or be unable to follow and participate in class discussions when hampered by these vocabulary deficits. This impacts overall learning and academic performance, not only in math but across disciplines.

Missing also is a basic understanding of the Latin and Greek roots of many of the terms they encounter in mathematics. When learning new terminology like "rotation" and "reflection", students would benefit from knowing that "rotate" comes from the Latin *rotare*, meaning "to turn around", and "reflect" comes from *reflecto* – "I turn back" in Latin. Being aware of the etymology can help terms stick better in one's mind and make their meanings more memorable. For example, recognizing that words like "polygon" and "pentagon" contain the Greek root *gon*, meaning "angle", builds intuition for what these shapes entail. Additionally, recognizing Greek and Latin roots builds connections between mathematical vocabulary and other subjects. With roots reinforced across the curriculum, from mathematics to science to humanities, term comprehension becomes an interdisciplinary asset. This contributes not only to conceptual knowledge within math but allows students to draw understanding between different fields of study through common word origins. Bolstering this broad foundational vocabulary with etymological examples leaves students better equipped to grasp complex geometric ideas, identify conceptual connections, and build skills as they progress in their mathematics education.

Encountering so many unfamiliar words hinders students' metacognition and self-regulation. When students do not comprehend key terms like "rotation" or "translation", for example, they often cannot recognize where their understanding breaks down. Confusion caused by misunderstood vocabulary impedes their ability to monitor comprehension and ask clarifying questions. Students passively listen without realizing content is not making sense (Abimbola, 2013).

This vocabulary disconnection leads to disengagement. Once students feel lost, they may tune out discussions and stop participating in activities. Lacking words to articulate their confusion, students may act out or withdraw rather than seeking help. Teachers may misinterpret this as disinterest or behavioral issues, rather than signaling a need for vocabulary scaffolding.

Why not feature literacy in all classes?

Considering the example of my geometry classes, I wondered why teachers aren't building literacy strategies into their content. Given that our program is well supported by instructional coaches, I asked them about this problem. Their response centered around the time-crunch involved in delivering the fast-paced curriculum with fidelity, a curriculum that rather unfortunately does not include literacy-building strategies.

Returning to class, I asked my colleague about this. He confided in me that teacher preparation programs for content areas like mathematics don't feature literacy development. That, he noted, was the job of the English department. If I believed that certain students needed more support, he trusted me to push into those tables on the fly to deliver that support. That, after all, is part of the role of the RSP teacher in inclusion settings.

But, I countered, what about those classes where an RSP is not present? What about chemistry, biology, and history … or the other sections of geometry that have no students with IEPs, and thus no RSP support? What about struggling students in these classes? I appreciated his honesty as he noted that he had enough to worry about with 6 classes to prepare for, which contain over 125 students in total. Ours is a magnet school, with small class sizes. There are usually no more than 25 students in our small classrooms. Elsewhere in our district, the big schools can have up to 50 students in a class. How do teachers manage?

Thinking further, I recalled my own teacher preparation and internship path. It really didn't feature a literacy component as such. Where RSP teachers are "globalists" in the academic subjects, English teachers are the language "specialists". The more I thought about it, the more I researched the problem, the more information I found that led me to see the rather siloed treatment of subjects in teacher preparation where teachers become masters of their very specific disciplines.

Yet literacy is fundamental to learning in every discipline, not just English language arts. However, as we've seen perhaps in our own practices, many content-area teachers in subjects like math and science do not sufficiently emphasize building students' literacy skills or integrate literacy into their instruction. Again, there are various reasons for this discrepancy, including beliefs that literacy is solely the English teacher's responsibility and lack of training in disciplinary literacy methods. But several major problems arise from treating literacy as a siloed skill.

First, overlooking literacy inhibits students from developing deep content mastery. As we can see from the introductory example, students cannot gain full understanding of subjects without the ability to comprehend, analyze, and respond to their textbooks. Interpreting graphics, diagrams, and mathematical language relies on specialized literacy techniques that must be explicitly taught. Writing genres like lab reports for a chemistry or biology class also follow subject-specific conventions that differ from narrative writing. Without explicit literacy development, students will lack the skills to fully engage with these genres (Laugksch, 2000).

Second, compartmentalizing literacy into a single class prevents students from transferring literacy abilities to new contexts. Literacy skills taught in isolation rarely span across subjects (McLean, 2022). Students may struggle to apply general reading approaches to technical texts or shift between varied discipline-specific writing styles. Broadening literacy instruction shows students how to utilize literacy flexibly.

Finally, literacy is inextricable from higher-order skills like critical thinking and problem-solving. Literacy provides the vehicle for unpacking complex ideas, self-monitoring understanding, communicating solutions, and constructing new knowledge. Restricting literacy to one class period limits development of these cognitive abilities, which are vital for all disciplines (García and Kleifgen, 2020).

To address these issues, teachers across subjects must share responsibility for literacy development and collaborate to promote cross-curricular literacy skills (Harris and Grenfell, 2004). Integrating relevant literacy activities into math, science, social studies, and other classes reinforces discipline-specific goals while building transferable skills. With training and support, teachers can adapt techniques like discussion, annotation, writing, and metacognition to fit their content areas. Embedding literacy universally promotes both subject mastery and broader literacy growth (World Bank, 2019).

Teacher preparation programs

It's not fair to put all the blame on teachers or the programs that prepare them for the classroom. Teacher preparation programs aiming to promote cross-curricular literacy integration face systemic barriers that reinforce subject-area isolation (Samuels, 2017). This begins with the structure of teacher education itself in the West. Programs are often segregated by content specialization, with teacher candidates earning degrees in subjects like math or history. Few opportunities exist for cross-disciplinary collaboration and modeling of integration (Wang, 2020).

Further isolation arises from emphasis on immersing candidates in content knowledge for their subject area. Teacher training prioritizes building deep expertise in the disciplinary content teachers will teach, leaving inadequate room for literacy pedagogy applicable across subjects (Chauvin and Theodore, 2015; McLean, 2022). Pressure can also come from accreditation and licensing requirements that focus teacher readiness on standards for their field rather than on cross-cutting competencies like literacy (NCTQ, 2020).

These divides are exacerbated by philosophical differences in views on teaching literacy. Some advocate embedding it within the content areas (Accurso and Gebhard, 2021). In this camp, you will find the advocates of systemic functional linguistics (SFL). The proponents of SFL argue that literacy instruction should be embedded across all school subjects, not just confined to English language arts lessons. They contend that each subject or discipline has its own specialized ways of using language to construct knowledge and meaning. For example, historical writing uses language to build explanations and arguments about the past, while mathematical writing uses language to describe numerical relationships and procedures. SFL advocates believe teachers need to make these disciplinary literacies explicit for students through functional language analysis. This involves examining the vocabulary, text structures, and language features typical of all the subjects usually found in schools. The goal is to apprentice students into using language in authentic ways for purposeful communication in each discipline. Rather than generic writing instruction, SFL calls for literacy teaching that helps students participate in the discourses of different school subjects. By taking an interdisciplinary approach, SFL aims to improve literacy development as well as deepen learning in specific content areas.

Others argue compellingly that literacy instruction should involve more than just embedding literacy teaching across the curriculum (Lawrence, Rabinowitz and Perna, 2008). While integrating literacy skills into content-area classes is valuable, they contend, focused literacy courses are also needed to truly develop students' advanced literacy abilities. They point out, for example, that the literacy demands placed on secondary students are far greater than those required of younger students, involving more complex texts and tasks. To handle this sophisticated content, adolescents require explicit instruction and extensive practice in specialized literacy skills. This camp believes that secondary schools should provide specific courses dedicated to developing literacy in context, such as reading and writing courses in the various subject areas found on campus. Through these discipline-specific literacy classes, students would get the opportunity to thoroughly learn literacy strategies and processes tailored to the particular texts and tasks encountered in each subject. With ample time and guided instruction focused narrowly on mastering the literacy requirements of individual subjects, students could develop the sophisticated reading, writing, speaking, and listening abilities necessary for success in secondary grades and beyond. Advocates here make a convincing case that a comprehensive secondary literacy program requires not just integration, but focused literacy instruction through subject-specific courses.

These divided perspectives can be reconciled. We'll get there shortly.

Continuing in our look at teacher preparation programs, these differing perspectives shape teacher training priorities and can inhibit a shared vision for cross-curricular literacy goals. Additionally, many teacher preparation faculty lack sufficient expertise in disciplinary literacy strategies to prepare content-area teachers for such an integration. Limited fieldwork and mentorship with teachers modeling effective cross-curricular literacy practices further hinders candidates (Shanahan, 2015). As such, teacher candidates may struggle to apply literacy techniques without sufficient exemplars.

Further to the point, assessments like standardized testing that separate literacy skills from content mastery provide additional disincentives. This constellation of barriers has entrenched the status quo of literacy as the sole domain of language arts (Afflerbach, 2017).

Making cross-disciplinary literacy central across teacher training requires addressing systemic divides between subjects, reconsidering policies, realigning standards, and providing faculty training. But improved integration holds potential benefits for teacher competence and student learning ... if we could only figure out how to pull it off.

What to do about the problem in the meantime?

Many teachers, of course, recognize the importance of literacy for student learning. But they still face challenges in successfully incorporating literacy work into their classes. They may lack training, worry about sacrificing content coverage for literacy, or hold misconceptions about literacy being a separate subject. Overcoming these barriers requires making a compelling case for cross-curricular literacy along with significant supports. The research shows that purposeful literacy integration not only builds reading and writing skills but deepens understanding of subject material (de Oliveira and Cheng, 2011). The key is framing literacy as an empowering tool for enhancing student outcomes, not an extra burden. With evidence, training, resources, and collaborative planning time, teachers can thoughtfully shift their instruction to highlight the natural intersections between literacy and content. Even starting small with subtle tweaks to existing lessons can pave the way for making literacy a shared priority across disciplines.

Consider the case of Jaime Escalante, a local hero in Los Angeles. Escalante, an East Los Angeles math teacher featured in the book and movie *Stand and Deliver*, achieved remarkable success inspiring at-risk students towards high achievement in math. A key factor in Escalante's teaching was explaining mathematical concepts using language students could comprehend, while also intentionally broadening their academic vocabulary. By highlighting relevant real-world applications in accessible terms, he made the value of math relatable. Escalante built up students' mathematical language over time by scaffolding new academic words and pushing them to engage with complex terminology.

Along with strategic language choices, Escalante motivated students by maintaining high expectations for their success. Rather than accepting assumptions that these students would drop out, he continually communicated his belief they could master challenging content (Mathews, 1989). Driven by Escalante's uplifting vision and their own desire to excel, his students reached exceptional levels of math proficiency. His ability to make math purposeful and comprehensible while expanding students' language abilities stands as an inspirational model for equitable math instruction (Chapman, 2013).

While inspirational, Escalante was not the sole exemplar of uplifting students through effective teaching. He serves as one of many models of educators who have transformed outcomes for their students and communities through dedication and innovative methods. Across the United States, for example, countless unsung teachers have similarly helped their marginalized or disadvantaged students thrive against the odds. Their grassroots work may not make headlines, but it creates meaningful change from within classrooms each day. For instance, teachers like Erin Gruwell (2007), Kyle Schwartz (2016), Rafe Esquith (2014), Vicki Abeles (Abeles and Rubenstein, 2015), and Vivett Dukes (Toch, Toppo and Napolitano, 2022) have used strategies from project-based learning to advocacy to culturally responsive pedagogy to dramatically empower their students. Their cases reinforce that with commitment and creativity, transformative teaching can occur in any school. Though perhaps not featured in movies, these everyday teachers quietly but profoundly lift their students in ways both academic and personal.

Many teachers of course recognize the merits of literacy integration, but still hesitate to shift their instructional focus toward cross-curricular literacy skills. Concerns about sacrificing content knowledge or lacking training in literacy techniques can discourage change. However, examples of transformative educators demonstrate how teaching literacy and uplifting students are intertwined goals. Jaime Escalante blended mathematical rigor with personal uplift to turn his students into math scholars. Erin Gruwell used writing to reshape her "unteachable" students' academic trajectories. Across subjects, inspiring teachers leverage literacy's power to make content relatable, build student confidence, and open doors to achievement. With the right support and vision, teachers can similarly guide students to success through intentional literacy instruction. Demonstrating literacy's role in mastering material and unlocking higher-order skills can motivate purposeful integration. Rather than an additional burden, literacy becomes the empowering tool teachers need to help students reach their potential. Just as Jaime Escalante demystified math through clear language, all teachers can make their subjects accessible and meaningful using strategic literacy strategies.

With these amazing examples in mind, here are some ways to help convince others to incorporate a focus on literacy into their classes.

- Provide clear evidence that literacy is critical for mastery of content knowledge (UNESCO, 1979). Teachers inherently want to see their students succeed. Most are driven by a fundamental desire to facilitate meaningful learning and growth. When teachers recognize that integrating literacy skills consistently improves student learning outcomes, comprehension, and higher-order abilities, they become intrinsically motivated to incorporate literacy-focused instruction. The key is connecting literacy to enhanced student achievement.
- Highlight research that reading and writing improves higher-order skills like critical thinking (Bouziane and Zohri, 2019; Herrington, 1981; Miterianifa et al., 2021; Thamrin and Widodo, 2019).
- Rather than simply mandating literacy integration, administrators should provide meaningful training and support, so teachers feel empowered to implement changes effectively. Top-down directives often breed resistance. Teachers need collaborative development of literacy integration skills guided by instructional coaches and teacher leaders. Job-embedded professional learning through modeling, co-teaching, and peer observation allow teachers to witness literacy strategies in action. Ongoing communities of practice sustain teacher growth and troubleshoot challenges together. Administrative backing comes through respecting teacher voice, offering flexibility to adapt techniques, and, importantly, providing planning time and resources. When teachers receive hands-on training and administrative support, they can integrate literacy in ways that enrich rather than overwhelm their instruction. The key is mutual investment in teachers' literacy growth (Gigante and Firestone, 2008).

- Literacy integration is most sustainable when teachers start small before making major instructional overhauls. Begin by incorporating minor enhancements like structured discussions of texts, brief writing prompts, or vocabulary journals. These manageable tweaks build teacher confidence with literacy techniques without major time investments. Over time, ramp up to fuller lesson redesigns applying a range of before / during / after reading strategies. By scaffolding literacy integration through incremental steps, teachers avoid burnout from drastic changes. Small starts allow refinement of techniques and set the stage for more ambitious integration. With an empowering cycle of small but deliberate improvements, teachers can lay the groundwork for literacy-rich instruction. (Graham, 2007; Macias, 2017).
- Professional development should highlight simple but effective ways for teachers to build literacy skills into existing lessons. Small tweaks like structured, social annotation of texts integrate literacy with minimal disruption (Hodgson, 2022). Teachers can add targeted reading strategies like predictions, clarifying questions, and summaries to spur engagement. Literacy extensions like journal responses, discussions, or graphic organizers also neatly align with current lessons. Rather than requiring stressful and time-consuming reinvention, these modest enhancements organically promote literacy development. When teachers realize literacy integration often means modification, not overhaul, they become more open to change. By providing bite-sized integration strategies, professional learning enables sustainable growth without drastic shifts. The focus is on creatively elevating lessons, not reinventing them.

- Professional learning should equip teachers with models of effective literacy integration specifically tailored to their grade level and subject area. Seeing concrete examples contextualized to their classroom needs makes implementation more tangible. After discussing principles, teachers could analyze a sample lesson plan, annotating the embedded literacy techniques. They might view video clips of literacy strategies being applied in a compatible classroom setting. Then teachers could draft lesson literacy integration plans using provided models as idea springboards. With directly applicable examples, teachers can make well-informed choices rather than guessing at what literacy might look like in their context. The goal is to empower teachers to craft creative literacy integration that feels right for their students. Tailored models pave the way by establishing a vision for possibilities (Snow, 2005).
- Like Escalante and Gruwell, teachers should have flexibility to adapt literacy initiatives to best serve their students. A core ingredient in those teachers' success was tailoring techniques to connect with their classes' unique needs and identities. Rigid, scripted literacy integration mandated by administrators often backfires by inhibiting teacher ownership. Instead, top-down policies should set literacy goals while welcoming local innovation. Within shared student literacy objectives, teachers can adjust strategies based on knowledge of their learners. They may modify texts to be culturally relevant, scaffold skills needing development, or enhance vocabulary instruction. When teachers like Escalante can flexibly retool literacy techniques, students meaningfully engage. Thus, top-down initiatives should

empower teachers with autonomy to customize integration approaches for their diverse contexts. Flexibility paired with support nurtures responsive, results-driven literacy instruction (Anders and Guzzetti, 2020).

- To facilitate collaborative literacy integration, structured planning time should allow for cross-disciplinary idea sharing. Content-area and literacy teachers can review upcoming units to identify opportunities for complementary literacy instruction. Special educators can contribute accommodations and scaffolds to promote accessibility. Beyond pairing classes studying related topics, creative projects crossing classroom divides can reinforce literacy goals (Letterman and Dugan, 2004). For instance, an economics and literature pairing could assign a persuasive essay on themes of money and morality in Steinbeck's *The Pearl*. A science and language arts unit might task students to create a children's book explaining a scientific concept like the water cycle. During collaborative sessions, teachers can brainstorm and provide constructive feedback on integrated projects and shared assignments. Rather than confining literacy to ELA classrooms, it becomes a unifying learning tool strengthened through teacher teamwork. Administrators empower this synergy by protecting designated co-planning time and fostering a collaborative culture across departments. When teachers collectively own literacy integration, students reap the interdisciplinary benefits.
- Professional development should also communicate that the goal of content literacy is not conventional reading and writing instruction, but strategically capitalizing on reading and writing to build knowledge. Direct literacy instruction is still vital, but content classes offer unique opportunities.

Teachers can use domain-specific texts to strengthen comprehension of complex materials through targeted strategies. Writing tasks can reinforce content learning while advancing communication skills. The aim is not to replicate English class, but to organically incorporate reading and writing to deepen engagement and understanding. Content literacy training should therefore focus on capitalizing on built-in opportunities for reading and writing rather than detracting from subject knowledge. When used as vehicles for learning, reading and writing become empowering rather than tangential. With this framing, teachers see literacy as amplifying rather than competing with content mastery (Fisher and Ivey, 2005).

- Misconceptions about literacy should be addressed not through top-down directives but sustained, collaborative dialogue. Literacy coaches might ask teachers to articulate their current understanding and pose clarifying questions. In team meetings, student work samples could illustrate literacy's interconnectedness across subjects. Teachers could share personal revelations that shifted their mindsets. Book studies on disciplinary literacy research can uncover new perspectives (Hinchman and O'Brien, 2019). Structured classroom observations followed by peer debriefs build shared philosophy. Through these reflective exchanges, teams can organically evolve restrictive mindsets that isolate literacy. Sustained collaboration transforms views by linking literacy tangibly to teacher and student experiences. Patience and partnership allow misconception shifting to be a communal, yet self-driven journey. Mandates engender resistance, but productive struggle together breeds shared commitments. With persistent team discourse, literacy ceases to be "someone else's subject" and becomes our collectively owned responsibility (Taylor and Kilpin, 2013).

- The most powerful advocacy for literacy integration comes directly from students sharing how literacy aids their learning. Teachers could directly survey students on techniques that help them engage with lessons. Student work could be analyzed for evidence of enhanced understanding from literacy strategies. Classes might track data before and after literacy integration to document impact. By speaking on panels, writing op-eds, or simply discussing with teachers, students give literacy efforts purpose and urgency. Rather than by decree, literacy becomes a grassroots call to action from those meant to benefit (Harklau, 2001). Just as transformative teachers stay grounded in student needs, professional development should regularly reflect student perspectives. At the heart of this endeavor are young people themselves – their voices must help guide the way. When students validate how literacy multimodalities make content stick, teachers listen and find inspiration to continue the work. For literacy integration to take hold, students must be partners, advocates, and change agents every step of the way.

The key to all of this is making a compelling case for literacy while providing significant support through training, models, resources, flexibility, and collaboration time. A supportive process focused on enhancing student outcomes will motivate change.

How I've done it

I will show you one of the educational tools I have developed for a course I assist with. What follows is a support document

I drafted to clarify the complex terminology and principles surrounding "regression" in the statistics class I co-teach.

I noticed that the book we were using did not explain the vocabulary and terms in a way that connected with students. Its examples were old and not relevant. Drawing on my experience in forensic science, I recognized the need to take complex processes and procedures and make them understandable to the judge and jury who serve as the trier of fact (Hoerricks, 2008). In this case, the triers of fact were the students. As I introduced my "explainer" to them, I modeled my thought process behind this approach. Connecting key terms together in a narrative form serves as a powerful way to create an anchor in the students' mind's eye. This mental scaffolding is crucial for them to build their understanding of the concepts step-by-step. The story provides a structure to hang the critical vocabulary and ideas on as we move through the material. In this way, the students can grasp the logical flow and interplay of the techniques and principles. By putting the terms in context, they gain meaning and stick in the students' memory. This method of conveying complex topics through narrative and visualization has proven highly effective for comprehension and retention, based on my experience (Simmons, 2015). The "explainer" offers an engaging, accessible entry point to guide the students into this new subject area.

Lesson 2.6 – Narrative text "explainer"

Note from Dr H: *Here's a peek into my process as a non-verbal autistic educator. As I don't work in the world of "words" as you likely know them and work with them, I need to build complex* *mental scripts (called gestalts) for my gestalt processing mind. These gestalts / scripts provide the structure upon which I can anchor definitions and concepts. Having the appropriate structure, I can then begin using the words in my work. If I don't have a "mental movie" of these important terms, my work in the text will suffer. I simply won't have the ability to understand what's being asked, how to perform the requested calculations, or why it's important that this information be processed in the first place. My mind will wander as it wonders what we're on about. So, I do, something like the below—tell the story of the concepts I wish to convey—for everything I must interact with professionally. This one, I share with you today.*

I use the example of "real estate" as it is a career in the US that is accessible to anyone, regardless of educational attainment, where true wealth can be amassed if one understands and can successfully employ the mathematics behind the business.

Molly's regression roundup

Meet Molly, a real estate agent trying to get better at pricing homes. First, she made a **scatterplot** showing each recently sold house as a dot with the x-position its size and y-position its price. She could immediately see larger homes cost more! Next, she calculated statistics like the **mean** price and size and **standard deviation**, to summarize typical houses.

Molly decided to make a model to predict prices from size. She calculated the **correlation**, which was very high – size had a strong link to price! Using **regression**, Molly related size and price with an equation. The **slope** showed how much more big houses cost per square foot. The **y-intercept** estimated the underlying land's base value.

Molly used the equation to **predict** prices for new listings, like a 1,800 sq ft house. She plugged in 1,800 for the size, did the math, and got an estimate! Some predictions were spot-on, but others had **residuals** – differences between her guess and the actual sale.

When a 12-bedroom mansion sold for way more than similar sized houses, Molly flagged it as an **outlier**. She decided to remove it when fitting the model since including outlier data could badly skew the equation.

By analyzing **residuals** and **outliers** and refining her model, Molly kept improving her pricing accuracy. Her clients loved her Regression 101 course and soon she was the top-selling agent in town!

Using stories and examples that students can relate to is an effective way to help them grasp complex topics, according to research, especially when done at students' instructional reading level. Pierce and Gilles (2021) found that when teachers connect abstract concepts to concrete situations familiar to students, the material becomes more meaningful and easier to understand. Rather than just textbook problems, students can link statistics back to real-world examples they already have some knowledge of or experience with. This allows them to build on their prior understanding when learning new ideas, instead of trying to comprehend them in isolation. Additionally, the narrative elements of stories make concepts more memorable, increasing the likelihood that students will recall the ideas later (Simmons, 2015). Relatable scenarios also help students envision how they might apply statistical concepts in practice, transitioning the subject from theoretical to applicable. Presenting intimidating topics like statistics through relatable everyday situations can further help to relieve some of the anxiety students feel. This leverages the human brain's innate preference and capacity for narrative-based learning, as Marunda-Piki (2018) demonstrated. By grounding the material in contexts linked to students' own aspirations and frames of reference, even very complex statistical subject matter can lead to deeper and longer-lasting learning.

Check for understanding

Let's pause to check our understanding as we integrate these new literacy concepts. First, review your notes and look up any unfamiliar terms like "disciplinary literacy", "metacognition", or "literacy multimodalities". Definitions for those and other key terms can be found at the end of this chapter. Clarify your notes and add any important vocabulary to your personal glossary.

Next, reflect on your reactions to the concepts presented so far. Did any spark memories from your own educational experiences? Are you noticing any common themes around your feelings regarding literacy across different subjects? Jot down these connections, questions, and reflections in your journal.

If you are engaging with this text as part of a course, take a moment to discuss with a classmate either in person or via chat in remote settings. Share an "a-ha" moment that resonated with you or an insight you gained. Explain what stood out and why. Then swap roles. Verbalizing our evolving understanding helps cement new learning and allows us to synthesize ideas. Through discussion and reflection, we actively integrate literacy into our own frameworks of knowledge. If you are reading this text independently to enrich your understanding, you can record these reflections in your notes or journal.

As we've seen throughout our journey together, capturing our thoughts at multiple points cements new learning and facilitates synthesis of concepts. By reflecting and discussing, we integrate literacy into our own understanding.

Some things that might trip you up

A key area that may trip you up in this chapter is the complex discussion of systemic barriers to literacy integration within teacher training and professional development. Several philosophical, political, and structural challenges were described, including siloed subject certifications, limited literacy pedagogy coursework, and conflicting literacy integration views. These dense paragraphs likely require careful unpacking, especially for non-educator audiences less familiar with the tensions in teacher preparation.

- Teacher training refers to the education and preparation programs that people must complete to become certified teachers. This includes both university-level coursework and supervised teaching experiences.

- Professional development refers to the ongoing learning and training teachers receive throughout their careers to improve their instructional skills. This can include workshops, coaching, courses, and collaboration with peers.
- Literacy integration means incorporating reading, writing, speaking, and listening instruction across all subject areas, like math, science, and history. This is also called cross-curricular literacy.
- Siloed subject certifications refers to teacher training programs focusing solely on one subject like math or chemistry. This means teachers do not get specific training in literacy skills or integrating literacy across subjects.
- Limited literacy pedagogy coursework means most teacher training programs require few if any courses on how to teach literacy skills like reading comprehension strategies or writing instruction. This coursework is seen as less important than content knowledge.
- Conflicting literacy integration views refers to differing opinions on whether literacy should be embedded within content classes or separated out and taught just in English / language arts classes. These unresolved philosophical divides about where literacy belongs inhibit unified teacher preparation approaches.

In addition, references to lesser-known instructional approaches may also require scaffolding for audiences unfamiliar with these methods. Project-based learning (PBL), for example, is an educational approach that involves students working together to solve real-world problems and apply their knowledge and skills. PBL allows for the integration of multiple subjects, including literacy skills, as students research, discuss, and present projects.

Here, students may be tasked with designing a sustainable community garden for their school. This would require research into gardening methods, budgeting, and proposals to the school administration. Students would need to use math, science, and literacy skills collaboratively to complete the project. PBL facilitates interdisciplinary learning in an engaging, student-driven format. Although PBL was only briefly mentioned before as a technique for literacy integration, it serves as a comprehensive example of how active, meaningful learning can promote the application of English and communication abilities (Almulla, 2020; Boss and Krauss, 2022).

In PBL, teachers guide students through extended inquiry processes to deeply engage with core academic content and skills as they complete projects. Hallmarks of PBL include driving questions, sustained inquiry, collaboration, critique and revision, and creating public products. In another example, an economics PBL unit might have students tackle the driving question "how can we reduce homelessness in our community?" by researching the problem, interviewing stakeholders, designing and pitching solutions to a panel of experts, testing ideas through simulations, and creating an action plan website to share their proposals. The teacher scaffolds literacy strategies like critical analysis of sources, synthesizing research, and persuasive writing to equip students with knowledge-building tools.

Unlike passive learning, PBL requires actively constructing and applying knowledge to dynamic situations. This aligns with the literacy integration goals of learning through authentic reading, writing, and communicating. However, without sufficient background knowledge, early references to PBL in this chapter may have been confusing rather than clarifying. Hopefully, in providing an overview and examples, we've clarified how PBL creates enriching project contexts to advance cross-curricular literacy abilities.

How might we fix it?

If you're not familiar with working across departments, or if you're reading this book to help yourself or your child, these brief overviews likely raised more questions than answers. That curiosity can energize your own investigatory journey into cross-curricular literacy. How might PBL projects address learning gaps students exhibit? What texts or topics most excite them? Every classroom dynamic differs, so use the questions and tensions outlined to spur exploration of your distinct context. Meet with faculty teaching the same students across subjects to map shared literacy opportunities, challenges, and ways content interconnects through projects. Parents, this can be accomplished within the context of "open house" or within IEP meetings. There, identify broader community issues, like food insecurity, to motivate real-world research and solutions.

See how cross-disciplinary methods like PBL breathe relevance into ELA standards through authentic expression, analysis, and dialogue. Let students self-direct literacy growth by selecting driving questions and sources. Guide them in sharpening communication skills to showcase findings through mediums they feel empowered choosing. Perhaps initial attempts only scratch the integration surface or miss key competencies. Yet reflection fuels revision and expansion of what works. Literacy blossoms when watered with practical usage beyond hollow skill drills alone.

Teachers, keep pressing fellow educators and administrators on why siloed content remains the norm when tools like PBL actively dismantle those barriers with such promise. Yes, modeling integration takes more initial effort, but shouldn't sparking students' knowledge-building passion be our purpose? Caution against quick fixes or superficial tweaks; this requires foundational change in institutional philosophy itself. Our end goal stays grounded in what students will be equipped to understand, analyze, evaluate, discuss, and share long after a test or worksheet gets recycled.

I hope these ideas ignite your own creative integrative sparks, both widening your visions and focusing approaches on your classroom's interests and dynamics. This exploration will doubtlessly have ups and downs, but students can create amazing things when guided to intersect literacy with purposeful content engagement.

Summary

PBL has gained attention as an instructional approach to develop twenty-first century skills in students. However, implementing PBL curriculum requires providing adequate teacher training and support. A recent study by Martinez (2022) investigated secondary school teachers' experiences in learning to teach twenty-first century skills through a graduate course focused on PBL curriculum design. The research highlighted both benefits and challenges teachers faced in applying their learning.

The study found teachers saw value in using PBL approaches to link classroom learning to real-world relevance and engagement. However, substantial obstacles remained regarding student attendance, classroom management, planning time, and collegial collaboration. The research underscores the need for sustained professional development to change classroom practices and successfully implement PBL on a wider scale.

The challenges teachers faced in implementing PBL approaches likely resonate with educators' own experiences of adapting instruction. Perhaps you have encountered similar obstacles in your own work when trying new activities or instructional formats like the end of chapter activity. For example, taking class time to have students work in groups or conduct projects often requires more involved planning and preparation. Traditional direct teaching can feel "easier" as it follows a more predictable pattern. Students, too, may initially resist participating more actively in their learning. And undertaking new teaching approaches without supportive colleagues can feel isolating. Yet the potential benefits to student engagement and depth of learning underscore why it is worthwhile to persist despite the challenges. With adequate training, support, and planning time, PBL and other student-centered approaches can be incorporated effectively. The key is providing teachers with the knowledge, resources, and collaborative communities to make fundamental changes in practice. Recognizing common barriers can help guide efforts to successfully implement innovative instruction.

The obstacles teachers face in adopting PBL mirror broader difficulties in making instructional changes to improve student outcomes. This includes efforts to incorporate more cross-curricular literacy instruction. Though literacy is a fundamental skill, enhancing reading, writing, and communication across subject areas can be hampered by similar barriers like insufficient planning time. Teachers may also lack training in literacy strategies beyond their content expertise. Here, too, collaboration is key, as teachers across disciplines must coordinate to consistently integrate literacy in their classrooms.

Yet research shows cross-curricular literacy initiatives can have significant benefits for student achievement when implemented effectively. Just as with PBL, the solution involves providing adequate professional development, planning resources, and collaborative structures. Teachers need knowledge, skills, and support to make meaningful shifts in instructional practice. By understanding common challenges, schools can proactively address conditions needed to ensure teachers have capacity to undertake literacy initiatives successfully. The potential gains for student learning warrant persistence through the initial growing pains of adopting new instructional approaches. With a concerted effort across subjects, students' essential literacy abilities can be enhanced.

7
Summary

Review

I hope you have found the information presented in this text to be helpful and informative as you pursue a greater understanding of human language acquisition and inclusive literacy instruction. Over the preceding chapters, we explored key concepts aimed at equipping educators, administrators, policymakers, parents, and care providers to effectively support all students in developing strong reading, writing, and communication abilities, regardless of language background or processing tendencies.

The ambitious learning goals set out at the start of each chapter provided meaningful targets for comprehending research-backed strategies and applying this knowledge to real-world classroom contexts. It is my sincere wish that working through this material has expanded your own perspectives regarding the diversity of language learners and given you renewed insight into nurturing literacy equitably.

In the introductory chapter, we covered key foundations regarding the diverse methods humans use to acquire language, including contrasting analytic and gestalt processing systems. We confronted flaws in the prevailing SOR paradigm that marginalizes those with differing learning needs. The reflections provided an opportunity to examine our own language experiences and biases.

Chapter 2 saw an in-depth exploration of the SOR, including its theoretical frameworks like Scarborough's Reading Rope. Using semiotic deconstruction, we analyzed how the SOR's technical focus often overlooks gestalt processors. Problematic issues around ethics and "evidence" claims in the SOR industry were raised as well.

In Chapter 3, we differentiated between the developmental stages of analytic versus gestalt language learners in early childhood and suggested targeted strategies for each group. The promise of translanguaging techniques to leverage multilingual students' diverse skills was highlighted next. Dramatization methods were also presented as tools to motivate young readers.

Moving up to the secondary grades, Chapter 4 confronted literacy gaps affecting struggling adolescent readers as well as approaches like RtI) and SRSD. My classroom-based research study on applying SRSD illustrated targeted literacy instruction in action.

In the key chapter on adult literacy, global illiteracy statistics set the stage for discussing marginalization issues in local communities. Drawing from my personal learning journey, the transformative potential of high-expectation mentoring was underscored as an avenue for expanding opportunity and achievement motivation.

Finally, in Chapter 6, barriers like teacher training siloes were analyzed regarding consistently integrating literacy across secondary subjects. Inspiring models of educators overcoming odds showed cross-disciplinary literacy enhancing accessibility, analytical skills, and higher achievement.

A cohesive view

By exploring diverse perspectives and weaving together research across multiple fields, I sincerely hope that a cohesive vision of effective, equitable English language instruction has emerged across these chapters. This text synthesizes vital insights from literacy development models, social learning theories, translanguaging frameworks, and deconstructive analysis, as well as the lived experience of an educator who fell through the cracks of the American educational system and found their way to literacy through a non-traditional path. Blending these lenses constructs a comprehensive case for responsive pedagogies attuned to analytic and gestalt learning variability among English language students.

Crucially, the array of practical strategies modeled provides actionable guidance for nurturing literacy inclusively in classrooms. From drama activities to self-regulation techniques, real-world exemplars demonstrate how research and passion can transform into practice accessible to all. Together these elements cohere into a unified instructional philosophy where flexibility, scaffolding, and multi-modality empower each unique learner.

Yet this text speaks not only to educators, but all invested in students' growth. The open questioning of long-held assumptions around skill hierarchies and literacy timelines invites families and caregivers to appreciate the diversity of language learning paths. Discussing marginalization issues underscores how pressure to conform to monolinguistic, monocognitive expectations hinders belonging for minorities. This catalyzes self-advocacy and allyship. Explaining brain differences normalized in some communities provides "mirrors" to validate learner identities. This representation seeds motivation and persistence.

In centering lived experiences alongside evidence, the hierarchies separating "researchers" from "subjects" blur. Instead, diversity of participants demonstrates equitable discovery of what pedagogies work for whom and why. This epitomizes the spirit of elevating formerly excluded voices to guide best practice. The text thus informs stakeholders at all levels of the factors influencing achievement.

Ultimately this resource coheres into a springboard for dialogue on how communities and schools can nurture the boundless potential of linguistically, culturally, and cognitively diverse students. Through coherence, inclusion, and partnership, it lights a path toward an education system where literacy fosters liberation.

Your charge

As I wrap up this book, I am thinking back to my life as a Freemason and what happens towards the end of the ritual of initiation. I'm thinking specifically of the charge given to all newly initiated members. A Masonic charge is a formal statement delivered by the Master of the Lodge that outlines the moral code, duties, and expectations for members of the Freemasons. Steeped in ceremonial language, the charge serves as a rite of passage for new initiates, cementing their commitment to upholding the principles of the centuries-old fraternal organization into which they are entering.

At its core, a Masonic charge impresses upon the newest members the high ethical standards by which Masons must conduct themselves, often emphasizing virtues like integrity, charity, selflessness, and trustworthiness. The charge reminds all Masons of their sworn obligation to safeguard the secrets, traditions, and landmarks of Freemasonry, which have been carefully preserved through the generations. Masons are admonished to faithfully fulfill their responsibilities within the Lodge, while avoiding any behavior that could damage Freemasonry's reputation in the outside world.

The charge also carries a degree of moral authority as it is formally delivered by the Master of the Lodge from their seat in the East. The Master bears solemn duties for setting an example of righteous leadership and steering the spiritual and philosophical direction of the Lodge. Therefore, the Master's pronouncement outlining standards of Masonic conduct carries special weight.

While espousing ancient wisdom, a Masonic charge additionally relates timeless expectations and lessons to present contexts and needs within the Lodge community. Although steeped in historic language and lore, the charge speaks to current times. Thus, it indelibly links new members to the heritage of Freemasonry while establishing guidelines for honorable conduct going forward as torchbearers of the enduring fraternity. Through words imbued with insight and authority, the Masonic charge indelibly sets every Mason on their path of committed service.

With this in mind and using the charge that I received during my initiation as my "mentor text", I present you with the following charge in relation to the work you have just completed.

The preceding chapters illuminate vital shortcomings in current literacy instruction models. Yet awareness alone cannot spark transformation without resolute activism. With conviction forged from new perspectives, we must rally stakeholders to enact equitable change classroom by classroom, and district by district. This charge is not issued lightly – the obstacles are formidable.

In an era of competing priorities and fiscal constraints, securing resources to actualize reform demands perseverance. Corporate encroachment into learning materials urges perpetual vigilance so financial motives do not eclipse pedagogical imperatives. Bureaucratic inertia resists deviation from entrenched systems, no matter how outdated. Some will defend dated paradigms and power structures rather than risk professional disruption.

Still truth compels action. We know one-size-fits-all literacy frameworks fail up to 40% of students, belying promises of empowerment through education. We recognize the perils of assessments valuing conformity over creativity, comprehension over connection. We have witnessed learners dulled by drills thrive under responsive guidance unlocking their potential. Yet responsibility now falls to us.

With courage and community, we must halt the machinery churning out disenfranchisement in the name of "achievement". Parent-educator partnerships can reform discussions on what society gains from graduates who "made the grade" yet lack holistic life skills. Grassroots advocacy gives voice to alternatives where libraries of knowledge pale beside the brilliance of youth guided to author their own futures.

The task seems thankless. The inertia discouraging. But imagine the inspiration of witnessing marginalized students grasp their limitlessness when schools celebrate, not constrain, their innate diversity. Envision generations of young people writing their destinies through schooling that teaches literacy as liberation. From this vantage, our shared responsibility snaps into focus – to ignite the spark of change so all students can illuminate their worlds. The uphill climb levels when we scale it together. If not us, then who will lead this charge? The future beckons us to find out.

Final thoughts

Writing a book aiming to change how literacy is taught when I struggled tremendously to become functionally literate feels rather ironic. My atypical autistic mind makes expressing ideas in writing very difficult. Yet I felt driven to create this resource because the current system failed me, and many students like me. If sharing my journey helps more students feel included and supported, it's worth the effort.

Progress on this book has not been quick or straightforward. My many underlying conditions make planning, focusing, and converting my thoughts into text an immense challenge. Communicating holistically through multimedia comes more naturally to me. Academic writing expects a linear format that I don't process well. It seems like I've spent ages staring at blank pages struggling to translate my insights appropriately.

Academia also favors affiliation and conformity over unique contributions. As an outsider questioning accepted ideas, I have faced many barriers. The intense stress has often overwhelmed me. I have only my internal motivation driving me. No established guideposts exist for this kind of advocacy work.

I found writing certain chapters smoother because their subjects align well with my autistic thinking. Other parts were painfully slow as I fought my own difficulties with writing and self-direction. During frustrating periods, remembering my own mentors' refusal to give up on me keeps me going. Their unrelenting investment enables my perseverance now when motivation evaporates. I just keep staring at the pages until this manuscript comes together bit by bit and panic attack after panic attack, my hard-won victory over immense obstacles.

Perhaps my stubborn perseverance stems from a history of otherness and being labeled with deficits. I want my hard-won knowledge to ease someone else's path. My goal is to help reshape literacy instruction to embrace diverse minds. If my insights can save one student from trauma, every exhausting hour will be worthwhile. I believe all young minds deserve support in reaching their potential with compassion and flexibility. My wish is that this text nudges us closer toward that goal.

> "But the opportunity to effect a great good does not often occur to any one. It is worse than folly for one to lie idle and inert, and expect the accident to befall him, by which his influences shall live forever. He can expect that to happen, only in consequence of one or many or all of a long series of acts. He can expect to benefit the world only as men attain other results; by continuance, by persistence, by a steady and uniform habit of laboring

for the enlightenment of the world, to the extent of his means and capacity.

"For it is, in all instances, by steady labor, by giving enough of application to our work, and having enough of time for the doing of it, by regular pains-taking, and the plying of constant assiduities, and not by any process of legerdemain, that we secure the strength and the staple of real excellence. It was thus that Demosthenes, clause after clause, and sentence after sentence, elaborated to the uttermost his immortal orations. It was thus that Newton pioneered his way, by the steps of an ascending geometry, to the mechanism of the Heavens, and Le Verrier added a planet to our Solar System." – Albert Pike, in *Morals and Dogma of the Ancient and Accepted Scottish Rite of Freemasonry*, 1871, p. 174, 10th Degree, Illustrious Elect of the Fifteen.

References

Chapter 1

Arnove, R. F. and Graff, H.J. eds. (1987). *National Literacy Campaigns: Historical and Comparative Perspectives* (New York: Plenum Press).

Berk, L. E. and Winsler, A. (1995). *Scaffolding Children's Learning: Vygotsky and Early Childhood Education*. Washington, DC: National Association for the Education of Young Children.

Blanc, M. (2012). *Natural Language Acquisition on the Autism Spectrum: The Journey from Echolalia to Self-Generated Language*. Communication Development Center, Inc. Madison, WI

Bodmer, F. (1944). *The Loom of Language: An Approach to the Mastery of Many Languages*. New York: WW Norton & Company.

Bourdieu, P., Coleman, J. S. and Coleman, Z. W. (2019). *Social Theory for a Changing Society*. Abingdon: Routledge.

California Commission on Teacher Credentialling (CTC). (2023). *Education Specialist Instruction Credential (CL-808CA)*. [Online] Available at: https://www.ctc.ca.gov/credentials/leaflets/Ed-Specialist-Instruction-Cred-(CL-808CA) [Accessed 22 April 2024].

Chidiac, N. (2019) On Writing Therapy. From Finding Forrester to Imre Kertész. *Annales Médico-Psychologiques, Revue Psychiatrique*, 177(5), pp. 394–403.

Comings, J. P. (1999). Literacy Skill Retention in Adult Students in Developing Countries. *International Journal of Educational Development*, 19(4), pp. 273–285.

Crystal, D. (2003). *English as a Global Language.* 2nd ed. Cambridge: Cambridge University Press.

Davidson, M. M. (2021). Reading Comprehension in School-Age Children with Autism Spectrum Disorder: Examining the Many Components that may Contribute. *Language, Speech, and Hearing Services in Schools*, 52(1), pp. 181–196.

Davis-McElligatt, J. and Roth, F. (2012). The words we write for ourselves: confronting the myths of race, education, and American genius in *Finding Forrester*. In: E. Janak and D. F. Blum, eds., *The Pedagogy of Pop: Theoretical and Practical Strategies for Success*. Lanham, MD: Rowman & Littlefield, pp. 61--80.

Dromi, E., Oren, A. and Mimouni-Bloch, A. (2021). Language comprehension and speech production in young children with autism spectrum disorder: Psycho-linguistic insights on restricted, repetitive behaviors and interests. In: E. Gal and N. Yirmiya, eds., *Repetitive and Restricted Behaviors and Interests in Autism Spectrum Disorders: From Neurobiology to Behavior.* New York: Springer Nature, pp. 143–157.

Eide, D. (2012). *Uncovering the Logic of English: A Common-Sense Approach to Reading, Spelling, and Literacy.* Rochester, MN: Logic of English, Inc.

Fay, W. H. (1969). On the Basis of Autistic Echolalia. *Journal of Communication Disorders*, 2(1), pp. 38–47.

Graff, H. J. (1987). *The Legacies of Literacy: Continuities and Contradictions in Western Culture and Society.* Bloomington: Indiana University Press.

Gredler, M. E. (2012). Understanding Vygotsky for the classroom: Is it too late?. *Educational Psychology Review*, 24, pp. 113–131.

Guthrie, J. W. and Kirst, M. W. (1985). *Conditions of Education in California*, 1985. Stanford: Policy Analysis for California Education.

Hoerricks, J. (2010). *Leadership in the Lodge of Perfection*. San Francisco: Blurb Publishing.

Hoerricks, J. (2023). *No Place for Autism? Exploring the Solitary Forager Hypothesis of Autism in Light of Place Identity*. New York: Lived Places Publishing.

Howatt, A. P. R. (2004). *A History of English Language Teaching*. 2nd ed. Oxford: Oxford University Press.

Jones, D. (1988). The genealogy of the urban schoolteacher. In: T Popkewitz, ed., *Cultural History and Education*. Abingdon: Routledge, pp.

Juel, C. (1988). Learning to Read and Write: A Longitudinal Study of 54 Children from First through Fourth Grades. *Journal of Educational Psychology*, 80(4), p. 437.

Kozulin, A., Gindis, B., Ageyev, V. S. and Miller, S. M. (2003). *Vygotsky's Educational Theory in Cultural Context*. Cambridge: Cambridge University Press.

Krashen, S. (1981) Second Language Acquisition. *Second Language Learning*, 3(7), pp. 19–39.

Lal, B. S. (2015) The Economic and Social Cost of Illiteracy: An Overview. *International Journal of Advance Research and Innovative Ideas in Education*, 1(5), pp. 663–670.

Lebedinsky, V.V. (2009). Autism as a Model of Abnormal Emotional Development. *Psychology in Russia*, 2, p. 404.

Lightbown, P. M. and Spada, N. (2021). *How Languages Are Learned*. 5th ed.. Oxford: Oxford University Press.

Loumbourdi, L. (2018). Communicative language teaching (CLT). In: J. I. Liontas, T. International Association, and M. DelliCarpini, eds., *The TESOL Encyclopedia of English Language Teaching*. Hoboken, NJ: Wiley, pp. 1–6.

Kinnaird, E., Stewart, C. and Tchanturia, K. (2019). Investigating Alexithymia in Autism: A Systematic Review and Meta-Analysis. *European Psychiatry*, 55, pp. 80–89.

Mason, J.M. and Sinha, S. (1992). *Emerging Literacy in the Early Childhood Years: Applying a Vygotskian Model of Learning and Development*. Urbana, IL: Center for the Study of Reading.

New, W. S. and Kyuchukov, H. (2022). Sukhareva's (1930) 'Toward the Problem of the Structure and Dynamics of Children's Constitutional Psychopathies (Schizoid Forms)': A Translation with Commentary. *European Child & Adolescent Psychiatry*, 32(8), pp. 1453–1461.

Ngulube, I. E. (2015). *Learn English Son: A Practical Approach to the English Language*. Port Harcourt, Nigeria: Ulamba Publishers.

Paulsrud, D. and Nilholm, C. (2023). Teaching for Inclusion– A Review of Research on the Cooperation between Regular Teachers and Special Educators in the Work with Students in Need of Special Support. *International Journal of Inclusive Education*, 27(4), pp. 541–555.

Piaget, J. (1959). *The Language and Thought of the Child (Vol. 5)*. London: Psychology Press.

Prizant, B. M. (1982). Gestalt Language and Gestalt Processing in Autism. *Topics in Language Disorders*, 3(1), pp. 16–23.

Prizant, B.M. (1983). Language Acquisition and Communicative Behavior in Autism: Toward an Understanding of the "Whole" of It. *Journal of Speech and Hearing Disorders*, 48(3), pp. 296–307.

Prizant, B. M. and Duchan, J. F. (1981). The Functions of Immediate Echolalia in Autistic Children. *Journal of Speech and Hearing Disorders*, 46(3), 241–249.

Prizant, B. M. and Rydell, P. J. (1984). Analysis of Functions of Delayed Echolalia in Autistic Children. *Journal of Speech and Hearing Research*, 27(2), 183–192.

Rees, J. (2019). *Tracing Boards of the Three Degrees in Craft Freemasonry Explained*. Bury St Edmunds: Arima Publishing.

Schuler, A. L. and Prizant, B. M. (1985). Echolalia. In: E. Schopler and G. B. Mesibov, eds., *Communication Problems in Autism*. Boston, MA: Springer US, pp. 163–184.

Scullin-Esser, K. (1988). Connecting the Self with What is Outside the Self in "The Thanatos Syndrome". *Renascence*, 40(2), p. 67.

Semingson, P. and Kerns, W. (2021). Where Is the Evidence? Looking Back to Jeanne Chall and Enduring Debates About the Science of Reading. *Reading Research Quarterly*, 56(S1), pp. S157–S169.

Simmonds, C. (2019). *GE Sukhareva's Place in the History of Autism Research: Context, Reception, Translation*. Wellington: Victoria University of Wellington.

Simpson, R. L., Ganz, J. B. and Mason, R. (2012). Social skills interventions and programming for learners with autism spectrum disorders. In: D. Zager, M. L. Wehmeyer, and R. L. Simpson, eds., *Educating Students with Autism Spectrum Disorders*. Abingdon: Routledge, pp. 207–226.

Skinner, B. F. (1957). *Verbal Behavior*. New York: Appleton-Century-Crofts.

Smagorinsky, P. (2013). What Does Vygotsky Provide for the 21st-Century Language Arts Teacher?. *Language Arts*, 90(3), pp. 192–204.

Sparks, J. E. (1968). *A State Legislates Improvement in Reading and the Miller-Unruh Act*. Washington, DC: ERIC Clearinghouse.

Stiegler, L. N. (2015). Examining the Echolalia Literature: Where Do Speech-Language Pathologists Stand? *American Journal of Speech-Language Pathology*, 24(4), 750–762. https://doi.org/10.1044/2015_AJSLP-14-0166.

Style, E. (1996). Curriculum as Window and Mirror. *Social Science Record*, 33(2), pp. 21–28.

Taylor, G.J. (1984). Alexithymia: Concept, Measurement, and Implications for Treatment. *The American Journal of Psychiatry*, 141(6), pp. 725–732.

Vágvölgyi, R., Coldea, A., Dresler, T., Schrader, J. and Nuerk, H.C. (2016). A Review about Functional Illiteracy: Definition, Cognitive, Linguistic, and Numerical Aspects. *Frontiers in Psychology*, 7, p. 1617.

Vasileva, O. and Balyasnikova, N. (2019). (Re) Introducing Vygotsky's Thought: From Historical Overview to Contemporary Psychology. *Frontiers in Psychology*, 10, p. 1515.

Vygotsky, L. S. (1962). *Thought and Language*. Cambridge, MA: MIT Press.

Vygotsky, L. S. (1978). *Mind in Society*. Cambridge, MA: Harvard University Press.

Vygotsky, L. S., van der Veer, R. E., Valsiner, J. E. and Prout, T. T. (1994). *The Vygotsky Reader*. Oxford: Basil Blackwell.

Vygotsky, L. S. (1987). *The Collected Works of LS Vygotsky: The Fundamentals of Defectology (Vol. 2)*. New York: Springer Science & Business Media.

Vygotsky, L. S. (2012). *The Collected Works of LS Vygotsky: Scientific Legacy*. New York: Springer Science & Business Media.

Walters, D. and Walters, L. (2002). *Speak and Grow Rich: Revised and Updated*. London: Penguin.

Wertsch, J. V. (1985). *Vygotsky and the Social Formation of Mind*. Cambridge, MA: Harvard University Press.

World Health Organization. (2021a). *International statistical classification of diseases and related health problems (ICD)*. [Online] Available at: www.who.int/standards/classifications/classification-of-diseases [Accessed 22 April 2024].

World Health Organization. (2021b). *2021 ICD-10-CM diagnosis code F84.0. ICD List.* [Online] Available at: https://icdlist.com/icd-10/F84.0 [Accessed 22 April 2024].

World Health Organization. (2021c). *ICD-11 for mortality and morbidity statistics: 6A02 Autism spectrum disorder.* [Online] Available at: https://icd.who.int/browse11/l-m/en#/http%3a%2f%2fid.who.int%2ficd%2fentity%2f437815624 [Accessed 22 April 2024].

Zachos, A. (2023). Gestalt Language Development: How Most Autistic Individuals Develop Language. *Autism Advocate Parenting Magazine*, January 2023, pp. 17–20.

Chapter 2

Aaron, P. G., Joshi, R. M., Ayotollah, M., Ellsberry, A., Henderson, J. and Lindsey, K. (1999). Decoding and Sight-Word Naming: Are They Independent Components of Word Recognition Skill?. *Reading and Writing*, 11, pp. 89–127.

Albright, E. D. and Harnett, S. M. (2022). An introduction to the Institutional Review Board and its role in human subject research. In: S. M. Harnett and L. P. Cantwell-Jurkovic, eds., *Finding Your Seat at the Table: Roles for Librarians on Institutional Regulatory Boards and Committees*. Lanham, MD: Rowman & Littlefield, pp. 3–14.

Alexander, A. W., Andersen, H. G., Heilman, P. C., Voeller, K. K. and Torgesen, J. K. (1991). Phonological Awareness Training and Remediation of Analytic Decoding Deficits in a Group of Severe Dyslexics. *Annals of Dyslexia*, 41, pp. 193–206.

Andreola, C., Mascheretti, S., Belotti, R., Ogliari, A., Marino, C., Battaglia, M. and Scaini, S. (2021). The Heritability of Reading and Reading-Related Neurocognitive Components: A Multi-Level Meta-Analysis. *Neuroscience & Biobehavioral Reviews*, 121, pp. 175–200.

Arkansas Department of Education (2018). *RISE Arkansas 2018 Report*. 1. [PDF] Arkansas: Arkansas Department of

Education. Available at: https://dese.ade.arkansas.gov/Files/ 20201207143440_RISE_Arkansas_2018_Report_REV2.pdf [Accessed 16 April 2024].

Bell, N. (1991). Gestalt Imagery: A Critical Factor in Language Comprehension. *Annals of Dyslexia*, 41, pp. 246–260.

Bindra, S., Sharma, D., Parameswar, N., Dhir, S. and Paul, J. (2022). Bandwagon Effect Revisited: A Systematic Review to Develop Future Research Agenda. *Journal of Business Research*, 143, pp. 305–317.

Blanc, M., Blackwell, A. and Elias, P. (2023). Using the Natural Language Acquisition Protocol to Support Gestalt Language Development. *Perspectives of the ASHA Special Interest Groups*, 8(6), pp. 1279–1286.

California Department of Education. (2018). *California Comprehensive State Literacy Plan*. 1. [PDF] California: California Department of Education. Available at: www.cde.ca.gov/pd/ps/documents/cacompstatelitplan.pdf [Accessed 16 Apr. 2024.]

California School Boards Association. (2020). *Getting reading right without the wars*. [Online] Available at: https://publications.csba.org/issue/fall-2020/getting-reading-right-without-the-wars/ [Accessed 16 April 2024].

California Teacher Credentialing Examinations. (2023). *About the RICA*. [Online] Available at: www.ctcexams.nesinc.com/PageView.aspx?f=GEN_AboutRICA.html [Accessed 16 April 2024].

Cano, R. (2020). California will pay millions to settle suit claiming it violated students' right to read. [Online] CalMatters. Available at: https://calmatters.org/education/2020/02/california-literacy-rights-lawsuit-settlement-teaching-students-read/ [Accessed 16 April 2024].

Caputo, J. D. ed. (1997). *Deconstruction in a Nutshell: A Conversation with Jacques Derrida (Vol. 53)*. New York: Fordham University Press.

Chall, J. S. (1976). *Reading and Development*. Newark, Del: International Reading Association.

Chall, J. S. (1977) *Reading 1967–1977: A Decade of Change and Promise. Fastback 97*. Bloomington, IN: Phi Delta Kappa Educational Foundation.

Chandler, D. (1994). *Semiotics for Beginners*. Aberystwyth: University of Wales.

Cunha, P., de Castro Silva, I. M., Neiva, E. R. and Tristão, R. M. (2019). Auditory Processing Disorder Evaluations and Cognitive Profiles of Children with Specific Learning Disorder. *Clinical Neurophysiology Practice*, 4, pp. 119–127.

Department for Education. (2006). *Independent Review of the Teaching of Early Reading: Final Report*. 1. [PDF] London: Department for Education. Available at: https://webarchive.nationalarchives.gov.uk/20100603160107/http://www.standards.dcsf.gov.uk/phonics/report.pdf [Accessed 16 Apr. 2024].

Derrida, J. (2020). *Deconstruction in a Nutshell: A Conversation with Jacques Derrida, with a New Introduction*. New York: Fordham University Press.

Double, K. S., McGrane, J. A., Stiff, J. C. and Hopfenbeck, T. N. (2019). The Importance of Early Phonics Improvements for Predicting Later Reading Comprehension. *British Educational Research Journal*, 45(6), pp. 1220–1234.

Duke, N. K. and Cartwright, K. B. (2021). The Science of Reading Progresses: Communicating Advances Beyond the Simple View of Reading. *Reading Research Quarterly*, 56, pp. S25–S44.

Ellis, G. and Bloch, C. (2021). Neuroscience and Literacy: An Integrative View. *Transactions of the Royal Society of South Africa*, 76(2), pp. 157–188.

Farrell, C. C., Penuel, W. R. and Davidson, K. (2022). "What Counts" as Research? Comparing Policy Guidelines to the Evidence Education Leaders Report as Useful. *AERA Open*, 8, p. 23328584211073157.

FindLaw. (2023). *California Code, Education Code - EDC § 44283*. [Online] Available at: https://codes.findlaw.com/ca/education-code/edc-sect-44283/ [Accessed 16 April 2024.]

Finnegan, E. G. and Accardo, A. L. (2018). Understanding Character Perspective: Strategies to Support Students with Autism Spectrum Disorder. *The Reading Teacher*, 72(1), pp. 71–80.

Ginsberg, Y. C., Hollands, F. M., Holmes, V. R., Shand, R., Evans, P., Blodgett, R., Wang, Y. and Head, L. (2022). Does ESSA Assure the Use of Evidence-Based Educational Practices?. *Educational Policy*, 38(1), p. 08959048221127989.

Glazzard, J. (2017). Assessing Reading Development through Systematic Synthetic Phonics. *English in Education*, 51(1), pp. 44–57.

Gough, P. B. and Tunmer, W. E. (1986). Decoding, Reading, and Reading Disability. *Remedial and Special Education*, 7(1), pp. 6–10.

Grady, C. (2015). Institutional Review Boards: Purpose and Challenges. *Chest*, 148(5), pp. 1148–1155.

Grigorenko, E. L., Compton, D. L., Fuchs, L. S., Wagner, R. K., Willcutt, E. G. and Fletcher, J. M. (2020). Understanding, Educating, and Supporting Children with Specific Learning Disabilities: 50 Years of Science and Practice. *American Psychologist*, 75(1), p. 37.

Hall, M., (1976). *Teaching reading as a language experience*.

Hobbs, G. (2022). Why some parents are eager for changes to Ontario's early reading curriculum. [Online] CBC News. Available at: www.cbc.ca/news/canada/right-to-read-inquiry-report-literacy-ontario-1.6378408 [Accessed 16 April 2024].

Hoerricks, J. (2023a). *No Place for Autism? Exploring the Solitary Forager Hypothesis of Autism in Light of Place Identity*. New York: Lived Places Publishing.

Hoerricks, J. (2023b). *Where's the science in the science of reading?*. [Blog] AutSide. Available at: https://autside.substack.com/p/wheres-the-science-in-the-science [Accessed 16 April 2024].

Hoerricks, J. (2023c). *What are "evidence mills?"*. [Blog] AutSide. Available at: https://autside.substack.com/p/what-are-evidence-mills [Accessed 16 April 2024].

Hoerricks, J. (2023d). *The autistic way of proceeding*. [Blog] Lived Places Publishing. Available at: https://livedplacespublishing.com/blog/the-autistic-way-of-proceeding [Accessed 17 April 2024].

Hoover, W.A. and Gough, P.B. (1990). The Simple View of Reading. *Reading and Writing*, 2, pp. 127–160.

Jackson Public School District. (2023) *Literacy-based promotion act*. [Online] Available at: www.jackson.k12.ms.us/LBPA [Accessed 16 April 2024].

Johann, V., Könen, T. and Karbach, J. (2020). The Unique Contribution of Working Memory, Inhibition, Cognitive Flexibility, and Intelligence to Reading Comprehension and Reading Speed. *Child Neuropsychology*, 26(3), pp. 324–344.

Jones, M. E. and Christensen, A. E. (2022). *Constructing Strong Foundations of Early Literacy*. Abingdon: Routledge.

Juul, H., Poulsen, M. and Elbro, C. (2014). Separating Speed from Accuracy in Beginning Reading Development. *Journal of Educational Psychology*, 106(4), p. 1096.

Kerns, W. (2021). A Historical and Sociocultural View of the Science of Reading Debate. *The Missouri Reader*, 44(3), pp. 10–16.

Kim, J.S. (2008). Research and the Reading Wars. *Phi Delta Kappan*, 89(5), pp. 372–375.

Kingston, A. J. (1968). Areas of Confusion in the Development of a Science of Reading. In: *1968 Yearbook of the National Reading Conference*, Paper presented at National Reading Conference, Los Angeles, Dec. 5-7, 1968

Knyazev, N. and Oosterhuis, H. (2022). The Bandwagon Effect: Not Just Another Bias. In: *Proceedings of the 2022 ACM*

SIGIR International Conference on Theory of Information Retrieval. New York: Association for Computing Machinery, pp. 243–253.

Lindamood, P. C., Bell, N. and Lindamood, P. (1992). Issues in Phonological Awareness Assessment. *Annals of Dyslexia*, 42, pp. 242–259.

Lindenmuth, S. (2023). RICA test pass rates & scoring information. [Online] Available at: https://study.com/academy/popular/rica-test-pass-rates-scoring-information.html [Accessed 16 April 2024].

MultiLit. (2023). *Programs & resources*. [Online] Available at: https://multilit.com/programs/ [Accessed 16 April 2024].

Musiek, F. (1999). Habilitation and Management of Auditory Processing Disorders: Overview of Selected Procedures. *Journal of the American Academy of Audiology*, 10(06), pp. 329–342.

Nation, K. (2019). Children's Reading Difficulties, Language, and Reflections on the Simple View of Reading. *Australian Journal of Learning Difficulties*, 24(1), pp. 47–73.

Noens, I. L. and van Berckelaer-Onnes, I. A. (2005). Captured by Details: Sense-Making, Language and Communication in Autism. *Journal of Communication Disorders*, 38(2), pp. 123–141.

NSW Education Standards Authority. (2023). *Phonics diagnostic assessment*. [Online] Available at: https://education.nsw.gov.au/teaching-and-learning/curriculum/literacy-and-numeracy/assessment-resources/phonics-diagnostic-assessment [Accessed 16 April 2024].

Ohio Department of Education. (2023). *Dyslexia*. [Online] Available at: https://education.ohio.gov/Topics/Learning-in-Ohio/Literacy/Dyslexia [Accessed 16 April 2024].

Palincsar, A. S. and Duke, N. K. (2004). The Role of Text and Text-Reader Interactions in Young Children's Reading Development and Achievement. *The Elementary School Journal*, 105(2), pp. 183–197.

Perdue, M. V., Mahaffy, K., Vlahcevic, K., Wolfman, E., Erbeli, F., Richlan, F. and Landi, N. (2022). Reading Intervention and Neuroplasticity: A Systematic Review and Meta-Analysis of Brain Changes Associated with Reading Intervention. *Neuroscience & Biobehavioral Reviews*, 132, pp. 465–494.

Prasad, S. and Sagar, R. (2021). Learning disorder (dyslexia): An overview description of the entity through available researches. In: S. Misciagna, ed., *Learning Disabilities-Neurobiology, Assessment, Clinical Features and Treatments*. London: IntechOpen, https://www.intechopen.com/chapters/79195.

Prizant, B.M. (1982). Gestalt Language and Gestalt Processing in Autism. *Topics in Language Disorders*, 3(1), pp. 16–23.

Prizant, B.M. (1983). Language Acquisition and Communicative Behavior in Autism: Toward an Understanding of the "Whole" of It. *Journal of Speech and Hearing Disorders*, 48(3), pp. 296–307.

Prizant, B. M. and Duchan, J. F. (1981). The Functions of Immediate Echolalia in Autistic Children. *Journal of Speech and Hearing Disorders*, 46(3), pp. 241–249.

Prizant, B. M. and Rydell, P. J. (1984). Analysis of Functions of Delayed Echolalia in Autistic Children. *Journal of Speech and Hearing Research*, 27(2), 183–192.

Robey, D. (1973). *Structuralism: An Introduction*. Oxford: Clarendon Press.

Rossi, J. and Schipper, B. (2012). *Case Studies in Preparation for the California Reading Competency Test*. London: Pearson.

Scarborough, H. S. (2001). Connecting early language and literacy to later reading (dis)abilities: Evidence, theory, and practice. In: S. B. Neuman and D. K. Dickinson, eds, *Handbook of Early Literacy Research*. New York: Guilford Press, pp. 23--38

Semingson, P. and Kerns, W. (2021). Where's the Evidence? Looking Back to Jeanne Chall and Enduring Debates about the Science of Reading. *Reading Research Quarterly*, 56(S1), pp. S157–S169.

Shanahan, T. (2012). Shanahan on literacy. [Online] Shanahan on Literacy. Available at: www.shanahanonliteracy.com/ [Accessed 16 April 2024].

Shanahan, T. (2020). What Constitutes a Science of Reading Instruction?. *Reading Research Quarterly*, 55, pp. S235–S247.

Spellecy, R. and Busse, K. (2021). The History of Human Subjects Research and Rationale for Institutional Review Board Oversight. *Nutrition in Clinical Practice*, 36(3), pp. 560–567.

Stammer, J. D. (1979). The Science of Reading. *Reading Horizons: A Journal of Literacy and Language Arts*, 19(4), p. 8.

Sturrock, J. (2008). *Structuralism*. Hoboken, NJ: John Wiley & Sons.

Tennessee Department of Education. (2023). *Tennessee Literacy Success Act Training and Licensure Requirements*. 1. [PDF] Tennessee: Tennessee Department of Education. Available at: www.tn.gov/content/dam/tn/education/licensure/TN_LSA_Training_and_Licensure_Requirements.pdf [Accessed 16 Apr. 2024].

Trassi, A. P. and Oliveira, K. L. D. (2019). Reading Comprehension, Learning Strategies and Verbal Reasoning: Possible Relationships. *Psico-USF*, 24, pp. 615–624.

UNESCO. (2023). *Adult literacy rate, population 15+ years (both sexes, female, male)*. [Online] Available at: https://data.uis.unesco.org [Accessed 22 April 2024].

Venezky, R. L. (2019). *Theoretical and Experimental Base for Teaching Reading (Vol. 9)*. Berlin: Walter de Gruyter GmbH & Co KG.

Vulchanova, M. and Vulchanov, V. (2022). Rethinking Figurative Language in Autism: What Evidence Can We Use for Interventions?. *Frontiers in Communication*, 7, p. 910850.

World Atlas. (2023). *List of countries by literacy rate*. [Online] Available at: www.worldatlas.com/articles/the-highest-literacy-rates-in-the-world.html#:~:text=Literacy%20Rate%20by%20Country%20%20%20%20%EF%BB%BFCountry,%20100.0%20%25%20%20106%20more%20rows%20 [Accessed 16 April 2024].

Zarrillo, J. (2017). *Ready for RICA: A Test Preparation Guide for California's Reading Instruction Competence Assessment.* London: Pearson.

Chapter 3

Angelopoulou, N. (2020). The effectiveness of translanguaging language practices in bilingual education: A literature review. In: B. Krzywosz-Rynkiewicz and V. Zorbas, eds., *Citizenship at a Crossroads: Rights, Identity, and Education.* Prague: Charles University and Children's Identity and Citizenship European Association, pp. 65–79.

Atmore, E. (2019). *An interpretive analysis of the early childhood development policy trajectory in post-apartheid South Africa.* Doctoral dissertation. Stellenbosch University.

Bai, Y., Ladd, H. F., Muschkin, C. G. and Dodge, K. A. (2020). Long-Term Effects of Early Childhood Programs through Eighth Grade: Do the Effects Fade Out or Grow?. *Children and Youth Services Review*, 112, p. 104890.

Bathgate, G. N. (2003). History of the development of whiskey distillation. In: G. Stewart and I. Russell, eds., *Whisky: Technology, Production and Marketing.* London: Elsevier, pp. 1–24.

Becker, F. da R. (2007). Early Childhood Education in Brazil: The Obstacles to a Successful Experience. *Revista Latinoamericana de Ciencias Sociales, Niñez y Juventud*, 5(2), pp. 515–537.

Bell, N. (2007). *Visualizing and Verbalizing for Language Comprehension and Learning.* Avila Beach, CA: Gander Publishing.

Berryman, M., Rameka, L. and Togo, T. (2022). Understanding Languaculture from an Indigenous Māori Worldview. *The Australian Journal of Indigenous Education*, 51(2).

Bloomfield, L. (1944) 'The Loom of Language'. *American Speech*, 19(3), pp. 211–213.

Bloch, B., Kuhn, M., Schulz, M., Smidt, W., and Stenger, U. eds. (2021). *Early Childhood Education in Germany: Exploring Historical Developments and Theoretical Issues* (Abingdon: Routledge).

Bodrova, E. and Yudina, E. (2018). Early childhood education in the Russian Federation. In: J. L. Roopnarine, J. E. Johnson, S. Flannery Quinn, M. M. Patte, eds., *Handbook of International Perspectives on Early Childhood Education*. Abingdon: Routledge, pp. 59–69.

Brannigan, G. G. and Decker, S. L. (2006). The Bender–Gestalt II. *American Journal of Orthopsychiatry*, 76(1), pp. 10–12.

Cenoz, J. and Gorter, D. (2020). Teaching English through Pedagogical Translanguaging. *World Englishes*, 39(2), pp. 300–311.

Duke, N. K., Purcell-Gates, V., Hall, L. A. and Tower, C. (2006). Authentic Literacy Activities for Developing Comprehension and Writing. *The Reading Teacher*, 60(4), pp. 344–355.

Dwivedi, Y. K., Kshetri, N., Hughes, L., Slade, E. L., Jeyaraj, A., Kar, A. K., Baabdullah, A. M., Koohang, A., Raghavan, V., Ahuja, M. and Albanna, H. (2023). "So What if ChatGPT Wrote It?" Multidisciplinary Perspectives on Opportunities, Challenges and Implications of Generative Conversational AI for Research, Practice and Policy. *International Journal of Information Management*, 71, p. 102642.

Edyburn, D. L. (2010). Would You Recognize Universal Design for Learning if You Saw It? Ten Propositions for New Directions for the Second Decade of UDL. *Learning Disability Quarterly*, 33(1), pp. 33–41.

Ellis, N. C. (2019). Essentials of a Theory of Language Cognition. *The Modern Language Journal*, 103, pp. 39–60.

Farrell, L., Osenga, T. and Hunter, M. (2013). *Comparing the Dolch and Fry High Frequency Word Lists*. Arlington, VA: Readsters, LLC.

Fishman, J. A. (1991). *Reversing Language Shift: Theoretical and Empirical Foundations of Assistance to Threatened Languages (Vol. 76)*. Bristol: Multilingual matters.

García, O., Kleifgen, J. A. and Falchi, L. (2008). *From English Language Learners to Emergent Bilinguals. Equity Matters: Research Review No. 1*. New York: Campaign for Educational Equity.

García, O. and Kleyn, T. (2016). Translanguaging theory in education. In: O. Garcia and T. Kleyn, eds., *Translanguaging with Multilingual Students: Learning from Classroom Moments*. Abingdon: Routledge, pp. 9–33.

García, O., Aponte, G. Y. and Le, K. (2019). Primary bilingual classrooms: Translations and translanguaging. In: S. Laviosa and M. González-Davies, eds., *The Routledge Handbook of Translation and Education*. Abingdon: Routledge, pp. 34–47.

Gleason, J. B. and Ratner, N. B. (2022). *The Development of Language*. San Diego: Plural Publishing.

Goodman, B. and Tastanbek, S. (2021). Making the Shift from a Codeswitching to a Translanguaging Lens in English Language Teacher Education. *TESOL Quarterly*, 55(1), pp. 29–53.

Goody, J. (1987). *The Interface between the Written and the Oral*. Cambridge: Cambridge University Press.

Graff, H. J. (1994). Literacy, myths and legacies: Lessons from the history of literacy. In: L. Verhoeven, ed., *Functional Literacy: Theoretical Issues and Educational Implications*. Amsterdam: John Benjamins, pp. 37–60.

Gweon, H. (2021). Inferential Social Learning: Cognitive Foundations of Human Social Learning and Teaching. *Trends in Cognitive Sciences*, 25(10), pp. 896–910.

Hannon, P. (2004). The history and future of literacy. In: T. Grainger, ed., *The RoutledgeFalmer Reader in Language and Literacy*. Abingdon: Routledge, pp. 19–32.

Harris, J. F., Coffield, C. N., Janvier, Y. M., Mandell, D. and Cidav, Z. (2021). Validation of the Developmental Check-In Tool for Low-Literacy Autism Screening. *Pediatrics*, 147(1).

Hoerricks, J. (2018). *Leadership in the Lodge of Perfection*. San Francisco: Blurb Publishing.

Hoerricks, J. (2023a). *No Place for Autism? Exploring the Solitary Forager Hypothesis of Autism in Light of Place Identity*. New York: Lived Places Publishing.

Hoerricks, J. (2023b). *What are "evidence mills?"*. [Blog] AutSide. Available at: https://autside.substack.com/p/what-are-evidence-mills [Accessed 16 April 2024].

Hung, M., Smith, W. A., Voss, M. W., Franklin, J. D., Gu, Y. and Bounsanga, J. (2020). Exploring Student Achievement Gaps in School Districts Across the United States. *Education and Urban Society*, 52(2), pp. 175–193.

Jiang, W. (2000). The Relationship between Culture and Language. *ELT Journal*, 54(4), pp. 328–334.

Johns, J. L. (1970). The Dolch Basic Word List—Then and Now. *Journal of Reading Behavior*, 3(4), pp. 35–40.

Kaestle, C. F. and Damon-Moore, H. (1991). *Literacy in the United States: Readers and Reading since 1880*. New Haven, CT: Yale University Press.

Karstens, B. (2012). Bopp the Builder. Discipline Formation as Hybridization: The Case of Comparative Linguistics. *The Making of the Humanities*, 2, pp. 103–127.

Kohfeldt, D. and Langhout, R.D. (2012). The Five Whys Method: A Tool for Developing Problem Definitions in Collaboration with Children. *Journal of Community & Applied Social Psychology*, 22(4), pp. 316–329.

LaBrant, L. (1947). Research in Language. *Elementary English*, 24(1), pp. 86–94.

Li, Y. and Vandenbroeck, M. (2020). Conceptualisations of Parent Involvement in Early Childhood Education in China. *Asia-Pacific*

Journal of Research in Early Childhood Education, 14(1), pp. 169–192.

Macedo, D. ed. (2019). *Decolonizing Foreign Language Education: The Misteaching of English and Other Colonial Languages*. Abingdon: Routledge.

Mazari, A. and Derraz, N. (2015). Language and Culture. *International Journal of Humanities and Cultural Studies*, 2(2), pp. 350–359.

Morris, D. (1983). Concept of Word and Phoneme Awareness in the Beginning Reader. *Research in the Teaching of English*, 17(4), pp. 359–373.

Mott, M. (2023). *Neurodiversity Affirming Education: A Handbook for Teachers and Classroom Professionals*. Sioux Falls, SD: AdaptEd 4 Special Ed.

Mulyadi, B. (2020). Early Childhood Character Education in Japan. In: The 5th International Conference on Energy, Environmental and Information System (ICENIS 2020). Diponegoro: E3S Web of Conferences, p. 07063.

Murphy, J. P. (2016) Poitín–a Spirit of Rebellion and Inspiration. In: *3rd Dublin Gastronomic Symposium*. Dublin: Technological University Dublin, pp. 1–16.

Musatti, T. and Picchio, M. (2010). Early Education in Italy: Research and Practice. *International Journal of Early Childhood*, 42, pp. 141–153.

Nxumalo, F. (2019). *Decolonizing Place in Early Childhood Education*. Abingdon: Routledge.

Parsons, S. A. and Ward, A. E. (2011). The Case for Authentic Tasks in Content Literacy. *The Reading Teacher*, 64(6), pp. 462–465.

Perlovsky, L. (2009). Language and Emotions: Emotional Sapir–Whorf Hypothesis. *Neural Networks*, 22(5–6), pp. 518–526.

Prizant, B. M. (1982). Gestalt Language and Gestalt Processing in Autism. *Topics in Language Disorders*, 3(1), pp. 16–23.

Prizant, B. M. (1983). Language Acquisition and Communicative Behavior in Autism: Toward an Understanding of the "Whole" of It. *Journal of Speech and Hearing Disorders*, 48(3), pp. 296–307.

Prizant, B. M. and Duchan, J. F. (1981). The Functions of Immediate Echolalia in Autistic Children. *Journal of Speech and Hearing Disorders*, 46(3), 241–249.

Prizant, B. M. and Rydell, P. J. (1984) Analysis of Functions of Delayed Echolalia in Autistic Children. *Journal of Speech and Hearing Research*, 27(2), 183–192.

Rana, M. V., Sharma, P., Tomar, M. N. and Atri, M. U. (2022). Aqua Vitae: Use for Disease Control and Prevention Benefits and Demerits. *Vegueta: Anuario de la Facultad de Geografía e Historia*, 22, p. 10.

Reetu, C., Renu, G. and Adarsh, S. (2017). Quality Early Childhood Care and Education in India: Initiatives, Practice, Challenges and Enablers. *Asia-Pacific Journal of Research in Early Childhood Education*, 11(1), pp. 41–67.

Rolstad, K. (2001). Language Death in Central Mexico: The Decline of Nahuatl and the New Bilingual Maintenance Programs. *Bilingual Review/La Revista Bilingüe*, 26(1), pp. 3–18.

Ryka, A. (2023). *Do English teacher practices involve translanguaging in English classes or are they English only?: A mixed-methods study about teachers' translanguaging patterns in EFL classrooms in Swedish lower secondary schools*. Independent Degree Project at Undergraduate Level. Stockholm University.

Sakai, K. L. (2005). Language Acquisition and Brain Development. *Science*, 310(5749), pp. 815–819.

Sapir, E. (1968). *Selected Writings of Edward Sapir*. Oakland, CA: University of California Press.

Saracho, O. N. (2019). Literacy in the twenty-first century: Children, families and policy. In: O. N. Saracho, ed., *Research in Young Children's Literacy and Language Development*. Abingdon: Routledge, pp. 332–345.

Saunders, M., Martínez, L., Flook, L. and Hernández, L. E. (2021). *Social Justice Humanitas Academy: A Community School Approach to Whole Child Education*. Palo Alto, CA: Learning Policy Institute.

Scribner, S. (1984). Literacy in Three Metaphors. *American Journal of Education*, 93(1), pp. 6–21.

Sweet, H. (2018). The practical study of language. In: A. P. R. Howatt and R. C. Smith, eds., *Early Years of Reform*. Abingdon: Routledge, pp. 137–161).

Tembo, S. (2021). Black Educators in (White) Settings: Making Racial Identity Visible in Early Childhood Education and Care in England, UK. *Journal of Early Childhood Research*, 19(1), pp. 70–83.

Tobin, J. (2005). Quality in Early Childhood Education: An Anthropologist's Perspective. *Early Education and Development*, 16(4), pp. 421–434.

Vogel, S. and García, O. (2017). Translanguaging. [Online] Oxford Research Encyclopedias, Education. Available at: https://oxfordre.com/education/display/10.1093/acrefore/9780190264093.001.0001/acrefore-9780190264093-e-181 [Accessed 22 April 2024].

Westerveld, M. F. and Paynter, J. (2021). Introduction to the Forum: Literacy in Autism—Across the Spectrum. *Language, Speech, and Hearing Services in Schools*, 52(1), pp. 149–152.

Xocoyotzin, N. H. (1996). Las Palabras Verdaderas. *Estudios de Cultura Náhuatl*, 26, pp. 290–298.

Chapter 4

Alexander, P. (1997). Mapping the multidimensional nature of domain learning: The interplay of cognitive, motivational, and strategic forces. In: M. Maehr and P. Pintrich, eds., *Advances in Motivation and Achievement*. Greenwich, CT: JAI Press, pp. 213–250).

Alexander, K., Entwisle, D. and Horsey, C. (1997). From First Grade Forward: Early Foundations of High School Dropout. *Sociology of Education*, 70, pp. 87–107.

Anderson, J. A., Kutash, K. and Duchnowski, A. J. (2001). A Comparison of the Academic Progress of Students with EBD and Students with LD. *Journal of Emotional and Behavioural Disorders*, 9, pp. 106–115.

Asaro-Saddler, K. (2016). Writing Instruction and Self-Regulation for Students with Autism Spectrum Disorders: A Systematic Review of Literature. *Topics in Language Disorders*, 36, pp. 266–283.

Bal, A. (2018). Culturally Responsive Positive Behavioural Interventions and Supports: A Process–Oriented Framework for Systemic Transformation. *Review of Education, Pedagogy, and Cultural Studies*, 40(2), pp. 144–174.

Banks, J. (2021). A Winning Formula? Funding Inclusive Education in Ireland. *Resourcing Inclusive Education*, 15, pp. 7–19.

Barrett, J. and Cocq, C. (2019). Indigenous Storytelling and Language Learning: Digital Media as a Vehicle for Cultural Transmission and Language Acquisition. In *Perspectives on Indigenous writing and literacies* (pp. 89–112). Brill.

Benner, G. J., Nelson, J. R., Ralston, N. C. and Mooney, P. (2010). A Meta-Analysis of the Effects of Reading Instruction on the Reading Skills of Students with or At Risk of Behavioural Disorders. *Behavioural Disorders*, 35(2), pp. 86–102.

Berger, M. (2005). Vygotsky's Theory of Concept Formation and Mathematics Education. *International Group for the Psychology of Mathematics Education*, 2, pp. 153–160.

Bloom, H. (2010). *Modern Regression Discontinuity Analysis.* New York: MDRC.

Bransford, J. and Johnson, M. (1972). Contextual Prerequisites for Understanding: Some Investigation of Comprehension and Recall. *Journal of Verbal Learning and Verbal Behavior*, 11, p. 722.

Brunzell, T., Stokes, H. and Waters, L. (2019). Shifting Teacher Practice in Trauma-Affected classrooms: Practice Pedagogy Strategies within a Trauma-Informed Positive Education Model. *School Mental Health*, 11(3), pp. 600–614.

Burke, M. D., Boon, R. T., Hatton, H. and Bowman-Perrott, L. (2015). Reading Interventions for Middle and Secondary Students with Emotional and Behavioural Disorders: A Quantitative Review of Single-Case Studies. *Behaviour Modification*, 39(1), pp. 43–68.

California Department of Education (Cal DOE) (2023). *Smarter Balanced Interim Assessments.* [Online] Available at: www.cde.ca.gov/TA/TG/sa/sbacinterimassess.asp [Accessed 22 April 2024].

Callahan, M. M., Fodstad, J. C. and Moore, J. W. (2023). History of applied behavior analysis. In: J. L. Matson, ed., *Handbook of Applied Behavior Analysis: Integrating Research into Practice.* Cham: Springer International Publishing, pp. 3–17.

Cheyne, J. A. and Tarulli, D. (1999). Dialogue, Difference, and Voice in the Zone of Proximal Development. *Theory & Psychology*, 9(1), pp. 5–28.

Coleman, M. and Vaughn, S. (2000). Reading Interventions for Students with Emotional/Behavioral Disorders. *Behavioral Disorders*, 25, pp. 93–104.

Costello, E. J., Angold, A., Keeler, G. P. (1999). Adolescent Outcomes of Childhood Disorders: The Consequences of Severity and Impairment. *Journal of the American Academy of Child and Adolescent Psychiatry*, 38, pp. 121–128.

Costello, E .J., Mustillo, S., Erkanli, A., Keeler, G. and Angold, A. (2003). Prevalence and Development of Psychiatric Disorders in

Childhood and Adolescence. *Archives of General Psychiatry*, 60, pp. 837–844.

Cuenca-Carlino, Y., Freeman-Green, S., Stephenson, G. W. and Hauth, C. (2016). Self-Regulated Strategy Development Instruction for Teaching Multi-Step Equations to Middle School Students Struggling in Math. *The Journal of Special Education*, 50, pp. 75–85.

Cuenca-Carlino, Y., Mustian, A. L., Allen, R. D. and Whitley, S. F. (2018). Writing for My Future: Transition-Focused Self-Advocacy of Secondary Students with Emotional/Behavioral Disorders. *Remedial and Special Education*, 40(2), pp. 83–96.

De Bruin, K. (2021). Response to Intervention (RTI) and Multi-Tiered Systems of Support (MTSS): An Introduction. *Learning Difficulties Australia Bulletin*, 53(3), pp. 15–18.

De Bruin, K., Kestel, E., Francis, M., Forgasz, H. and Fries, R. (2023). *Supporting Students Significantly Behind in Literacy and Numeracy: A Review of Evidence-Based Approaches.* [Online] Melbourne: Australian Education Research Organisation/Monash University. Available at: www.edresearch.edu.au/research/research-reports/supporting-students-significantly-behind-literacy-numeracy [Accessed 18 April 2024].

The Education Endowment Foundation (EEF). (2023). *Testing a whole-school improvement programme, focused on improving leadership, teaching and engagement with parents.* [Online] Available at: https://educationendowmentfoundation.org.uk/projects-and-evaluation/projects/achievement-for-all [Accessed 18 April 2024].

Ennis, R. P. and Jolivette, K. (2014). Existing Research and Future Directions for Self-Regulated Strategy Development with Students with and At Risk for Emotional and Behavioural Disorders. *The Journal of Special Education*, 48, pp. 32–45.

Fields, V. L., Soke, G. N., Reynolds, A., Tian, L. H., Wiggins, L., Maenner, M., DiGuiseppi, C., Kral, T. V., Hightshoe, K. and Schieve, L. A. (2021). Pica, Autism, and Other Disabilities. *Pediatrics*, 147(2).

Fien, H., Chard, D. J. and Baker, S. K. (2021). Can the Evidence Revolution and Multi-Tiered Systems of Support Improve Education Equity and Reading Achievement?. *Reading Research Quarterly*, 56, pp. S105–S118.

Fisher, D. and Frey, N. (2013). *Gradual Release of Responsibility Framework*. 1. [PDF] Newark, DE: International Reading Association. Available at: https://keystoliteracy.com/wp-content/uploads/2017/08/frey_douglas_and_nancy_frey-_gradual_release_of_responsibility_intructional_framework.pdf [Accessed 18 April 2024].

Gagnon, J. C., Sylvester, F. J. and Marsh, K. (2021). Alignment of School Discipline with Positive Behavioural Interventions and Supports: The Case of One Disadvantaged Urban South African Primary School. *South African Journal of Childhood Education*, 11(1), pp. 1–9.

Garwood, J. D. (2018). Literacy Interventions for Secondary Students Formally Identified with Emotional and Behavioural Disorders: Trends and Gaps in the Research. *Journal of Behavioural Education*, 27, pp. 23–52.

Gillon, G. (2023). Supporting Children who are English Language Learners Succeed in Their Early Literacy Development. *Folia Phoniatrica et Logopaedica*, 75(4), pp. 219–234.

Glasser, W. (1998a). *Choice Theory: A New Psychology of Personal Freedom*. New York: HarperCollins.

Glasser, W. (1998b). *The Quality School: Managing Students without Coercion*. New York: HarperCollins.

Glasser, W. (1998c). *The Quality School Teacher: A Companion Volume to The Quality School*. New York: HarperCollins.

Glasser, W. (2001). *Counseling with Choice Theory*. New York: HarperCollins.

Glasser, W. (2003). *Warning: Psychiatry Can Be Hazardous to Your Mental Health*. New York: HarperCollins.

Glasser, W. (2008). *Every Student Can Succeed*. New York: HarperCollins.

Graham, S., McKeown, D, Kiuhara, S. and Harris, K. R. (2012). A Meta-Analysis of Writing Instruction for Students in the Elementary Grades. *Journal of Educational Psychology*, 104, pp. 879–896.

Harris, K. R. and Graham, S. (1999). Programmatic Intervention Research: Illustrations from the Evolution of Self-Regulated Strategy Development. *Learning Disability Quarterly*, 22, pp. 251–262.

Harris, K. R., Graham, S., Mason, L. H. and Saddler, B. (2002). Developing Self-Regulated Writers. *Theory Into Practice*, 41, pp. 110–115.

Harris, K. R., Graham, S., Mason, L. H. and Friedland, B. (2008). *Powerful Writing Strategies for All Students*. Baltimore, MD: Brookes.

Hendren, R. L., Haft, S. L., Black, J. M., White, N. C. and Hoeft, F. (2018). Recognizing Psychiatric Comorbidity with Reading Disorders. *Frontiers in Psychiatry*, 9, p. 101.

Hingstman, M., Doolaard, S., Warrens, M. J. and Bosker, R. J. (2021). Supporting Young Struggling Readers at Success for All Schools in the United States and the Netherlands: Comparative Case Studies. *Research in Comparative and International Education*, 16(1), pp. 22–42.

Hinshaw, S. P. (1992). Externalizing Behavior Problems and Academic Underachievement in Childhood and Adolescence: Causal Relationships and Underlying Mechanisms. *Psychological Bulletin*, 111(1), pp. 127–155.

Hoerricks, K. J. (2018). *Higher education support strategies: An evaluation of needs satisfaction on autistic college student retention*. Doctoral Dissertation. Trident University International.

Hoerricks, K. J. (2022a) *Classroom management and alexithymia: Understanding how classroom energy states affect autistic student behaviour.* [Blog] The AutSide. Available at: https://autside.substack.com/ [Accessed 15 January 2024].

Hoerricks, K. J. (2022b). *It's time to reduce prompt dependence.* [Blog] The AutSide. Available at: https://autside.substack.com/p/its-time-to-reduce-prompt-dependence [Accessed 18 April 2024].

Hoerricks, K. J. (2022c.) *The challenge of learning to comprehend language.* Unpublished. Loyola Marymount University School of Education.

Hoerricks, J. (2023). *No Place for Autism? Exploring the Solitary Forager Hypothesis of Autism in Light of Place Identity.* New York: Lived Places Publishing.

Hoffman, A. R., Jenkins, J. E. and Dunlap, S. K. (2009). Using DIBELS: A Survey of Purposes and Practices. *Reading Psychology,* 30(1), pp. 1–16.

Joffe, V. L. and Black, E. (2012). Social, Emotional, and Behavioral Functioning of Secondary School Students with Low Academic and Language Performance: Perspectives from Students, Teachers, and Parents. *Language, Speech, and Hearing Services in Schools,* 43(4), pp. 461–473.

Jones, M. M., Lignugaris/Kraft, B. and Peterson, S. M. (2007). The Relation Between Task Demands and Student Behaviour Problems During Reading Instruction: A Case Study. *Preventing School Failure: Alternative Education for Children and Youth,* 51(4), pp. 19–28.

Kazdin, A. E. (1982). The Token Economy: A Decade Later. *Journal of Applied Behavior Analysis,* 15(3), pp. 431–445.

Kestner, K. M., Peterson, S. M., Eldridge, R. R. and Peterson, L. D. (2019). Considerations of Baseline Classroom Conditions in Conducting Functional Behavior Assessments in School Settings. *Behavior Analysis in Practice,* 12, pp. 452–465.

Khan, O. (2020). *Experiences with and conceptions of school discipline and PBIS implementation: A phenomenography of fifteen students with disabilities in one Title I middle school*. Doctor of Education in Special Education. Kennesaw State University.

Levy, S. and Chard, D. J. (2001). Research on Reading Instruction for Students with Emotional and Behavioural Disorders. *International Journal of Disability, Development and Education*, 48(4), pp. 429–444.

Losinski, M., Cuenca-Carlino, Y., Zablocki, M., and Teagarden, J. (2014). Examining the Efficacy of Self-Regulated Strategy Development for Students with Emotional or Behavioral Disorders: A Meta-Analysis. *Behavioral Disorders*, 40, pp. 52–67.

Lundqvist, J. (2023). Putting Preschool Inclusion into Practice: A Case Study. *European Journal of Special Needs Education*, 38(1), pp. 95–109.

Mason, L. H. (2004). Explicit Self-Regulated Strategy Development versus Reciprocal Questioning: Effects on Expository Reading Comprehension among Struggling Readers. *Journal of Educational Psychology*, 96, pp. 283–296.

Mason, L. H. (2013). Teaching Students who Struggle with Learning to Think Before, While, and After Reading: Effects of Self-Regulated Strategy Development Instruction. *Reading & Writing Quarterly*, 29, pp. 124–144.

Mason, L. H., Davidson, M. D., Scheffner Hammer, C., Miller, C. A. and Glutting, J. J. (2013). Knowledge, Writing, and Language Outcomes for a Reading Comprehension and Writing Intervention. *Reading and Writing: An International Journal*, 26, pp. 1133–1158.

Mason, L. H., Snyder Hickey, K. Sukhram, D. P. and Kedem, Y. (2006). TWA+PLANS Strategies for Expository Reading and Writing: Effects for Nine Fourth-Grade Students. *Exceptional Children*, 73, pp. 69–89.

Mastropieri, M. A. and Scruggs, T. E. (2014). Intensive Instruction to Improve Writing for Students with Emotional and Behavioral Disorders. *Behavioral Disorders*, 40, pp. 78–83.

Mathews, H. M., Lillis, J. L., Bettini, E., Peyton, D. J., Pua, D., Oblath, R., Jones, N. D., Smith, S. W. and Sutton, R. (2021). Working Conditions and Special Educators' Reading Instruction for Students with Emotional and Behavioural Disorders. *Exceptional Children*, 87(4), pp. 1–21.

Mesibov, G. B., Shea, V. and Schopler, E. (2004). *The TEACCH Approach to Autism Spectrum Disorders*. New York: Springer Science+Business Media Inc.

Morgan, P. L., Farkas, G., Tufis, P. A. and Sperling, R. A. (2008). Are Reading and Behaviour Problems Risk Factors for Each Other?. *Journal of Learning Disabilities*, 41(5), 417–436.

The National Assessment of Educational Progress (NAEP). (2023). *NAEP report card: Reading*. [Online] Available at: www.nationsreportcard.gov/reading/?grade=12 [Accessed 22 April 2024].

Richards-Tutor, C. and Solari, E. J. (2022). Evidence-based, culturally responsive interventions to improve academic outcomes for English learners with reading difficulties. In: C. J. Lemons, S. R. Powell, K. L. Lane and T. C. Aceves, eds., *Handbook of Special Education Research (Vol. II)*. New York: Routledge, pp. 150–162.

Roos, H., Fälth, L., Karlsson, L., Nilvius, C., Selenius, H. and Svensson, I. (2023). Promoting Basic Arithmetic Competence in Early School Years–Using a Response to Intervention Model. *Journal of Research in Special Educational Needs*, 23(4), pp. 313–322.

Sanders, S., Hart Rollins, L., Michael, E. and Jolivette, K. (2022). "TRAP is Legit!" Using Self-Regulated Strategy Development to Teach Reading Comprehension in a Residential Treatment Facility. *Preventing School Failure: Alternative Education for Children and Youth*, 66(1), 89–98.

Sanders, S., Jolivette, K., Rollins, L. H. and Shaw, A. (2021). How to "TRAP" Information: A Reading Comprehension Strategy for Students with Emotional and Behavioural Disorders. *TEACHING Exceptional Children*, 53(6), pp. 450–458.

Sanders, S., Ennis, R. P. and Losinski, M. (2018). Effects of TWA on Science Text Comprehension of Students with Emotional and Behavior Disorders in a Special Day School. *Education and Treatment of Children*, 41, pp. 483–506.

Sanders, S., Losinski, M., Ennis, R. P., White, W., Teagarden, J. and Lane, J. (2019). A Meta-Analysis of Self-Regulated Strategy Development Reading Interventions to Improve the Reading Comprehension of Students with Disabilities. *Reading & Writing Quarterly*, 35, pp. 1–15.

Sanders, S., Rollins, L. H., Mason L. H., Shaw, A., and Jolivette, K. (2021). Intensification and Individualization of Self-Regulation Components within Self-Regulated Strategy Development. *Intervention in School and Clinic*, 43, 131–140.

Sandhaug, M., Palmu, I., Jakobsen, S., Friberg, P., Berg, J., Fensbo, L., Sjöström, J. and Thastum, M. (2022). Recording, Reporting, and Utilizing School Attendance Data in Sweden, Finland, Denmark, and Norway: A Nordic Comparison. *Orbis Scholae*, 16(2), pp. 173–186.

Schlinger, H. (2021). The impact of B. F. Skinner's science of operant learning on early childhood research, theory, treatment, and care. *Early Child Development and Care*, 191, 1089–1106. https://doi.org/10.1080/03004430.2020.1855155.

Scruggs, T. E. and Mastropieri, M. A. (2007). *The Inclusive Classroom: Strategies for Effective Instruction*. London: Pearson.

Smarter Balanced. (2018). *2018–19 Summative Technical Report*. [Online] Santa Clara, CA: Smarter Balanced. Available at: https://technicalreports.smarterbalanced.org/2018-19_summative-report/_book/report-interp.html [Accessed 22 April 2024].

Smarter Balanced. (2021). *Interpretive guide for English language arts / literacy and mathematics assessments*. Available at: https://portal.smarterbalanced.org%2Flibrary%2Fen%2Freporting-system-interpretive-guide.pdf [Accessed 22 April 2024].

Smith, W. S., Cumming, M. M., Merrill, K. L., Pitts, D. L. and Daunic, A. P. (2015). Teaching Self-Regulation Skills to Students with Behaviour Problems: Essential Instructional Components. *Beyond Behaviour*, 24, pp. 4–13.

Spear-Swerling, L. (2019). Structured Literacy and Typical Literacy Practices: Understanding Differences to Create Instructional Opportunities. *Teaching Exceptional Children*, 51(3), pp. 201–211.

Sullo, B. (2011). Choice Theory. [Online] Funderstanding. Available at: www.funderstanding.com/educators/choice-theory/ [Accessed 18 April 2024].

Thomas, M. S., Crosby, S. and Vanderhaar, J. (2019). Trauma-Informed Practices in Schools across Two Decades: An Interdisciplinary Review of Research. *Review of Research in Education*, 43(1), pp. 422–452.

Van der Veer, R. (2014). *Lev Vygotsky*. London: Bloomsbury Publishing.

Vaughn, S., Levy, S., Coleman, M. and Bos, C. S. (2002). Reading Instruction for Students with LD and EBD: A Synthesis of Observation Studies. *The Journal of Special Education*, 36(1), pp. 2–13.

Vygotsky, L. (1978). *Mind in Society: The Development of Higher Psychological Processes*. Cambridge, MA: Harvard University Press.

What Works Clearinghouse (WWC). (2017). *Self-Regulated Strategy Development: What Works Clearinghouse Intervention Report*. Washington, DC: US Department of Education. Available at: https://files.eric.ed.gov/fulltext/ED577336.pdf [Accessed 18 April 2024].

Whitley, J. and Hollweck, T. (2020). Inclusion and Equity in Education: Current Policy Reform in Nova Scotia, Canada. *Prospects*, 49(3–4), pp. 297–312.

Chapter 5

Adler, M. J. and Van Doren, C. (1972). *How to Read a Book*. London: Simon and Schuster.

Aikens, N. L. and Barbarin, O. (2008). Socioeconomic Differences in Reading Trajectories: The Contribution of Family, Neighborhood, and School Contexts. *Journal of Educational Psychology*, 100(2), p. 235.

Allison, H. G. (2011). *Roots of Stone: The Story of Those who Came Before*. New York: Random House.

Børdahl, V. (1996). *The Oral Tradition of Yangzhou Storytelling (Vol. 73)*. London: Psychology Press.

Barrett, J. and Cocq, C. (2019). Indigenous storytelling and language learning: digital media as a vehicle for cultural transmission and language acquisition. In: C. Cocq and K. Sullivan, eds., *Perspectives on Indigenous Writing and Literacies*. Leiden: Brill, pp. 89–112.

Barrett, G. F. and Riddell, W. C. (2019). Ageing and Skills: The Case of Literacy Skills. *European Journal of Education*, 54(1), pp. 60–71.

Barron, K. (2022). Literacy in America: The facts and consequences. [Online] TCK Publishing. Available at: www.tckpublishing.com/literacy-in-america [Accessed 18 April 2024].

Borgia, L. (2009). Enhanced Vocabulary Podcasts Implementation in Fifth Grade Classrooms. *Reading Improvement*, 46(4), pp. 263–273.

Boyce, M. (1957). The Parthian Gōsān and Iranian Minstrel Tradition. *Journal of the Royal Asiatic Society*, 89(1–2), pp. 10–45.

Bulajić, A., Despotović, M. and Lachmann, T. (2019). Understanding Functional Illiteracy from a Policy, Adult Education, and Cognition Point of View: Towards a Joint Referent Framework. *Zeitschrift für Neuropsychologie*, 30(2), pp. 109–122.

Burritt, A. M. and Massam, K. T. (2020). Interreligious Dialogue, Literacy and Theologies of Storytelling: Australian Perspectives. *Teaching Theology & Religion*, 23(4), pp. 265–275.

Byrne, C. (1983). *The Vernacular Tradition in Atlantic Canada. Acadiensis*, 13(1), pp. 142–149.

Carlson, C. L. (2010.). Adolescent Literacy, Dropout Factories, and the Economy: The Relationship between Literacy, Graduation Rates, and Economic Development in the United States. *Journal of Education and Human Development*, 2(1), pp. 1–8.

Carter-Black, J. (2007). Teaching Cultural Competence: An Innovative Strategy Grounded in the Universality of Storytelling as Depicted in African and African American Storytelling Traditions. *Journal of Social Work Education*, 43(1), pp. 31–50.

Chafe, W. (1988). Punctuation and the Prosody of Written Language. *Written Communication*, 5(4), pp. 395–426.

Chall, J. S., Heron, E. and Hilferty, A. (1987). Adult Literacy: New and Enduring Problems. *The Phi Delta Kappan*, 69(3), pp. 190–196.

Chandler, M. C., Gerde, H. K., Bowles, R. P., McRoy, K. Z., Pontifex, M. B. and Bingham, G. E. (2021). Self-Regulation Moderates the Relationship between Fine Motor Skills and Writing in Early Childhood. *Early Childhood Research Quarterly*, 57, pp. 239–250.

Chard, B. J. T. D. J. (2000). Focus on Inclusion: Using Readers Theatre to Foster Fluency in Struggling Readers: A Twist on the Repeated Reading Strategy. *Reading & Writing Quarterly*, 16(2), pp. 163–168.

Common Core State Standards Initiative (CCSSI). (2023). *Common Core State Standards for English Language Arts & Literacy in History/Social Studies, Science, and technical subjects*. 1. [PDF] United States: CCSSI. Available at: https://corestandards.org/wp-content/uploads/2023/09/ELA_Standards1.pdf [Accessed 19 April 2024].

Culham, R. (2023). *Writing Thief: Using Mentor Texts to Teach the Craft of Writing*. Abingdon: Routledge.

Curtis, M. E. (2005). *Teaching Adults to Read: A Summary of Scientifically Based Research Principles*. Washington, DC: National Institute for Literacy.

Cushing, E., English, D., Therriault, S. and Lavinson, R. (2019). *An Analysis of ESSA, Perkins V, IDEA, and WIOA*. Washington, DC: College & Career Readiness & Success Center at American Institutes for Research. Available at: https://files.eric.ed.gov/fulltext/ED602409.pdf [Accessed 18 April 2024].

Cvorovic, J. and Coe, K. (2022). *Storytelling around the World: Folktales, Narrative Rituals, and Oral Traditions*. New York: Bloomsbury Publishing USA.

Diehl, J. J. and Paul, R. (2012). Acoustic Differences in the Imitation of Prosodic Patterns in Children with Autism Spectrum Disorders. *Research in Autism Spectrum Disorders*, 6(1), pp. 123–134.

Egan, G. and Gurr, A. (2002). Prompting, Backstage Activity and the Openings onto the Shakespearian Stage. *Theatre Notebook*, 56, pp. 138–142.

Ellis, C. (2021). Remembering the Vikings: Ancestry, Cultural Memory and Geographical Variation. *History Compass*, 19(4), p. e12652.

Foster, S. M. (2020). *A Historiography of Literacy Policy: Analyzing Ideological Positionings in Race to the Top Fund and Every Student Succeeds Act*. Carbondale, IL: Southern Illinois University at Carbondale.

Gallagher, K. (2023). *Write Like This: Teaching Real-World Writing through Modeling and Mentor Texts*. Abingdon: Routledge.

Garagozov, R. (2008). Historical Narratives, Cultural Traditions, and Collective Memory in the Central Caucasus [Continued]. *Journal of Russian & East European Psychology*, 46(2), pp. 3–57.

Hale, T. A. (1985). Islam and the Griots in West Africa: Bridging the Gap between Two Traditions. *Africana Journal*, 13(1–4), pp. 84–90.

Hale, T. A. (1997). From the Griot of Roots to the Roots of Griot: A New Look at the Origins of a Controversial African Term for Bard. *Oral Tradition*, 12(2), pp. 249–278.

Hargis, C. H., Gickling, E. E. and Mahmoud, C. C. (1975). The Effectiveness of TV in Teaching Sight Words to Students with Learning Disabilities. *Journal of Learning Disabilities*, 8(1), pp. 37–39.

Harman, D. (1970). Illiteracy: An Overview. Harvard Educational Review, 40(2), pp. 226–243.

Hertel, R. and Johnson, M. M. (2013). How the traumatic experiences of students manifest in school settings. In. E. Rosen and R. Hull, eds., *Supporting and Educating Traumatized Students: A Guide for School-based Professionals*. Oxford: Oxford University Press, pp. 23–35.

Hilvert, E., Davidson, D. and Scott, C. M. (2019). An In-Depth Analysis of Expository Writing in Children With and Without Autism Spectrum Disorder. *Journal of Autism and Developmental Disorders*, 49, pp. 3412–3425.

Hoerricks, J. (2007). *Learning to tell your story*. [Blog] Forensic Multimedia Analysis Blog. Available at: https://forensicphotoshop.blogspot.com/2007/12/learning-to-tell-your-story.html [Accessed 22 April 2024].

Hoerricks, J. (2008). *Book publishing*. [Blog] Forensic Multimedia Analysis Blog. Available at: https://forensicphotoshop.blogspot.com/2008/02/book-publishing.html [Accessed 22 April 2024].

Hoerricks, J. (2017). *What you know vs. what you can prove*. [Blog] Forensic Multimedia Analysis Blog. Available at: https://forensicphotoshop.blogspot.com/2017/09/what-you-know-vs-what-you-can-prove.html [Accessed 22 April 2024].

Hoerricks, K. J. (2018a). *Higher education support strategies: An evaluation of needs satisfaction on autistic college student retention*. Doctoral Dissertation. Trident University International.

Hoerricks, J. (2018b). *Report writing in forensic multimedia analysis.* [Blog] Forensic Multimedia Analysis Blog. Available at: https://forensicphotoshop.blogspot.com/2018/05/report-writing-in-forensic-multimedia.html [Accessed 19 April 2024].

Hoerricks, J. (2019a). *Retrieval / seizure of electronic evidence from crime scenes.* [Blog] Forensic Multimedia Analysis Blog. Available at: https://forensicphotoshop.blogspot.com/2019/06/retrieval-seizure-of-electronic.html [Accessed 22 April 2024].

Hoerricks, J. (2019b). *Leadership in the Lodge of Perfection.* San Francisco: Blurb Publications.

Hoerricks, J. (2023). *Where's the science in the science of reading?.* [Blog] AutSide. Available at: https://autside.substack.com/p/wheres-the-science-in-the-science [Accessed 16 April 2024].

Hogg, U. and MacGregor, M. (2018) Historiography in Highlands and Lowlands. In: N. Roya, ed., *The International Companion to Scottish Literature 1400–1650.* Glasgow: Scottish Literature International, pp. 100–123.

Johnson, K. (2019). Chronic Poverty: The Implications of Bullying, Trauma, and the Education of the Poverty-Stricken Population. *European Journal of Educational Sciences*, (Special), pp. 76–101.

Kapur, R. (2014). Growth and Regional Inequality in Literacy in India. *International Journal of Transformations in Business Management*, 4(II), pp. 1–7.

Kaschula, R. H. (1999). Imbongi and Griot: Toward a Comparative Analysis of Oral Poetics in Southern and West Africa. *Journal of African Cultural Studies*, 12(1), pp. 55–76.

Keefe, E. B. and Copeland, S. R. (2011). What is Literacy? The Power of a Definition. *Research and Practice for Persons with Severe Disabilities*, 36(3–4), pp. 92–99.

Kirsch, I., Yamamoto, K. and Khorramdel, L. (2020). Design and key features of the PIAAC survey of adults. In. D. B. Maehler and

B. Rammstedt, eds., *Large-Scale Cognitive Assessment: Analyzing PIAAC Data*. New York: Springer, pp. 7–26.

Krenzke, T., Mohadjer, L., Li, J., Erciulescu, A., Fay, R., Ren, W., Van de Kerckhove, W., Li, L. and Rao, J. N. K. (2020). *Program for the International Assessment of Adult Competencies (PIAAC): State and County Estimation Methodology Report.* [Online] Washington, DC: National Center for Education Statistics. Available at: https://nces.ed.gov/pubs2020/2020225.pdf [Accessed 18 April 2024].

Kroeber, A. L. (1925). *Handbook of the Indians of California*. Washington: Government Printing Office.

Kruidenier, J. (2002). *Research-Based Principles for Adult Basic Education Reading Instruction*. Washington, DC: National Institute for Literacy.

Le, T. T. H., Tran, T., Trinh, T. P. T., Nguyen, C. T., Nguyen, T. P. T., Vuong, T. T., Vu, T. H., Bui, D. Q., Vuong, H. M., Hoang, P. H. and Nguyen, M. H. (2019). Reading Habits, Socioeconomic Conditions, Occupational Aspiration and Academic Achievement in Vietnamese Junior High School Students. *Sustainability*, 11(18), p. 5113.

Lewis, T. (1997). America's Choice: Literacy or Productivity?. *Curriculum Inquiry*, 27(4), pp. 391–421.

MacLean, J. P. (2009). *A History of the Clan MacLean from Its First Settlement at Duard Castle, in the Isle of Mull, to the Present Period, Including a Genealogical Account of Some of the Principal Families Together with Their Heraldry, Legends, Superstitions, Etc.* Berwyn Heights, MD: Heritage Books.

Macpherson, A. G. (1966). *An Old Highland Genealogy and the Evolution of a Scottish Clan*. Edinburgh: Oliver and Boyd Limited.

Malo, E. and Bullard, J. (2000). Storytelling and the Emergent Reader. In: 18th International Reading Association World Congress on Reading. Auckland: International Reading Association, pp. 1–18.

Mani, A., Mullainathan, S., Shafir, E. and Zhao, J. (2013). Poverty Impedes Cognitive Function. *Science*, 341(6149), pp. 976–980.

McCabe, A. (1997). Cultural Background and Storytelling: A Review and Implications for Schooling. *The Elementary School Journal*, 97(5), pp. 453–473.

McGinn, C. (2011). Vehement celebrations: The global celebration of the Burns Supper since 1801. In: M. Pittock, ed., *Robert Burns in Global Culture*. Lewisburg, PA: Bucknell University Press, pp. 189–203.

McShane, S. (2005). *Applying Research in Reading Instruction for Adults: First Steps for Teachers*. Washington, DC: National Institute for Literacy.

Mraz, M., Nichols, W., Caldwell, S., Beisley, R., Sargent, S. and Rupley, W. (2013). Improving Oral Reading Fluency through Readers Theatre. *Reading Horizons: A Journal of Literacy and Language Arts*, 52(2), p. 5.

Næss, M. S. (2016). *A case study of readers theatre with minority background adult learners of English in Norway*. Master's thesis. University of Stavanger, Norway.

Newton, M. (2015). *Seanchaidh Na Coille / The Memory-Keeper of the Forest*. Sydney, Nova Scotia: Cape Breton University Press.

NoackLeSage, F., Shaheen, G. L., Davis, T. E., Castagna, P. J., Kaskas, M. M., Ryan, P. and Lilly, M. E. (2019). Predicting Reading, Writing, and Mathematics Achievement: Do Anxiety and ADHD Symptoms Add to the Variance Explained by Working Memory and Verbal Reasoning Alone?. *Current Psychology*, 38, pp. 792–802.

OECD. (2021). *OECD Skills Outlook 2021: Learning for Life*. [Online] Paris: OECD Publishing. Available at: https://doi.org/10.1787/0ae365b4-en [Accessed 18 April 2024].

Ozdowska, A., Wyeth, P., Carrington, S. and Ashburner, J. (2021). Using Assistive Technology with SRSD to Support Students on the Autism Spectrum with Persuasive Writing. *British Journal of Educational Technology*, 52(2), pp. 934–959.

Phillips, L. G. and Nguyen, T. T. P. (2022). Introduction: The what, how, and why of storytelling pedagogy. In: L. G. Phillips and T. T. P. Nguyen, eds., *Storytelling Pedagogy in Australia & Asia*. Singapore: Springer Singapore, pp. 1–19.

Rigg, P. and Kasemek, F. E. (1983). Adult Illiteracy in the USA: Problem and Solution. *Convergence*, 16(4), p. 24.

Ritchey, K. D. and Goeke, J. L. (2006). Orton-Gillingham and Orton-Gillingham—Based Reading Instruction: A Review of the Literature. *The Journal of Special Education*, 40(3), pp. 171–183.

Ross, A. (2000). *Folklore of the Scottish Highlands*. Cheltenham: The History Press.

Rupley, W. H., Nichols, W. D., Rasinski, T. V. and Paige, D. (2020). Fluency: Deep Roots in Reading Instruction. *Education Sciences*, 10(6), p. 155.

Samuelson, B. L., Park, G. Y. and Munyaneza, S. P. (2018). Cultural Imaginaries and Oral Traditions as Creative Resources for Connecting Home Storytelling to English Learning. *TESOL Journal*, 9(4), pp. 1–11.

Sanchez, H. (2021). *The Poverty Problem: How Education Can Promote Resilience and Counter Poverty's Impact on Brain Development and Functioning*. Thousand Oaks, CA: Corwin.

Selvaraj, M. and Aziz, A. A. (2019). Systematic Review: Approaches in Teaching Writing Skill in ESL Classrooms. *International Journal of Academic Research in Progressive Education and Development*, 8(4), pp. 450–473.

Sherman, J. (2015). *Storytelling: An Encyclopedia of Mythology and Folklore*. Abingdon: Routledge.

Shoulders, J. (2022). Are Podcasts a Return to Oral Storytelling?. *Ashen Egg*, 10, pp. 63–68.

Singh, C. K. S., Singh, T. S. M., Ja'afar, H., Tek, O. E., Kaur, H., Moastafa, N. A. and Yunus, M. (2020). Teaching Strategies to Develop Higher-Order Thinking Skills in English Literature. *International Journal of Innovation, Creativity and Change*, 11(80), pp. 211–231.

Solovyeva, A. (2019). Men's Business? Two Female Skalds of the Uppsala Edda and the Origins of Poetry. *Kyngervi*, 1, pp. 16–36.

Soto, E. F., Irwin, L. N., Chan, E. S., Spiegel, J. A. and Kofler, M. J. (2021). Executive Functions and Writing Skills in Children With and Without ADHD. *Neuropsychology*, 35(8), p. 792.

Stantcheva, S. (2022). Inequalities in the Times of a Pandemic. *Economic Policy*, 37(109), pp. 5–41.

Stevens, E. A., Austin, C., Moore, C., Scammacca, N., Boucher, A. N. and Vaughn, S., 2021. Current State of the Evidence: Examining the Effects of Orton-Gillingham Reading Interventions for Students With or At Risk for Word-Level Reading Disabilities. *Exceptional Children*, 87(4), pp. 397–417.

Sticht, T. (2022). Adult literacy and basic education in the United States. In: *Oxford Research Encyclopedia of Education*. Oxford: Oxford University Press, pp.

Szasz, M. (2007). *Scottish Highlanders and Native Americans: Indigenous Education in the Eighteenth-Century Atlantic World*. Norman, OK: University of Oklahoma Press.

Teaching Tolerance. (2016). *Reading Diversity: A Tool for Selecting Diverse Texts*. 1. [PDF] Montgomery, AL: Southern Poverty Law Center. Available at: www.learningforjustice.org/sites/default/files/2017-10/Teaching-Tolerance-Reading-Diversity-Extended-Edition-2016-VFF.pdf [Accessed 22 April 2024].

Turner, III, H. M. (2008). This Systematic Review Empirically Documents that the Effectiveness of Orton-Gillingham and Orton-Gillingham-Based Reading Instruction Remains to be Determined. *Evidence-Based Communication Assessment and Intervention*, 2(2), pp. 67–69.

UNESCO. (1979). *Records of the General Conference, 20th Session, Paris, 24 October to 28 November 1978, v. 1: Resolutions*. Paris: UNESCO. Available from: https://unesdoc.unesco.org/ark:/48223/pf0000114032 [Accessed 19 April 2024].

Vágvölgyi, R., Bergström, K., Bulajić, A., Klatte, M., Fernandes, T., Grosche, M., Huettig, F., Rüsseler, J. and Lachmann, T. (2021). Functional Illiteracy and Developmental Dyslexia: Looking for Common Roots. A Systematic Review. *Journal of Cultural Cognitive Science*, 5(2), pp. 159–179.

Wright, I. (2007). The Diaspora and Its Writers. *The Edinburgh History of Scottish Literature: Modern Transformations: New Identities (from 1918)*, 3, p. 304.

Young, C., Durham, P., Miller, M., Rasinski, T. V. and Lane, F. (2019). Improving Reading Comprehension with Readers Theater. *The Journal of Educational Research*, 112(5), pp. 615–626.

Young, C. and Rasinski, T. (2009). Implementing Readers Theatre as an Approach to Classroom Fluency Instruction. *The Reading Teacher*, 63(1), pp. 4–13.

Zajic, M. C., Solari, E. J., McIntyre, N. S., Lerro, L. and Mundy, P. C. (2020). Overt Planning Behaviors during Writing in School-Age Children with Autism Spectrum Disorder and Attention-Deficit/Hyperactivity Disorder. *Research in Developmental Disabilities*, 100, p. 103631.

Chapter 6

Abeles, V. and Rubenstein, G. (2015). *Beyond Measure: Rescuing an Overscheduled, Overtested, Underestimated Generation*. New York: Simon and Schuster.

Abimbola, I. O. (2013). The Misunderstood Word in Science: Towards a Technology of Perfect Understanding for All. Available at: https://citeseerx.ist.psu.edu/document?repid=rep1&type=pdf&doi=742101131ee00bb617df3243b38edf3a4ea36bf9 [Accessed 19 April 2024].

Accurso, K. and Gebhard, M. (2021). SFL Praxis in US Teacher Education: A Critical Literature Review. *Language and Education*, 35(5), pp. 402–428.

Afflerbach, P. (2017). *Literacy Leadership Brief: The Roles of Standardized Reading Tests in Schools*. 1. [PDF] Newark, DE: International Literacy Association. Available at: www.literacyworldwide.org/docs/default-source/where-we-stand/ila-roles-standardized-reading-tests-in-schools.pdf?sfvrsn=c6ada58e_4 [Accessed 19 April 2024].

Almulla, M. A. (2020). The Effectiveness of the Project-Based Learning (PBL) Approach as a Way to Engage Students in Learning. *Sage Open*, 10(3), p. 2158244020938702.

Anders, P. L. and Guzzetti, B. J. (2020). *Literacy Instruction in the Content Areas*. Abingdon: Routledge.

Anderson, J. C. (2007). *Effect of problem-based learning on knowledge acquisition, knowledge retention, and critical thinking ability of agriculture students in urban schools* (Doctoral Dissertation). University of Missouri--Columbia.

Barnes, J. (2015). An introduction to cross-curricular learning. In: P. Driscoll, A. Lambirth and J. Roden, eds., *The Primary Curriculum: A Creative Approach*. Los Angeles: Sage Publications, pp. 260–282.

Barron, B. J., Schwartz, D. L., Vye, N. J., Moore, A., Petrosino, A., Zech, L. and Bransford, J. D. (1998). Doing with Understanding: Lessons from Research on Problem-and Project-Based Learning. *Journal of the Learning Sciences*, 7(3–4), pp. 271–311.

Boaler, J. (2002). Learning from Teaching: Exploring the Relationship between Reform Curriculum and Equity. *Journal for Research in Mathematics Education*, 33(4), pp. 239–258.

Boss, S. and Krauss, J. (2022). *Reinventing Project-Based Learning: Your Field Guide to Real-World Projects in the Digital Age*. Arlington, VA: International Society for Technology in Education.

Bouziane, A. and Zohri, A. (2019). The Effect of Explicit Instruction in Critical Thinking on Higher-Order Thinking Skills in Reading Comprehension: An Experimental Study. *European Journal of English Language Teaching*, 5(1), pp. 114–126.

Chapman, S. L. (2013). *The Applied Scholastics Study Technology – A Definition and Brief Description with Comments on the Need for Comprehension Strategy Instruction*. 1. [PDF] St Louis, MO: Applied Scholastics International. Available at: https://citeseerx.ist.psu.edu/document?repid=rep1&type=pdf&doi=f1a56fa7fa1543edff0293af8aec39cfb7234f57 [Accessed 19 April 2024].

Chauvin, R., and Theodore, K. (2015). Teaching Content-Area Literacy and Disciplinary Literacy. *SEDL Insights*, 3(1), pp. 1–81

Cornell University Center for Teaching Innovation. (2023). *Social annotation*. [Online] Available at: https://teaching.cornell.edu/learning-technologies/collaboration-tools/social-annotation [Accessed 22 April 2024].

de Oliveira, L. C. and Cheng, D. (2011). Language and the Multisemiotic Nature of Mathematics. *Reading Matrix: An International Online Journal*, 11(3), pp. 255–268.

Ediger, M. (1993). The Affective Domain, Science, and the Middle School Student. *Journal of Instructional Psychology*, 20(4), p. 314.

Esquith, R. (2014). *Real Talk for Real Teachers: Advice for Teachers from Rookies to Veterans: "No Retreat, No Surrender!"*. London: Penguin.

Fang, Z. and Coatoam, S. (2013). Disciplinary Literacy: What You Want to Know about It. *Journal of Adolescent & Adult Literacy*, 56(8), pp. 627–632.

Fisher, D. and Ivey, G. (2005). Literacy and Language as Learning in Content-Area Classes: A Departure from "Every Teacher a Teacher of Reading". *Action in Teacher Education*, 27(2), pp. 3–11.

García, O. and Kleifgen, J. A. (2020). Translanguaging and Literacies. *Reading Research Quarterly*, 55(4), pp. 553–571.

Gigante, N. A. and Firestone, W. A. (2008). Administrative Support and Teacher Leadership in Schools Implementing Reform. *Journal of Educational Administration*, 46(3), pp. 302–331.

Graham, P. (2007). Improving Teacher Effectiveness through Structured Collaboration: A Case Study of a Professional Learning Community. *RMLE Online*, 31(1), pp. 1–17.

Graham, S., Kiuhara, S. A. and MacKay, M. (2020). The Effects of Writing on Learning in Science, Social Studies, and Mathematics: A Meta-Analysis. *Review of Educational Research*, 90(2), pp. 179–226.

Gruwell, E. (2007). *The Freedom Writers Diary: How a Teacher and 150 Teens Used Writing to Change Themselves and the World Around Them*. New York: Crown.

Harklau, L. (2001). From High School to College: Student Perspectives on Literacy Practices. *Journal of Literacy Research*, 33(1), pp. 33–70.

Harris, V. and Grenfell, M. (2004). Language-Learning Strategies: A Case for Cross-Curricular Collaboration. *Language Awareness*, 13(2), pp. 116–130.

Hayes, D. (2010). The seductive charms of a cross-curricular approach. *Education 3–13*, 38(4), pp. 381–387.

Herrington, A. J. (1981). Writing to Learn: Writing across the Disciplines. *College English*, 43(4), pp. 379–387.

Hinchman, K. A. and O'Brien, D. G. (2019). Disciplinary Literacy: From Infusion to Hybridity. *Journal of Literacy Research*, 51(4), pp. 525–536.

Hodgson, J., Kalir, J. R. and Andrews, C. (2023). Social annotation as writing: Promising technologies and practices in writing. In: O. Kruse, C. Rapp, C. Anson, K. Benetos, E. Cotos, A. Devitt and A. Shibani, eds., *Digital Writing Technologies in Higher Education*. New York: Springer, pp. 141–155.

Hoerricks, J. (2008). *Forensic Photoshop, a Comprehensive Imaging Workflow for Forensic Professionals*. San Francisco: Blurb Publishing.

Kirsten, N. (2019). Improving Literacy and Content Learning across the Curriculum? How Teachers Relate Literacy Teaching to School Subjects in Cross-Curricular Professional Development. *Education Inquiry*, 10(4), pp. 368–384.

Laugksch, R. C. (2000). Scientific Literacy: A Conceptual Overview. *Science Education*, 84(1), pp. 71–94.

Lawrence, S. A., Rabinowitz, R. and Perna, H. (2008). Reading Instruction in Secondary English Language Arts Classrooms. *Literacy Research and Instruction*, 48(1), pp. 39–64.

Letterman, M. R. and Dugan, K. B. (2004). Team Teaching a Cross-Disciplinary Honors Course: Preparation and Development. *College Teaching*, 52(2), pp. 76–79.

Livingston, J. A. (2003). Metacognition: An Overview. Psychology, 13, pp. 259–266.

Macias, A. (2017). Teacher-Led Professional Development: A Proposal for a Bottom-Up Structure Approach. *International Journal of Teacher Leadership*, 8(1), pp. 76–91.

Martinez, C. (2022). Developing 21st Century Teaching Skills: A Case Study of Teaching and Learning through Project-Based Curriculum. *Cogent Education*, 9(1), p. 2024936.

Marunda-Piki, C. J. (2018). The Impact of Narrative-Based Learning in Classroom. *Research in Drama Education: The Journal of Applied Theatre and Performance*, 23(1), pp. 107–113.

Mathews, J. (1989). *Escalante: The Best Teacher in America*. New York: Henry Holt (OWL).

McLean, E. (2022). *Writing and Writing Instruction: An Overview of the Literature*. [Online] Melbourne: Australian Educational Research Organization, pp. 1–27. Available at: https://apo.org.au/sites/default/files/resource-files/2022-10/apo-nid322989.pdf [Accessed 19 April 2024].

Miller, S. M., Thompson, M. K., Lauricella, A. M., Boyd, F. B. and McVee, M. B. (2013). A literacy pedagogy for multimodal composing: Transforming learning teaching. In: S. M. Miller and M. B. McVee, eds., *Multimodal Composing in Classrooms*. Abingdon: Routledge, pp. 114–129.

Miterianifa, M., Ashadi, A., Saputro, S. and Suciati, S. (2021). Higher Order Thinking Skills in the 21st Century: Critical Thinking. In: *Proceedings of the 1st International Conference on Social Science, Humanities, Education and Society Development*. Tegal, Indonesia: ICONS, pp. 1–10.

Moffett, J. (1968). *Teaching the Universe of Discourse*. Boston, MA: Houghton Mifflin Company.

National Council on Teacher Quality (NCTQ). (2020). *State of the states 2021: Teacher preparation policy*. [Online] Available at: www.nctq.org/publications/State-of-the-States-2021:-Teacher-Preparation-Policy [Accessed 19 April 2024].

Newell, G. E. (2006). Writing to learn. In: C. A. MacArthur, S. Graham and J. Fitzgerald, eds., *Handbook of Writing Research*. New York: Guilford Press, pp. 235–247.

Nuntasane, J., Tawnonngiew, B. and Nuangchalerm, P. (2020). Developing Scientific Writing of Lower Secondary Students through Inquiry and Science Writing Heuristic Learning. *Jurnal Penelitian dan Pembelajaran IPA*, 6(2), pp. 180–193.

Pierce, K. M. and Gilles, C. (2021). Talking about Books: Scaffolding Deep Discussions. *The Reading Teacher*, 74(4), pp. 385–393.

Rowley, C. and Cooper, H. eds. (2009). *Cross-Curricular Approaches to Teaching and Learning* (Los Angeles: Sage).

Rutherford, F. J. and Ahlgren, A. (1991). *Science for All Americans: Project 2061*. Oxford: Oxford University Press.

Samuels, A. J. (2017). Exploring Culturally Responsive Pedagogy: Teachers' Perspectives on Fostering Equitable and

Inclusive Classrooms. *Journal of Educational Research and Practice*, 7(2), pp. 1–14.

Schwartz, K. (2016). *I Wish My Teacher Knew: How One Question Can Change Everything for Our Kids*. Boston, Ma: Da Capo Lifelong Books.

Shanahan, C. (2015). *Disciplinary Literacy Strategies in Content Area Classes*. 1. [PDF] Newark, DE: International Literacy Association. Available at: www.literacyworldwide.org/docs/default-source/member-benefits/e-ssentials/ila-e-ssentials-8069.pdf [Accessed 19 April 2024].

Simmons, A. (2015). *Whoever Tells the Best Story Wins: How to Use Your Own Stories to Communicate with Power and Impact*. New York: Amacom.

Snow, M.A. (2005). A model of academic literacy for integrated language and content instruction. In: E. Hinkel, ed., *Handbook of Research in Second Language Teaching and Learning*. Abingdon: Routledge, pp. 693–712.

Taylor, R. and Kilpin, K. (2013). Secondary School Literacy in the Social Sciences: An Argument for Disciplinary Literacy. *New Zealand Journal of Educational Studies*, 48(2), pp. 130–142.

Thamrin, N. R. and Widodo, P. (2019). Developing Higher Order Thinking Skills (HOTS) for Reading Comprehension Enhancement. *Journal of Physics: Conference Series*, 1179(1), p. 012073.

Toch, T., Topp, G. and Napolitano, J. (2022). Beyond Bake Sales. *Education Next*, 22(4), pp. 28–37.

UNESCO. (1979). *Records of the General Conference, 20th Session, Paris, 24 October to 28 November 1978, v. 1: Resolutions*. Paris: UNESCO. Available from: https://unesdoc.unesco.org/ark:/48223/pf0000114032 [Accessed 19 April 2024].

Walsh, M. (2010). Multimodal Literacy: What Does It Mean for Classroom Practice?. *The Australian Journal of Language and Literacy*, 33(3), pp. 211–239.

Wang, H. H., Charoenmuang, M., Knobloch, N. A. and Tormoehlen, R. L. (2020). Defining Interdisciplinary Collaboration Based on High School Teachers' Beliefs and Practices of STEM Integration Using a Complex Designed System. *International Journal of STEM Education*, 7, p. 3. https://doi.org/10.1186/s40594-019-0201-4

World Bank. (2019). *Ending Learning Poverty: What Will It Take?*. [Online] Washington, DC: World Bank. Available at: https://documents.worldbank.org/curated/en/395151571251399043/pdf/Ending-Learning-Poverty-What-Will-It-Take.pdf [Accessed 19 April 2024].

Index

Alexithymia 7, 131, 169

Autism 2, 6, 7, 8, 23, 47, 72, 103, 143, 191, 270

Echolalia 6, 7, 8, 20, 64, 99, 102, 103, 104, 118, 186

Evidence mills 68, 107

Evidence-based 38, 70, 75, 106, 108, 109, 128, 138, 147, 164, 207

Executive functioning 191, 192

Freemasonry 17, 18, 19, 80, 179, 183, 187, 243, 247

Masonic 18, 20, 80, 81, 179, 180, 187, 242, 243

Functional literacy 17

Gestalt language processing 5, 22, 26, 31, 47, 48, 51, 59, 69, 70, 73, 83, 85, 95, 99, 102, 105, 114, 115, 117, 118, 120, 123, 142, 163, 167, 182, 186, 187, 190, 191, 198, 201

Language acquisition 3, 21, 22, 23, 24, 25, 36, 48, 76, 94, 95, 104, 176, 239

Mentor text 193, 194, 195

Multi-Tiered System of Supports 170

MTSS. 135, 136, 137, 138, 139, 164, 165, 166, 170

Non-verbal 2, 5, 20, 70, 227

Pedagogy 83, 87, 127, 215, 219, 231, 232

Reading instruction 39, 40, 42, 79, 130

Response to Intervention 135, 137, 138, 170, 240

RtI. 135, 136, 137, 138, 139, 164, 166, 170, 240

Science of Reading 21, 27, 35, 36, 39, 40, 43, 48, 62, 72, 102, 239

Specific learning disability 21, 46, 47, 143

Universal Design for Learning 25, 69, 70, 94, 126, 200

Writing instruction 195, 203, 216, 224, 232

www.ingramcontent.com/pod-product-compliance
Lightning Source LLC
Chambersburg PA
CBHW070754230426
43665CB00017B/2348